477-3187

The HOUSE *that* BOGLE BUILT

How John Bogle and Vanguard Reinvented the Mutual Fund Industry

LEWIS BRAHAM

New York   Chicago   San Francisco   Lisbon   London
Madrid   Mexico City   Milan   New Delhi   San Juan   Seoul
Singapore   Sydney   Toronto

1 2 3 4 5 6 7 8 9 10 11 12 13 14 15   QFR/QFR   1 6 5 4 3 2 1

ISBN   978-0-07-174906-0 (print book)
MHID   0-07-174906-3

ISBN   978-0-07-175115-5 (e-book)
MHID   0-07-175115-7

This publication is designed to provide accurate and authoritative information in regard to the subject matter covered. It is sold with the understanding that neither the author nor the publisher is engaged in rendering legal, accounting, securities trading, or other professional services. If legal advice or other expert assistance is required, the services of a competent professional person should be sought.
> —*From a Declaration of Principles Jointly Adopted by a Committee of the American Bar Association and a Committee of Publishers and Associations*

Library of Congress Cataloging-in-Publication Data

Braham, Lewis.
    The house that Bogle built : how John Bogle and Vanguard reinvented the mutual fund industry / by Lewis Braham.
        p.   cm.
    Includes bibliographical references and index.
    ISBN: 978-0-07-174906-0 (alk. paper)
    1. Bogle, John C.   2. Vanguard Group of Investment Companies.   3. Mutual funds—United States.   I. Title.
    HG4530.B694   2011
    332.63'27092—dc22   2010047474

This book is based on Robert Slater's *John Bogle and the Vanguard Experiment.*

McGraw-Hill books are available at special quantity discounts to use as premiums and sales promotions or for use in corporate training programs. To contact a representative, please e-mail us at bulksales@mcgraw-hill.com.

This book is printed on acid-free paper.

To my wife and family—
we are without beginning or end.

CONTENTS

Contents

PREFACE

I first met Jack Bogle in November of 2009 at his office in Malvern, Pennsylvania. I'd seen the founder of Vanguard Funds before on television a few times and heard him talk once at a conference, but I had never actually spoken to him face to face. So I was nervous.

It isn't often in this life one gets to meet a legend. And I knew that as Bogle's biographer, I would have to say some unpleasant things about him, that part of my unenviable job would be to see the clay in the hero's feet. What's more, the greatest advocate of shareholder democracy in the history of Wall Street was known for his autocratic personality and intolerance of dissent.

This, after all, was the same man who in his *The Battle for the Soul of Capitalism* railed against "a system of dictatorship in corporate America . . . in which the power of the CEO seems virtually unfettered,"[1] and yet, during our first interview at Vanguard, told me, "If someone says when I was running this place, I was a dictator, I would say, man, you've got that right!"

Of course, I was also intrigued. A complicated soul who often contradicts himself, Bogle embodies that much abused and overused term "maverick." In many ways he resembles my late father. Both grew up in the shadow of the Great Depression to Scottish American families. Both were born well-off and then lost it all. Both had fathers who were absent, and as a result had to become men when they were much too young. I'm not going to make any exaggerated claims that Jack Bogle *c'est moi*. My father never had the opportunity to go to the Blair Academy or to Princeton. Nor did he launch the world's largest mutual fund company.

Yet the similarities were enough to pique my interest and terrify me at the same time. As it turned out, my journey to Malvern put me in the right mood to meet the king of the penny-pinching fund companies, as I didn't have much of a kitty for travel expenses. Consequently, I had to take a seven-hour Amtrak train from my home in Pittsburgh instead of a plane. I later told Jack I was "living the Vanguard way."

Roaring through the blighted hinterlands of Pittsburgh on a gray, drizzly day with my Dell Precision M4300 and a stack of articles about Bogle balanced precariously on my lap, I couldn't help feeling like Marlowe going after Kurtz in the Congo, hoping to find a voice of reason in the dark heart of Wall Street, yet dreading that, when I finally reached Bogle, he'd just gasp, "The horror, the horror!"

Since no train goes all the way to Malvern and I couldn't afford a taxi, my in-laws, who live nearby, had to give me a lift from the Exton station. The long, tortuous drive through multiple checkpoints onto the Vanguard campus did little to assuage my nerves. At the end of a tree-lined Vanguard Boulevard, the campus felt more like a remote military compound than the collegial edifice of financial wisdom the company would have investors believe. Although Vanguard houses none of its $1.4 trillion in assets here, its guards recently started carrying guns just in case—of what I'm not exactly sure. They seemed out of place in a region of Pennsylvania known more for its Amish whoopie pies and giant King of Prussia shopping mall.

Bogle is no longer in the C-suite after being forced to retire as Vanguard's chairman in 1999. His office as the titular president of the Bogle Financial Research Center is now on the same floor as the legal department of what can only ironically be called the Victory Building. It overlooks the main square of the Vanguard campus and a bronze statue of him. "I guess in certain ways I like this much better," he says, smiling uncomfortably. "Instead of overlooking the parking lot, I am overlooking this place out there. I can see my statue over there. I can see the crew members walking back and forth. I feel much more a part of things."

Lest anyone at Vanguard forget, the office serves as a reminder that Jack Bogle is still very much part of everything. It is crammed with accolades and Vanguard memorabilia. In one corner, a stack of Bogle books is piled on top of a cardboard Vanguard-opoly, the "one of a kind property trading game." On the floor, an election placard—Jack Bogle for President—is propped up against a rather garish rosy-hued life-sized portrait of Bogle grinning before an American flag. There are also several honorary degrees and pictures of Jack with actual presidents—Bill Clinton and George Herbert Walker Bush. (W. is conspicuously absent.)

Mounted on a tripod by the window is perhaps the pièce de résistance, a long brass spyglass, which I imagine Bogle sometimes used to survey the movements of his frenemy Jack Brennan on the campus. Since Brennan replaced Bogle as CEO, the two haven't been on speaking terms.

Despite his overt success, at age 80 Bogle is physically a shadow of the man he once was. Stooped, he walks with his head down, one foot turned slightly inward as he hobbles around the Vanguard campus greeting everyone whose name he can remember. He has had both his heart and a shoulder replaced. In 2008, his body started to reject the transplant he'd received in 1996, and he had to change his medication. In 2009, he had a bacterial infection that nearly killed him.

Even Bogle's clothes have suffered. "My father likes Brooks Brothers suits off the rack," says his eldest daughter, Barbara Renninger. "But for the past 15 years his health has been so precarious he always says, 'I'm not going to buy any clothes because I won't be around long enough to wear them.' As things get rattier and rattier, we have undertaken a mission to upgrade his wardrobe a little bit." Recently she took him to the Brook Brothers Outlet and convinced him to buy two shirts and a pair of pants only because it was the outlet's after-Christmas sale.

And yet Bogle's wit and intelligence remain. Or, as he likes to put it in his usual aphoristic way, "There is this wonderful story about John Quincy Adams. Somebody comes to see him in his very late years and asks, 'How is John Quincy Adams doing today?' Adams replies: 'John Quincy Adams is fine. John Quincy Adams has probably never been better in his entire life. But the house John Quincy Adams lived in is falling apart.'"

In Jack's case, the house he lived in may be crumbling, but the house he built is stronger than ever. With a 13 percent market share,[2] Vanguard is the largest fund company in the United States and one of the largest asset managers in the world. But in many ways it doesn't resemble his original creation. The foundation of a low-cost mutualized fund company owned by its shareholders is still there, but what's being built on top of it seems irreconcilable with Bogle's long-term buy-and-hold philosophy—exchange traded funds you can buy at 10 a.m. and sell at 2:30 p.m., a high-turnover hedged mutual fund, narrowly focused sector funds, high-tech online brokerage trading platforms.

Perhaps most troubling of all to Bogle is Vanguard's titanic size. "We have two things going for us here," he says. "One is the investment side, which we have a lock on; and two is the human side. We started with 28 people, and we now have 12,300, and it is that side that is the biggest challenge to Vanguard's future. How do you keep people motivated? How do you get people to feel like they are not just cogs in a machine? How do you keep the human element? It gets more and more difficult every step of the way as you get bigger and bigger."

When I looked at Vanguard's campus, it was easy to see how Bogle might think this crucial human element was dying. The image of the low-slung brown factory-like buildings where 12,300 "crew members" work was not the wholesome one I had envisioned for a company with such a cheery nautical theme. Vanguard always had a military ethos (supposedly, from an aerial view, the campus even resembles a battleship), but in the past it seemed more of a genial affectation, a romanticized allusion to a nineteenth-century war engaged in by distinguished gentlemen such as the Duke of Wellington and General Blucher, who shook hands on the field at Waterloo and then fought Napoleon side by side. But the campus I encountered seemed grim and industrial; the workers there as anonymous as shares of an index fund.

If Bogle is the deposed dictator of this financial republic, surely he is a benevolent one. He ambles around the campus greeting crew members by their first names and eats in Vanguard's rather drab cafeteria like an average schmo. At lunch, Erica, the sandwich lady at the deli counter, always welcomes him with a, "How you doin', young man?" In his office, he barks out orders to his assistants Emily and Kevin like a drill sergeant: "Emily, get me the transcript of my interview with Don Phillips at Morningstar, will ya!" And yet he does so with genuine affection. In fact, he sometimes mistakenly replaces Emily's name with his wife's. He has recently even been grieving the death of his barber, who cut his hair for the past 35 years. "To me he was always Mr. Ron and I was Mr. B.," he says. "When he died, I was totally devastated. How many people do you know that you've seen for 35 years, 10 hours a year?"

And that perhaps is Bogle's most appealing quality. Despite his evident skill in mathematics—he still reckons complex sums on his slide rule—he's a humanist at heart. He often laments the use of such short-term numbers as quarterly earnings to measure the long-term viability of companies and prefers instead to search for signs of individual integrity. "Human beings are the prime instruments for implementing a corporation's strategy," he writes. "Other things being equal (of course they never are), if those who serve the corporation are inspired, motivated, cooperative, diligent, ethical and creative, the stockholders will be well served."[3]

All of which relates to Bogle's primary gripe against the mutual fund industry—that it's more interested in gathering assets than in being a good steward of capital. Good stewards care about their clients, get to know them. But how do you get to know $1.4 trillion worth of your clients when you don't even know the names of all of your employees? Or as Bogle puts it: "How do you keep Vanguard a place where judgment has at least a fighting chance to triumph over process?"

Bogle recognizes the need for bureaucracy that comes with running a big financial institution, but he doesn't like it. In his view, money management should be a profession with high ideals, not a mercenary business that treats its clients as customers to exploit and its employees as replaceable parts. Being a true fiduciary—perhaps Bogle's favorite word in the English language—requires a relationship of trust—his second favorite. And it's easy for that sense of individual trust to erode when a money manager becomes a gigantic institution like Vanguard.

Bogle's humanism, of course, has limits. He can also be fiercely competitive. During our first lunch together with my editor Gary Krebs, I mentioned that I'd recently written a story about Pimco Total Return, the world's largest mutual fund. Jack paused from eating his roast beef sandwich, and with a serious stare said, "I would think if you combined all the accounts of our Total Stock Market Index product, we would be the biggest." He looked to his assistant Kevin for help at the other end of the table, but Kevin only smiled wryly and shook his head: "They've got $200 billion. We've got only 125." The expression of pure irritation on Bogle's face was unmistakable.

But on the whole it is safe to say that Bogle is a good man in a bad industry. "The interesting philosophical question is what kind of a different company would Vanguard have been if it had had someone in charge over the last 15 years who fought back against process every step of the way instead of someone who loved process and pushed it forward every step of the way," Bogle says with more than a little wistfulness. "I certainly would be the former, and Brennan would be closer to the latter."

Looking around the campus, it is clear to me that this is not quite Jack Bogle's Vanguard anymore. Nor is it fair to say that it's really Jack Brennan's or even the more recently installed Bill McNabb's. A more accurate assessment would be that Vanguard is not really anyone's anymore. It has grown beyond individuality to become much bigger than the sum of its parts. About the only vestige of Bogle's belief in individual achievement in this institutional behemoth is the statue of him at its center: a larger-than-life bronze Bogle in a suit with his square Scotsman's jaw and beetling brow stepping boldly onto what appears to be Plymouth Rock, evoking Jack's favorite saying—*press on regardless*. There is a picture of a much frailer-looking flesh-and-blood Bogle standing side by side in the same pose with the statue in his office. "I feel like Dorian Gray when I look at it," Bogle says.

The statue seems both a consolation and an act of revenge on Bogle's part. One can only imagine what Chairman Brennan felt walking by it every day on his way to work. And yet until he retired in 2009, Brennan was on the top of the Victory Building, while Bogle was on its bottom. "We've become more like a typical mutual fund company, more of a marketing company, more of a business instead of a profession," Bogle admits. When he dies, it is possible that Vanguard will become just another factory of finance in which dollars roll in and out like widgets on an assembly line. One hopes that it doesn't, and energetic leaders such as Bill McNabb are striving to prevent that from happening, but without Bogle's outsized personality, in many ways it seems like it already has.

Yet perhaps this book will go a little way toward preserving some of Bogle's legacy, recounting for posterity at least a portion of some of this titan of finance's greatest individual accomplishments while accurately recording and fairly assessing some of his missteps. With that in mind, I welcome you to *The House That Bogle Built*.

CHAPTER 1

The Sopwith Camel

Tucked away on a bookshelf in Jack Bogle's office beside a copy of Kahlil Gibran's *The Prophet* and Michael Novak's *Business as a Calling* is a scale model of a Sopwith Camel. The World War I biplane seems out of place in a room full of nineteenth-century naval artifacts and Vanguard memorabilia. As it turns out, it was this specific make of plane that Bogle's father, William Yates Bogle, Jr., flew for the Royal Flying Corps and crashed in the Great War.

And yet this biographical fact does little to answer the mystery of the Camel's presence. Reading the published history of Bogle's childhood in books like *Enough*, one might think it has an almost storybook rags-to-riches quality, but there are parts of his youth that he often finds painful to discuss. Truth be told, the Bogle family and its paterfamilias were on hostile terms during the final years of William's life because of his persistent alcoholism. And perhaps it is easier for Jack to focus on this bit of heroism on his father's part than to dwell on more unpleasant aspects of his past. It would go against his philosophy of *press on regardless* to do otherwise.

William Yates Bogle, Jr., was born in Montclair, New Jersey, in 1896. In 1920 he married Josephine Lorraine Hipkins, born in Brooklyn, also in 1896. Both came from wealthy, respected Scottish American families, in Josephine's case dating all the way back to the eighteenth century, when her mother's family, the Armstrongs, immigrated to the United States to farm here.

Bogle often cites his great grandfather Philander Banister Armstrong as his "spiritual progenitor."[1] Armstrong was in the insurance industry and was a bit of a firebrand. He made speeches urging the industry to lower its costs and also penned a 268-page screed called *A License to Steal: How the Life Insurance Industry Robs Our Own People of Billions.* In it, Armstrong asks readers to contribute $2.50 each to join the "Policyholders' Alliance," which would strive to force insurance companies to "disgorge three billion six hundred million dollars stolen from policyholders by dishonest laws and dishonest accountings, dishonest mortality, dishonest 'profits,' dishonest forfeitures and dishonest premiums."[2]

Interestingly enough, Armstrong also once got in trouble with the law. A 1907 article in the *New York Times* titled "Says Insurance Co. Was Built on Wind" describes how the New York State attorney general put the Excelsior Fire Insurance Company, of which Armstrong was president, into receivership after alleging that $137,500 of $300,000 invested in the company was never deposited in the bank and that instead fictitious credits were created.[3] Armstrong later wrote a letter to Governor Hughes asking for the removal of the state superintendent of insurance and accusing him of ruining Excelsior's reputation. But the damage to his credibility was enough that when his book came out in 1917, *The Insurance Monitor*, an industry publication, wrote a scathing review titled "A License to Bunk."[4] No doubt this was partially an act of retribution on the *Monitor's* part. Like Bogle, Armstrong's critique of his industry made him few friends.

In the early years of their marriage, the Bogles lived a well-to-do existence in a spacious home in Verona, New Jersey, a bedroom community not far from New York City. Though their first two children, twins Josephine and Lorraine, died at birth, they had a son, William Yates Bogle, III, in 1927. Then, on May 8, 1929, Josephine again gave birth to twins—John Clifton and David Caldwell, named after their maternal grandfather and great-grandfather. Despite the stuffiness of their namesakes, the three Bogle boys were informally nicknamed Bud, Jack, and Dave or more affectionately known as Bud-Ro, Jack-Ro, and Dave-Ro among friends. "My mother called me Jack," Bogle says. "My grandmother thought we should've stuck with John, which basically is a better name, not slangy. But Jack it is."

The Bogles had a glamorous life their children never experienced. "They were Scott and Zelda [Fitzgerald] of the '20s," Jack says. "My father was a very handsome man. They used to call him the Prince of Wales who would later become king. And my mother was glamorous and charming, and everybody loved her." The fact that his father was a war hero only added to his romantic allure. "There was a lot of patriotism back then," Bogle says. "In 1916 my father would have been 19 years old. And there was a great feeling in America that 'I want to get into this fight.' As I understand this story, my father went to Canada, joined the Royal Canadian Air Force, got transferred to the Royal Flying Corps, now the RAF, and went over to England."

Jack's first model of a successful businessman, though, was his grandfather, William Yates Bogle, Sr., who had founded the American Brick Corporation and cofounded the Sanitary Can Company, which was eventually acquired by the American Can Company in 1908 after getting into financial trouble during the crash of 1907. William, Sr., was a heroic figure in the canning industry, having been one of the first industrialists to develop and promote the sanitary double-seamed can. Previously, soldered cans would often have black flakes inside of them, a residue of the soldering process that caused fruits and vegetables to carbonize.[5] (Ironically, American Can would eventually be run in the 1980s by Gerald Tsai, a famous ex-manager of Vanguard's arch-nemesis Fidelity Funds, who would somehow turn what was once America's premier canning concern into Primerica, a financial services company that would later be acquired by Sandy Weill and the company that is now Citigroup—a sentence which perhaps encapsulates the sad history of American industry more than any other on earth.)

When Jack's father returned from the war, he worked in sales and marketing, first for American Brick, and then for American Can. In both these jobs he prospered, and the family enjoyed a genteel life. Then came the 1929 stock market crash, which had a nearly disastrous effect on the Bogles, wiping out the family's inheritance. "Their friends didn't desert them when it happened," Bogle says. "But it was a different kind of life. We never saw that first life. We saw photographs of it. They would say, 'This is how we lived before.'"

Because of their financial problems, the Bogle boys all had to go to work at a very young age to help support the family, and it was this specific period in their lives that instilled in them a powerful work ethic and belief in frugality. By age 10, Jack was delivering newspapers and magazines (*The Ladies' Home Journal, Collier's,* and *The Saturday Evening Post*) and working at an ice-cream parlor. Among his numerous other "pre-Vanguard" positions were waiter, pollster, brokerage securities runner, night reporter at the *Philadelphia Bulletin,* and pins setter in a bowling alley. The last position Bogle always said was the hardest job he ever had, resetting the pins after each crash being a dull, Sisyphean task.

Yet Bogle says he relished the learning experience and actually found an environment of growing up surrounded by wealthy, educated people yet still having to work hard to be ideal for building character. "I don't think there is anything healthier than learning that you have to earn what you want to spend," he says. "It's a great blessing. When you are working at a young age, particularly when you are dealing with the public, you learn about human relations. You learn about dealing with people; you learn about getting to work on time; you learn that sometimes bosses are really tough; you learn the customer is always right." And that goes a long way to explain why, at ages 80 and 82, respectively, Jack and his brother Bud are still working.

Though hard work didn't trouble the Bogle boys, their father's carousing did. "It always fell upon me to be the leader and to protect my younger brothers and myself against whatever kind of bad things my father got into, which was too much wine, women, and song," says Jack's older brother Bud. "I could see the damage way before they realized what was going on. And I was the guy who had to find the damn bottles of booze and break them in front of him and cry. It was horrible. It affected my mother, and it affected everybody. My father was a wonderful sentimental man, and he would cry when I'd do that, but I didn't realize that alcohol is a disease."

Eventually, their father's behavior cost him his job at American Can in the early 1940s, and that caused the family additional financial hardship, forcing them to move out of their house in Verona. For a while the Bogles house-hopped around the Jersey coast. "We went from a lovely house that my parents had built to a house we rented [in Lakewood] from my grandparents on my mother's side, probably for nothing, and then we couldn't even afford that as my father lost his job, so we had to move down to the Jersey shore," says Bud.

And yet William, Jr., was always able to find a job somewhere, as he was a very charming, talented salesman, and the boys would pitch in to make ends meet. His behavior ultimately was probably more damaging emotionally to Bud than to Jack. "I won a scholarship to Montclair Academy, which was a prestigious boys' school," he says. "My brothers weren't even aware that I'd won a full scholarship because I was the smartest kid in my eighth-grade class. And that's when we had to leave town. I tried to live with my cousin, but there was no room for me. So I lost that scholarship, and as opposed to Jack, I never studied seriously again. I was a sore loser."

Winning was always essential to Jack and Bud, and they were extremely competitive with each other. While Jack's fraternal twin, David, was more studious, artistic, and gentle, the other two boys were sports fanatics who played war games and generally spent a lot of time roughhousing. "You know we would always fight, and it was for real," says Bud. "We were really serious. I remember once we went up on a hill across from where we lived, and we started dropping rocks on each other for some reason. I mean, thick stones. We came home bloody. Another time in our basement we even took hammers and started banging on each other's heads. It was really weird, the violence."

Surely the turmoil at home must have sparked all sorts of animosity. When he was 16, Bud was so upset by having to give up his scholarship and by his father's behavior that he moved out of the house for a year to live with his uncle Clifton Armstrong Hipkins, a successful investment banker in Greenwich, Connecticut. While the twins stayed with their parents in Spring Lake, New Jersey, and attended Manasquan High School, Bud went to Greenwich High School. "I was so unhappy at home," says Bud. "To see what was going on was too much for me. So my uncle said, 'He needs a better life for a while. Maybe I can get him straightened out here.'"

Jack doesn't really like to discuss or remember the family's struggles, although he seems to have handled them better by turning inward and remaining focused on his goals. "I was a very introverted person, and I had a huge imagination," he says. "The world could revolve around me. My brothers had more friends than I did—no question about it. And I was in a lot of ways to myself. I had things I wanted to accomplish, and I accomplished them." About the problems at home he says: "I always thought that we had a wonderful, wonderful background, and having a challenged family life is a—you survive that or you don't. You survive that and you are stronger than a person who goes breezing through life thinking the world is their oyster."

By 1945, financial hardship had forced the family to move into a two-room apartment on the third floor of a modest house in Ardmore, a Philadelphia suburb. There was a master bedroom, a living room, and in between a flat expanse with a coffeemaker and a hot plate, and that was about it. Because the cooking facilities were so crude, most nights the family ate its dinners at a Horn & Hardart around the corner. "That was a cheap dining place, most famous for having automats," Bogle says. "We didn't go to the automat part. They had a restaurant, and we sat down for dinner." Anyone who has seen Edward Hopper's *Automat* painting of a woman drinking coffee alone in an empty restaurant knows how dreary such a dining experience can be.

And yet Josephine Bogle was determined that her children have a better life. With her brother Clifton's assistance, she helped her sons win scholarships to Blair Academy, a prestigious boarding school in Blairstown, New Jersey. The lovely 423-acre hilltop campus was just the right environment for the boys to escape their troubled home life. Bud went for one year and graduated in 1945, and then Jack and David followed him for two years, graduating in 1947. "My mother came to my graduation, but she was crying, and I didn't realize that she had my orders to report to the Marine Corps the very next week," says Bud. "The war was still going on." Meanwhile, when David graduated, he also enlisted and was stationed in Japan. Neither son ever saw any action.

While both Bud and David enjoyed their stay at Blair, for Jack it was truly a transformative experience. He later would say about the school, "Virtually everything I've achieved in life began with my few years there."[6] Founded in 1848, Blair Academy was an all-boys school with an enrollment of 300 during Jack's junior and senior years. Although Blair was no boot camp in Jack's day, it had some of the ambience of a military school. Students rose at 6 a.m., attended classes, worked at part-time jobs on campus, and hurried to complete their homework before lights out at 10 p.m.

Pampered students would have found Blair stifling, but Jack thrived in the atmosphere. He got his first chance to show what he could do—in academics, athletics, and the jobs he took to maintain his scholarship— and he was determined to make the most of the experience. He was driven to make his mark at Blair, to attain good grades, to please his parents, and to attend college.

That's not to say that it was easy for him at first. "While Blair was a great leap forward in our lives, the academic demands were large and the transition painful," he later remarked. "But the outcome was commensurately rewarding. I started with a miserable grade of 40 in Jesse Witherspoon Gage's algebra class, but my final grade of 100 was then thought to be the only perfect score he had ever awarded. And in Marvin Garfield Mason's English class, this demanding master drummed into me an inspirational sentence from Macaulay's essay on Samuel Johnson that I have never forgotten: 'The force of his mind overcame his every impediment.'"[7]

Jack had a particular aptitude for math. Numbers fascinated him; he could look at a stack of figures and point out an error in the computation before anyone else had started to work on the problem. He could analyze mathematical problems in his head and arrive at answers long before other students, using pencil and paper, could. His ability to use a slide rule became his trademark.

In 1947 Jack graduated from Blair cum laude. Although his senior classmates voted him most likely to succeed as well as best student, he failed by a fraction of a percentage point to be named class valedictorian. Jack was so determined to succeed that he regarded being number two (he was named class salutatorian) as a stinging defeat. He visited several of his teachers and urged them to reconsider his grades so that he could graduate number one. None would. (Even now, he does not think number two is good enough, often citing the crossword puzzle definition of "came in second," which is "lost.")

Bogle came to believe that he owed his greatest debt to Blair Academy. His success there enabled him to attend a top-ranking college, without which he may not have accomplished as much as he did in later life. As a result, repaying Blair became of great importance to him, and the bulk of his charitable contributions would be directed to Blair, eventually making him the largest single contributor in Blair's 148-year history. In 1972 he joined the board of trustees of Blair and served as its chairman from 1984 through 2001.

"Blair gave him a stable place to grow up at a time when his life wasn't so stable at home," says Chandler Hardwick, Blair's current headmaster. "It gave him a scholarship to attend. And since Jack was the beneficiary of someone else's philanthropy, one part of our endowment he created is a scholarship fund that pays for a lot of kids to come here." When Bogle became Blair's chairman in 1984, its endowment was a mere $900,000, while now it is estimated to be in excess of $61 million, thanks in no small part to his contributions and fund-raising efforts. His brothers have also donated to the school, and today there is a Bogle Hall and an Armstrong-Hipkins Hall at Blair named in the family's honor.

And yet despite all the benefits Blair provided, because of the family's limited finances, only one of the Bogle boys could attend college. The two other brothers would have to work to help support the family. With little discussion, it was understood that Jack would be the one to attend, while David and Bud would help the Bogle family stay afloat financially. Against this backdrop of responsibility and guilt, Jack became even

THE TWINS

Throughout their adult lives, the Bogle twins remained close. They engaged in friendly competition over who could complete the Sunday *New York Times* crossword puzzle first, one often phoning on Monday morning to help the other finish. Long after he graduated from college, Jack felt grateful for David's sacrifice, even mentioning it when he eulogized David, who died suddenly in December 1994. In the eulogy, Jack described himself as "the more competitive, determined, egocentric, introverted twin" and David as "the warmer, more caring, outgoing soul who seemed to place everyone else's concerns ahead of his own." Bogle went on to say, "By reason of family circumstances, David did not go on to college. But let me make it clear to you, as I always did to him, that he was more intelligent and, finally, better educated—a self-taught scholar, a voracious reader, a competent writer—than most of us who had the advantages of a Princeton education." He went on to muse about success, implicitly comparing himself with his twin: "Success is an elusive concept. David was wise enough to realize that success has little to do with money, with starting a business that grows . . . or even with writing a book. What success has to do with, I think, is personal integrity, good citizenship, giving joy and comfort and support to others . . . On all counts, David was an extraordinary success. I know that he was proud of me; you should know that I was even more proud of him."

more motivated, more determined that nothing should interfere with his success.

Bogle ultimately decided on Princeton University for his college choice because it offered a generous scholarship and student jobs that together would cover all his expenses. In his determined frame of mind, he sifted through the Princeton curriculum, majoring in economics but discovering Shakespeare, English history, and, for the first time, art history. A few courses gave him trouble. Despite his aptitude for mathematics, he found calculus a challenge, and a course in international trade was no snap. (In later years, he quipped that perhaps he owed his skepticism about investing in foreign markets to the troubles he encountered in that course.)

He particularly enjoyed the introductory economics course. Paul Samuelson's now-classic textbook *Economics: An Introductory Analysis,* published in 1948 when Bogle was a sophomore, affected him more than any other textbook. He recalled, "It opened my eyes to the world of economics, a world I never knew existed. I knew what earning and saving money was, but I never thought about economics as a body of lore, quasi-scientific or scientific." As it happened, in 1993 Professor Samuelson would write the foreword to Bogle's bestselling book *Bogle on Mutual Funds: New Perspectives for the Intelligent Investor.*

Unfortunately, while Jack was away at Princeton and his brother David was in Japan, conditions continued to deteriorate at home. Josephine Bogle was beginning to experience the symptoms of what would later be diagnosed as cervical cancer. And her husband was becoming increasingly difficult to manage. Having just been discharged from the Marines, Bud Bogle was finally forced to confront his father. "I had taken the liberty of telling my father he had to leave because I was the only one at home at that point," he says. "We had rented a little place, sharing a house, and I said one day to him, 'My mother, your wife, and I can't take it anymore.' So I cried and put him on the train to New York. Later, I would meet him over there sometimes, and he got another job. He was always able to get some kind of a job. I even visited him when he was at a dry-out place in Staten Island."

Jack tells a different, slightly more sanitized version of this story: "They never divorced. They separated—it wasn't working out well. We lived in Philadelphia, and somewhere along the way, my father left for New York. I think it was mutual consent. So we just had to struggle. By that time my brother William was out of the service, and he was able to help support my mother. I went off to Princeton and supported myself."

By his junior year, Bogle had stepped up his search for something that would set him on a path to success. The search bore fruit when he began thinking about a topic for his senior thesis in fulfillment of his economics major. He was determined to tackle a subject that had not been analyzed to death by hundreds of other econ students. One day he was browsing through magazines in the university library when he came upon an article headlined, "Big Money in Boston" in the December 1949 issue of *Fortune*. The article examined Massachusetts Investors Trust, which, with assets of $100 million, was then the largest mutual fund in the United States.

Few people at that time had heard of the mutual fund industry. Small and centered in Boston, it had only $2 billion in assets under management. Noting that the industry represented only about 1 percent of the total savings of American families, the article acknowledged that "mutual funds may look like pretty small change." But *Fortune* concluded that the mutual fund industry was "a rapidly expanding and somewhat contentious industry of great potential significance to U.S. business." Bogle was intrigued by the combination of a bland present ("small change") and a bright future ("great potential significance"); he decided that he had found his thesis topic. The thesis would give him the opportunity to conduct original research, apply his writing skills, and learn in depth about an emerging industry. In retrospect, he later said about his fortuitous finding of such a provocative topic: "I thought I was in heaven."

Bogle spent his junior and senior years working on the project. During his senior year he had an A average, and in June 1951 he graduated from Princeton magna cum laude, in large part because his 123-page thesis, "The Economic Role of the Investment Company," received a grade of A+. Not only did he demonstrate a grasp of how the industry worked, but he knew enough of its strengths and weaknesses to offer prescriptions for its future. It was as if the thesis had been drafted not by a college student but by the head of a mutual fund company.

Although some have called the thesis prescient, in many ways it revealed more about Bogle's idealistic character and the future of Vanguard than it did about the fund industry at large and the speculative miasma it would eventually become. Among the five future economic roles the thesis ascribed to the mutual fund industry, three were to be a source of venture capital for businesses to help the economy grow, a positive influence on corporate management, and a stabilizing factor on securities exchanges. By and large, none of these predictions would come true, and as Bogle himself would later reveal in books such as *The Battle for the Soul of Capitalism,* quite the opposite has become the case. Mutual funds are now an endless source of speculation and the primary enablers allowing some of the worst corporate excesses to occur.

Yet the thesis provided an early glimpse of the principles that would serve as the intellectual contours for Jack's Vanguard. Even in its very first chapter, Bogle noted that "funds can make no claim to superiority over the market averages, which are in a sense investment trusts with fixed portfolios; e.g., the stocks composing the particular 'average.'"[8] He also would write, "Management can scarcely be expected to buy so that the fund can stay ahead of the market when the very securities that it buys are a part of that market."[9] Already the germ of the idea for the low-cost index fund was planted with these statements.

Bogle went on in his thesis to chastise mutual fund companies for concentrating their efforts on marketing their funds rather than on serving the interests of investors. He recommended curtailing advertising abuses and focusing on costs as a crucial factor in the choice of an investment. He finished this argument, as if anticipating his later concern that the industry's interest in asset gathering was supplanting its focus on its responsibility of trusteeship, with this citation: "The principal function of investment companies is the management of their portfolios. Everything else is incidental to performance of this function." The Bogle philosophy was in place, etched by a 21-year-old who was preaching to an industry he knew only as an outsider.

Unfortunately, neither of Jack's parents lived to see him put his theories into practice at Vanguard. After graduating from Princeton in 1951, Jack returned to Philadelphia to work and live with his mother. Once more the Bogle boys were together under the same roof, but within a year their mother was dead of cervical cancer. "I couldn't help my mother until I graduated, but I graduated in '51 and she died in February of '52," Bogle says. "It was really kind of tragic."

Surely, Josephine's final months were anything but pleasant. "The shocking thing was when she was bedridden for the last year, the three of us had to give her injections of Demerol," says Bud. "In those days that was the drug for pain. We would have to wake her up in the night and give it to her, and it wasn't much fun. We had a two-bedroom apartment, and one of us slept in her room, and we finally had to hire a nurse so we could go to work."

All three Bogle boys idolized their mother. It didn't help that in the same year their father also died in Bellevue Hospital of a stroke. Jack was only 23 at the time, and for him talking about this period of his life is almost too painful for words. When I asked if his father was helping out financially during Josephine's final months, he said, "I don't know, but I don't think he was able to. I think he would have if he could have. You know when you're a kid you don't—I wish I had done a better job." And then he started crying.

On the surface, neither Jack nor Bud blames their father for what happened to the family. If anything, they still love and miss him and have some genuinely fond memories of him. "Every Christmas my father would scrabble together presents," says Bud. "It was often used stuff, not the greatest, but we never knew. We never felt deprived. Christmas was always wonderful, and we remember how much he loved setting up the railroad tracks and the Lionel trains and stuff."

Or as Bogle puts it: "I think he was a man who was not very strong, but who did his best. What are you supposed to say about that?" Not a lot, apparently, if you ask him. Bogle believes instead in focusing on the good that his father brought into the world and pressing on regardless. And that's probably the reason why until this day he has a model of the Sopwith Camel on a shelf next to his desk.

CHAPTER 2

The Mutual Fund Pioneer

John Bogle's first employer in the mutual fund business was Walter L. Morgan, who began his career in the 1920s when he founded the Wellington organization, the forerunner of Vanguard. By the time he stepped down as chairman of Wellington Management Company in 1967 and then three years later as chairman of Wellington Fund, he had become one of the longest-serving leaders in the mutual fund industry and one of the longest-serving presidents of any U.S. corporation. For years, almost up until his death at the age of 100 in September 1998, he continued to work twice a week at what would ultimately be renamed the Morgan Building in his honor at Vanguard's Malvern campus. The only mutual fund pioneer who lived longer was Philip L. Carret, founder of the Pioneer Fund in 1928; he died at the age of 101, also in 1998.

Born in Wilkes-Barre, Pennsylvania, on July 23, 1898, to a storied eighth-generation Welsh American family—which included Daniel Boone among its ancestors—Morgan learned at an early age what a miserable experience it was to lose money when he borrowed some from a family member to buy some oil stock that proved worthless. Adding salt to the wound were his father's losses in the stock market and his grandfather's losses in a Montana gold-mining company and a trolley line. Morgan promised himself that, whatever he did later in life, he would do his best to protect his earnings. He would never veer from that conservative philosophy.

In 1920, Morgan graduated from Princeton University, where he majored in money and banking. But even a Princeton education did not impress his uncle, Charles Loxley, who worked in a brokerage office. "You're not worth a damn to anybody," Loxley told his nephew. "I want you to go out and learn something." Morgan obliged, but only because his uncle found him work at the Philadelphia office of the accounting firm of Peat, Marwick, and Mitchell. There, for $28 a week, Morgan learned as much as he could about how financial statements were produced.

A few years later, Morgan asked for a raise. When he was turned down, he began his own accounting firm, giving investment advice to its numerous clients. Morgan came to believe that he could provide investment guidance more efficiently and profitably by combining accounts into a single large fund. Through such a fund, he could offer potential investors a wider range of securities than they could otherwise afford to hold. With the mutual fund industry still in its infancy, Morgan had few colleagues with whom he could converse about his ideas. One was W. Wallace Alexander, the Philadelphia investment counselor who, in 1907, began the Alexander Fund, the progenitor of the mutual fund in the United States.

In the late 1920s, most investment companies were closed-end funds. They pooled money from a group of investors and issued a fixed number of shares at an initial offering. Once the initial offering was completed, investors could neither purchase additional shares nor sell their existing shares through the fund company. Instead, they had to buy or sell shares in the stock market through a stockbroker.

The founding of Massachusetts Investors Trust (MIT) in March 1924 marked a radical departure from the closed-end concept. As an "open-end" fund—later called a mutual fund—it continuously offered new shares to investors and redeemed existing shares at their net asset value. This open-end feature gave investors daily liquidity to convert their investments into cash. More important, it gave smaller investors, with little money and expertise, the ability to enjoy the same returns as larger investors by pooling their money and investing it under the watchful eye of a professional investment adviser.

Investors were slow to accept Massachusetts Investors Trust; only some 200 people invested in MIT during its first year of operation. But as other funds appeared, including Incorporated Investors and State Street Investment Trust, Walter Morgan began to get the itch to join this new industry by starting his own mutual fund firm. With encouragement from his grandfather, who told him he was better off starting his own business "even if it was a peanut stand," Morgan raised $100,000 to form a mutual fund by pooling his own savings of $25,000 with funds from friends and family. He incorporated his new mutual fund on December 28, 1928, and opened for business the following July.

Morgan was helped in those early days by investment banker A. Moyer Kulp and by Brandon Barringer, head of the investment management division of First Pennsylvania Bank in Philadelphia. Morgan first called his fund the Industrial & Power Securities Company, but then changed its name to Wellington Fund in 1935, a designation reflecting Morgan's love of British history and his admiration for the "Iron Duke" of Wellington, who had defeated the French at Waterloo in 1815.

Thus the three existing funds—MIT, State Street, and Incorporated Investors, all equity funds—were now joined by Morgan's Wellington Fund. Morgan's fund, though, was unique among the open-end funds in that, for safety's sake, it provided substantial allocations (30 percent at the outset) to high-quality corporate and government bonds, rather than investing primarily in common stocks. Hence, it was known as a "balanced" fund; at the time, it was the only one of its kind offered to the public. By committing a portion of its portfolio to bonds, which were less risky than equities, the balanced fund was meant to appeal to the cautious investor. Adding to the conservative hue of Wellington Fund was Morgan's policy, in contrast to that of the closed-end funds, of avoiding leverage (borrowing against fund assets to magnify its gains or losses), a move aimed at discouraging speculation and risk taking.

In early 1929, hundreds of closed-end investment firms were managing most of the investing public's assets—roughly $7 billion. In contrast, there were only 19 open-end funds like Morgan's, managing a mere

$140 million in assets. Many of the closed-end funds, however, were time bombs. Directed by professional managers who were expected to produce miraculous returns, most closed-end funds traded at premiums of 100 percent or even 200 percent over the actual market value of their investments. When the stock market collapsed, many of the funds' premiums quickly turned into discounts, with the funds' shares selling for less than the market value of the investments they held. Compounding the problem was the excessive use of leverage by closed-end managers, which amplified losses when the crash occurred. By 1933, the share prices of closed-end investment firms had plummeted, on average, by 90 percent. Many went bankrupt.

In retrospect, Morgan had chosen the worst time in U.S. financial history to launch a new investment firm. However, because Wellington Fund's investment policies entailed less risk than those of its competitors, to say nothing of the closed-end funds, they mitigated the effects of the crash on the fund's investors. Three factors in particular benefited Wellington Fund: (1) as an unleveraged fund, it did not rely on borrowed money; (2) as an open-end fund, it could redeem shares on demand, eliminating speculative swings from premium to discount; and (3) as a balanced fund, it had a large position in bonds and cash reserves, which cushioned the fund from the steep stock market drop. In fact, during the summer of 1929, Kulp and Barringer, who were the principal investment consultants to the Wellington Fund, had urged Morgan to reduce the company's common stock allocation from 75 percent of its assets to 33 percent. Taking their advice, Morgan sold, for example, Curtis Publishing at $124 per share; three years later, the stock was worth $5 a share.

While other investment firms fared miserably in the three-year stock market crash—MIT, for instance, lost more than 60 percent of its asset value—Wellington Fund lost far less and attracted modest public attention. Its assets grew from $100,000 in July 1929 to $500,000 at the end of 1933. Never doubting that his mutual fund was a wise investment choice, Morgan exuded self-confidence: "I knew we could do a better job of investment management for most people than they could do for themselves,"[1] he said. Because of the success of funds like Wellington in combating the worst effects of the Great Crash of 1929, most new investment companies founded after that debacle were open-end.

The growth of Wellington Fund led to some changes at Morgan's firm. Its management, which had been handled by W. L. Morgan & Co. from 1929 to 1933, was now in the hands of the newly created Wellington Management Company. Morgan also hired a distribution and management team. As investment dealers in Philadelphia, and then on the rest of the East Coast, began to learn about Wellington Fund and its impressive performance record, its assets started to grow. By December 1934, the fund's assets had reached $600,000; a year later, they passed $1 million; four years later, they topped $5 million.

World War II brought new investment opportunities. When Germany moved into Poland in 1939, Morgan purchased a number of stocks that he correctly predicted would benefit from the fighting. By the end of the war, Wellington Fund's assets had grown to $25 million. With this impressive growth, Morgan needed new staff. He hired Kulp to head the investment management division full time, and Alvin J. Wilkins, whose firm had been the leading seller of Wellington Fund shares since 1935, to head the national sales and distribution team. Joseph E. Welch, who had been associated with Wellington Management Company since 1937, became executive vice president. (He would become president in 1959.) Under the leadership of this team of senior executives, the fund's growth continued. In 1949 the fund's assets reached $100 million; within two years, assets had nearly doubled, reaching $190 million.

By mid-1951, Wellington Fund was the fourth largest mutual fund in the United States, and Walter Morgan was clearly established as a pioneer and an industry leader. While Morgan could not have known it at the time, the young fellow Princetonian he was about to hire would, in time, step into his shoes as an industry leader and become a pioneer of a very different sort.

CHAPTER 3

"He Knows More About the Fund Business than We Do"

After graduating from Princeton in 1951, Jack Bogle narrowed his career options to banking and investments. He was finding it difficult to choose between offers from the Philadelphia National Bank and Boenning & Company, an old-line Philadelphia brokerage firm, when a third offer arose. During Bogle's senior year at Princeton, Walter M. Geisler, the manager of the Elm Club, Bogle's campus dining club, encountered Princeton graduate Walter Morgan and suggested that he hire Bogle, mentioning Bogle's thesis on the mutual fund industry. Initially, Morgan resisted, believing that Princeton students were spoiled, but eventually he agreed to have his staff interview Bogle—still with no intention of hiring him.

The interview was conducted by two senior Wellington executives, A. Moyer Kulp and Joseph Welch. They were impressed enough by Bogle's thesis to suggest that Morgan read it as well. Morgan was fascinated by Bogle's astute observations on the industry, still a tiny one with just 100 funds and roughly $2.5 billion in assets. Morgan observed to his associates, "He knows more about the fund business than we do."[1]

Morgan marked the thesis with notations and sent it to Wellington's 50 employees, urging them to pay attention to Bogle's views.

Bogle was coy during the interview process, letting the firm know that others were courting him and that he had a solid offer from a bank. Morgan, in turn, toyed with Bogle, saying, "I don't know what we're going to do with you. We don't need anybody." But he had already decided to hire Bogle, so at last he pulled out all the stops: "Jack, you'll never get anywhere in a bank. Join us. We're a growing company. You'll be one of the top guys eventually."

Bogle was in a quandary. He was flattered by Morgan's interest, but he thought that a banking career offered greater stability, believing that in 5 or 10 years the bank would still be there, and so would his job, important considerations for someone who valued stability as much as he did. (Ironically, Philadelphia National Bank would eventually be merged out of existence in the 1980s.) Some also considered the little-known mutual fund industry disreputable because of those risky, highly leveraged closed-end funds that had collapsed with the stock market in 1929. But Bogle also had some reservations about taking the bank job. The bank seemed old-fashioned, and although he had conservative instincts dating back to his childhood experiences in the Depression era, Bogle had an adventuresome streak. He longed for the chance to be creative and entrepreneurial, and a bank was unlikely to give him a chance like that.

Hoping for clarity, he talked to his cousin, Edward L. Winpenny, who worked as a research analyst and broker, but instead he got the ambiguity he deserved: "You wrote a thesis about the mutual fund business," his cousin reminded him. "So you ought to be able to figure out if you want to be in the business or not. You should be able to figure out better than anyone else how to deal with the risk." The more Bogle contemplated his options, the less concerned he became about the risks of accepting Morgan's offer. Bogle began to see the mutual fund industry as brimming with opportunity, and although Wellington was a small company, it seemed poised to expand and diversify. He decided to accept the Wellington offer.

In mid-1951, the entire mutual fund industry had only 1 million shareholder accounts and managed just $3 billion in assets. The industry was small in comparison with the $54 billion in life insurance reserves, $74 billion in savings deposits, and $50 billion in U.S. savings bonds. Put differently, mutual funds managed only about 1.5 percent of the $178 billion total of these savings programs. Just two top funds at the time—Massachusetts Investors Trust and Investors Mutual—accounted for 25 percent of the industry's assets.

Bogle went to work for Wellington on July 5, 1951. At the time, the company managed only Wellington Fund, with net assets of $194 million and a 6.2 percent share of the industry's assets. He initially worked at the Wellington organization's office on Walnut Street in Philadelphia. Still not quite sure what to do with him, Morgan stuck him, in Morgan's words, over in the corner.[2] Bogle needed little time, though, to get Wellington's senior management to take notice of him. He was intelligent, he understood the functions of each of the departments, and he showed no hesitation about busying himself in the work of those departments.

James C. French, who would later rise to be senior vice president for equity trading, joined Wellington just days before Bogle did. When Bogle arrived, he took an empty desk in French's office. Joseph Welch, Wellington's executive vice president, gave the two some clerical work to do. At the time, in an effort to boost fund sales, Wellington Fund had just begun to offer a program that permitted shareholders to automatically reinvest their dividends at the fund's net asset value. Welch assigned to Bogle and French the task of demonstrating the plan's benefits by showing, for example, what a $10,000 investment made 15 years earlier would have been worth in 1951 with all dividends reinvested. As they went through the calculations, Bogle made a bet that he could perform the calculations more quickly with his slide rule than "Frenchy" could with his state-of the-art rotary calculator. Bogle won the bet.

Bogle and French were responsible as well for calculating the average cost of each investment held by Wellington Fund. To calculate the fund's net asset value, brokers phoned twice a day—once at midday and again when the markets closed—and gave the prices of each of the fund's investments to the accounting department. At the end of each week, French, using his calculator, would calculate the average costs, while

Bogle checked the calculations with his slide rule. After a few months of this kind of clerical work, Bogle was promoted; he was given the task of assisting Morgan with writing fund reports, corresponding with shareholders, and carrying out a variety of administrative chores.

By 1953, Bogle was becoming a public relations voice for the company, speaking to sales representatives and industry groups. But Morgan knew that slotting Bogle as the head of a department would prove too limiting for someone with his wide-ranging abilities. In 1955, therefore, he formally made Bogle his assistant, a position he held for the next seven years, using the post to learn all aspects of the business. Morgan gave his protégé a long leash, and Bogle thrived on the independence. He ranged throughout the company, dabbling in analyzing stocks and bonds alongside the investment department staff, number crunching with the accounting department, writing letters for Morgan, and preparing annual reports and memos to the sales department. He knew how to wander through the thicket of charts and graphs and put together statistics that shed the best light on the company. Morgan and Welch were sometimes harsh taskmasters, scrutinizing Bogle's work until they felt it was perfect, making him correct letters as many as five times. With these role models, it is little wonder that, when he ran the company in later years, Bogle was the same kind of tough boss.

By the late 1950s, Bogle had enough self-confidence to try to persuade Morgan to adopt a new investment strategy. For years, the Wellington formula had been a success; its conservative strategy had helped it survive the 1929 crash and the Depression of the 1930s. The distribution system that Morgan built up after World War II, combined with the rapid expansion in the mutual fund industry, enabled Wellington Fund's assets to grow to $280 million by December 1953 and to $600 million by December 1957.

By the late 1950s, however, the Wellington Fund formula was being questioned. Bogle believed that balanced funds were losing their attraction and that Wellington Management Company should branch out by introducing new funds. Rival funds were riding the bull market in stocks and making much more money for their shareholders than Wellington was.

THE SUMMER OF 1956

In the summer of 1956, Bogle invited friends to join him and his brothers at their Bay Head, New Jersey, summer cottage. The play *My Fair Lady* had opened that spring and taken Broadway by storm. Bogle sat glued to the hi-fi listening to the show's tunes. When he was not listening to music or Giants baseball games, he generally was out on the basketball court tossing a ball around with his brothers, or playing a "vicious" game of Ping-Pong with his Princeton schoolmate and good friend John J. F. (Jay) Sherrerd. Bogle was also around the Sherrerd home in Merion, Pennsylvania, a good deal of the time. He was captivated by Sherrerd's sister, Eve. (They had met when he was 20 and she was 15; he was especially impressed that she shined her brother's saddle shoes.) Eve had graduated from Shipley School in 1951 and Smith College in 1955. Shortly after her college graduation, Bogle began courting her. They became engaged in July 1956 and were married on September 22 of the same year. They built a solid family life with six children: Barbara, born in 1957; Jean, 1958; John, Jr., 1959; Nancy, 1961; Sandra, 1967; and Andrew, 1971.

It would not be easy to persuade Morgan to change. He had always considered it an advantage to focus the business on a single fund—and a balanced fund at that—and he had always been able to convince brokers that balanced funds minimized the risks of investing. Morgan's associates, too, genuinely believed that selling a fund composed of only stocks was too risky and therefore might breach their fiduciary duty to shareholders. As evidence, they pointed to the lackluster performance of firms that ran common stock funds, noting that their share of mutual fund assets was not rising. Morgan's team also argued that running more than one fund would increase the firm's expenses. Because few firms had experience operating a fund family, the conventional wisdom was that if the management company doubled the number of funds it ran, its expenses would automatically double. A second fund, for example, might require a second portfolio management team, and so on.

Bogle, though, looked into the future and saw risks for Wellington Management Company if it clung to a one-fund strategy. He believed that the firm should have not only a balanced fund but a growth fund, an income fund, and several bond funds as well. But it was still too early for him to have much of an impact on Morgan and the other senior executives at Wellington; to them, the balanced fund was gospel, and the idea of starting new funds was heresy. (Later, Vanguard officials liked to say that Morgan's strategy of concentrating all resources on a single product was similar to Henry Ford's market approach: "You can have any color car you want, just so long as it is black.")

Wellington Management Company was not alone in its resistance to new funds; few other fund companies at that time were prepared to branch out and start additional funds. Even those that did, did so cautiously. Bogle laughed when he recalled Massachusetts Investors Trust's early decision to start a second fund. Typical of the industry's lack of creativity in those days, it chose the name Massachusetts Investors Second Fund. (Later it was renamed Massachusetts Investors Growth Stock Fund.)

Bogle was determined to get his point across: if in later years the industry was to innovate to attract new customers, Bogle reasoned, a single-fund strategy represented burying its collective head in the sand. In his Princeton thesis, he had identified many potential new funds, including "funds composed of tax-exempt securities, funds with the securities of industries in given geographical areas, and special investment Companies to serve the specialized demands of pension and trust funds." Picking up on this theme, he wrote a rudimentary business plan for his company, envisioning the day when Wellington would sponsor a range of funds, becoming a sort of fund supermarket.

Even as Bogle was trying to make his case for expanding Wellington Management Company's operations, it was becoming clear that Morgan was grooming Bogle to become his successor. The promotion would have to be earned, though, and Bogle would have to demonstrate initiative and creativity. Despite his own reluctance to change, Morgan wanted his replacement to be an activist. In seeking to transform Wellington's corporate strategy, Bogle was meeting the activist test.

Bogle repeatedly heard all the arguments against change, but he also listened to investors and dealers urge Morgan to develop a stock fund. By 1958, Bogle was convinced that it was time to act, so he suggested to Morgan that Wellington sponsor a pure equity fund.

By this time, Morgan was ready for a change as well, sensing that balanced funds were indeed losing popularity, that the public had been enticed by higher-risk equity funds, and that risk was no longer the ugly word it had been in the post-Depression era. Making such a fund more appealing to him was the fact that a few recent Wall Street underwritings of new mutual funds had succeeded in raising substantial initial capital. An initial public offering for the new mutual fund would help it to quickly accumulate "seed capital" to achieve economies of scale, the better to enhance Wellington Management Company's profits.

Concluding that there was money to be made—by shareholders and by sponsors—in managing equity funds, Morgan gave his blessing to Bogle, who labored with great urgency on the prospectus for the Wellington Equity Fund. (Bogle and Morgan were hardly more imaginative than their rivals at MIT when it came to choosing the name for their new fund; it would be renamed Windsor Fund in 1963.) To Morgan's credit, when Bogle proposed taking the company down what was then considered a revolutionary path in 1958, Morgan agreed that changes were necessary, although he portrayed the new fund in less-than-revolutionary terms, noting that its purpose was simply to provide a managed common stock program for those investors who believed that they had enough fixed-income investments.

The creation of the new fund was a turning point in Bogle's career at Wellington Management Company. He had gone out on a limb and succeeded, and now Morgan was telling others that Jack was on the fast track to lead the company some day. Meanwhile, the birth of the new fund meant that Bogle was given his first fund officer title: secretary of Wellington Equity Fund. Along with the title came some mundane tasks, such as keeping minutes, helping with correspondence, and hanging pictures. Leading a revolution was not all fame and glory.

CHAPTER 4

A Marriage Made in Heaven

lthough many observers had their doubts as to whether Wellington Equity Fund would be successful, it got off to a very good start. Buoyed by a sharply rising stock market, the fund's original underwriting proved to be one of the three largest mutual fund underwritings up to that time, raising initial assets of more than $33 million, a sum that Wellington Fund had taken 17 years to reach, and totaling $44 million by the end of 1959. This favorable beginning established Wellington Equity Fund as a major new entrant into the industry and carried Wellington Management Company's total assets under management across the $1 billion threshold at year-end, helping to maintain the Wellington organization's standing as one of the largest mutual fund firms in the nation.

Despite Wellington Equity Fund's auspicious beginning, the early 1960s were not kind to the Wellington organization. A new generation of investors was emerging, with more money at its disposal and a greater inclination to take risks with that money. Wellington Management Company, though, was still heavily dependent on the conservative

Wellington Fund—regarded as following an increasingly archaic style of investing—which produced 95 percent of the company's revenue. If balanced funds, with their heavy bond component, had made sense to a generation for whom the 1929 crash was still a vivid memory, the new generation thumbed its nose at bonds. Less concerned about preserving its hard-earned money than the previous generation, new investors looked at the hot new "high-performance" funds and dreamed of making a killing despite the risks. Out of step with the new, aggressive style of investing, Wellington Fund's share of industry assets declined, as the market share of balanced funds in the aggregate fell from 30 percent in 1955 to 20 percent in 1964.

HEART TROUBLES

Just as his career was switching into high gear, Jack Bogle suffered a major personal setback. For most of his life he had enjoyed good health; in 1956, he had a physical examination, and the physician described his heart as normal[1]—undoubtedly the last time such an assertion was made about his heart. On a cool Labor Day weekend in 1960, Bogle was playing tennis with his brother-in-law, Jay Sherrerd. Bogle was 31, Sherrerd 30, so there was no reason to believe that a simple tennis game might cause either of them physical harm.

Yet as Bogle was starting to serve in the middle of the first set, he suddenly felt pain and saw a large flash of light before him.

"Are you all right?" Sherrerd asked his brother-in-law, who looked dazed.

Bogle whispered, "Jay, I have to stop a minute." After he caught his breath, he said, "You're not going to believe me, but I think I just had a heart attack." Both men laughed, because the idea seemed preposterous.

Incredibly, the two men resumed play. Bogle even won the set, the first time that summer he had beaten Sherrerd. But he began to feel ill again, so they retired from the court, chatting about business as Bogle leaned against a tree. Bogle improved enough to drive home, but once there, he again began to feel worse, so his wife, Eve, took him to a doctor, who diagnosed the problem as a heart attack and put him in the hospital, where he remained for six weeks. "I was in a decent amount of trouble,"[2] Bogle recalled.

Bogle would later suffer five more serious heart attacks. Once, while he was playing squash, his heart suddenly stopped. His opponent, Philadelphia brokerage executive Raymond H. Welsh, revived him by pounding on his chest. Another time he collapsed in a Philadelphia train station after leaving a meeting, leading to another stay in the hospital. He also had a cardiac arrest in a school auditorium; two doctors were present and used CPR to get his heart beating again. Living on borrowed time became routine, for the doctors had gloomily predicted in private that his chances of long-run survival were small.

Although his colleagues were worried about him, Bogle continued to function at full throttle. He had always been a driven, determined man, but now he had something to be truly driven about. He now knew that his life was precarious, but he was not prepared to retire from business and sit at home. "It's something that has made life . . . rather difficult for me, although I've always plunged into everything I had to do with great enthusiasm and concentration, and that probably ain't bad if you've got a malady," he says. "It's certainly better than doing absolutely nothing, waiting for the Grim Reaper to come."[3]

The addition of Wellington Equity Fund in 1958 had not improved the company's bottom line very much. Although it had done well in its first three years, the new fund met with disaster in 1962, when the fund lost a quarter of its value. The portfolio manager was replaced in June 1964 by John B. Neff, who would serve in that capacity until his retirement 32 years later, all the while building a reputation as a true investment guru, along with Peter Lynch and Warren Buffett. But at the time about the only passion Wellington Equity Fund aroused came from several Wellington Fund shareholders who sued the fund, claiming that it had capitalized unfairly on the Wellington name and insisting that Wellington Fund had exclusive rights to the name. The suit was settled in 1963, when Wellington Equity Fund agreed to change its name to Windsor Fund.

Although Wellington Management Company crossed the $2 billion mark in assets under management in 1965, sales of its funds' shares continued to decline in 1965 and 1966. To remedy this situation, the company enlisted one portfolio manager after another, but investment performance continued to lag, purchases of fund shares continued to fall, and share redemptions remained dangerously high. Bogle believed that the company needed something new to boost its assets, and there was no question in his mind what that something was. High-performance ("go-go") funds had taken hold in the industry, climbing from 21 percent of new sales in 1955 to more than 40 percent in 1964 and 64 percent in 1966. Bogle knew, however, that growing a performance fund in-house would not be easy, as the experience in building Windsor Fund had proved.

From Bogle's vantage point, one viable alternative was to buy the adviser to an already existing fund and merge it into Wellington Management Company. At the time, it seemed like a novel idea. Bogle had already tried to grow the company when he helped to develop Windsor Fund, but a merger would represent a far more sweeping change. As a result of a series of promotions, Bogle wielded a big enough stick to hope to pull it off. In 1962, Morgan had promoted him to the position of administrative vice president; then, in 1965, Bogle was named executive vice president and was told by Morgan and Welch to do whatever it took to turn the company around.

Bogle was excited at the prospect of a merger. A merger could provide what Wellington was sorely lacking—investment management talent. By getting the company out of its conservative rut, a merger could boost sales and assets and quickly turn the company around. It might even help move the company beyond mutual funds, allowing Wellington Management Company to break into the institutional investment counsel business. Bogle saw no downside to the idea. "If you're stupid as well as impatient," he said later with a touch of bitterness in his voice, "you say, 'Let's merge. We'll solve all the problems at once. It will be a marriage made in heaven.' It actually isn't that simple. Basically, mergers are always bad for one side or the other."[4] In fact, a favorite mantra of Bogle's in subsequent years would become, "Growth must be earned, not bought."

Unfortunately, Bogle arrived at this conclusion only with the benefit of hindsight. One day over lunch with John C. Jansing, the national fund sales manager for Bache & Co., one of the largest brokerage firms of the day and Wellington's major distributor, Bogle casually mentioned that Wellington Management Company was having difficulties and that he wanted to acquire a firm with investment talent and a high-powered performance fund. Jansing knew of a group of investment advisers who might fit the bill. "If you are really thinking of doing a merger with a 'hot' fund, there's a group in Boston," Jansing said. "They also have a good counseling business run by four people you'll be very comfortable with."

The phrase *hot fund* was one that Bogle would grow to detest, running counter as it did to his conservative, stay-the-course philosophy. His ears perked up, however, when he realized that Jansing was talking about the Ivest Fund, the hottest fund in the business; it had been the number one performing fund for the previous five years, but was still relatively unknown to most investors. The fund had been enormously successful almost from the very start, accumulating $1 million in assets by the end of its first year of operations in 1959. Over the next six years, it enjoyed a total return of 389 percent—as its assets under management grew to $17 million—while the Standard & Poor's 500 index rose by only 94 percent during the same period. Ivest's investment strategies were decidedly more aggressive than either Wellington Fund's or Windsor Fund's, but that might be the key to a turnaround for the Wellington organization.

Managing Ivest Fund was a counseling firm called Thorndike, Doran, Paine & Lewis, Inc. (TDP&L). Its four partners were all under the age of 35, but the firm's total assets under management had already reached $200 million. In addition to Ivest Fund, TDP&L had built a thriving counseling business, including among its clients corporate pension funds, college endowments, religious institutions, and labor unions. Wellington Management Company had not been in the booming pension fund management business, but Bogle thought that its synergies with the mutual fund industry might benefit the firm. The partners of TDP&L were soon to be featured in a book by Martin Mayer, *The New Breed on Wall Street,* which was subtitled, ironically (as later events would prove), *The Men Who Make the Money Go.*

A courtship of TDP&L began in late 1965. Bogle negotiated the details of the merger opposite Robert W. Doran and W. Nicholas Thorndike, who represented the four partners of TDP&L. If matching personalities mattered, the merger negotiations should have failed before they even started. Bogle was outgoing, exuberant, and brimming with self-confidence; Doran, on the other hand, was quiet to the point of shyness, not given to emotion, and reluctant to stand in the spotlight. Unlike Bogle, he was not inclined to insist that only he knew what was right. As someone who preferred to paint a problem in broad strokes and leave the details to others, Thorndike was also very different from Bogle, a hands-on man who made sure he grasped every detail.

Oddly enough, however, Bogle and Doran instantly felt a good chemistry. "I liked him," Doran said later. "I found him very bright, very enthusiastic. He was vital, alive. Those initial conversations were very, very positive."[5] Doran had a huge stake in getting along with Bogle because, despite the high-performing Ivest Fund, TDP&L was relatively small and lacked a powerful distribution system for marketing its fund. Wellington Management Company, in contrast, was strong in distribution, offering administrative and marketing capabilities that would mesh with the Boston firm's investment management skills. A merger between Wellington Management Company and TDP&L could produce a powerful new force in the mutual fund industry.

The Boston partners were flattered to be courted by a giant in the field, and they enjoyed the prestige of being in the same room with the legendary Walter Morgan. Then aged 67, Morgan felt that Wellington had to become a more aggressive enterprise. Nearing retirement and proud of Bogle's achievements, Morgan made a point of attending cocktail parties with the Boston group, regaling them with tales of the mutual fund industry from the 1920s and 1930s. With his shock of wavy white hair, Morgan exuded a mixture of self-confidence and stability, of conservatism and maturity, that put the Boston partners' minds at ease about the merger. Yet the Bostonians had their own confidence that they could provide the ailing Wellington and Windsor Funds with a shot in the arm. Robert Doran, for one, told Bogle, "I can't wait to get my hands on Wellington Fund." At least for the time being, those words were music to Bogle's ears.

In the spring of 1966, following nine months of negotiations, the merger with TDP&L was moving toward a positive conclusion. In response to a comment that the merger seemed out of character for him, Bogle simply said, "Everyone likes a deal."[6] Bogle was so confident that the merger would be free of conflict that he agreed to a division of Wellington Management Company's shares that granted the four Boston partners a 40 percent ownership position of the company's voting power, greater than his own 28 percent position. In his eagerness to complete the merger, Bogle underestimated the peril he had placed himself in by relinquishing so much voting power. "I had this naive idea that I could always persuade one of them to my position and that would give me 38 percent to the three others' 30 percent," Bogle later said. "Naive? Stupid might be more like it."[7]

As the merger talks between Wellington Management Company and TDP&L proceeded, Walter Morgan arranged it so that he would retain control of Wellington Management Company, at least for the time being. Rather than give Bogle and the Boston partners part ownership immediately, he determined that they would be given such ownership only after the merger was five years old. During that five-year period, the voting shares that would give them partial ownership were to be placed in what Morgan described as a voting trust. This plan would give the directors a chance to consider whether or not the merger was working. So while the merger agreement was reached on June 6, 1966 (in retrospect, it probably should've been considered an omen that the date of a merger that was supposed to be a marriage made in heaven is commonly referred to in popular culture as the birthday of Satan), the voting trust would terminate on April 1, 1971, at which point the shares would be distributed according to plan—40 percent for the Boston partners, 28 percent for Bogle, with the remainder owned by public shareholders.

These shares, of course, represented ownership in Wellington's management company, not the Wellington funds. As it would turn out, that distinction would prove critical to Bogle's future. Most mutual fund companies effectively have two boards of directors, one for the management company and one for the funds themselves. Inevitably this leads to a conflict of interest between what is best for the management company and what is best for fund shareholders. Often management's desire to maximize profits is literally at the expense of fund shareholders, who are overcharged. Fund directors are supposed to act as a check on managerial abuses, but since a mutual fund is little more than a corporate shell with no employees or officers, fund boards generally behave like lackeys to the management company. The management company establishes the fund and handpicks the fund's board, and these handpicked and often very well-compensated fund directors authorize the management company by contract to provide all the services required by the fund. It is in their capacity to make such authorizations, as we shall soon see, that fund directors have a great, albeit rarely utilized, power.

After the merger was completed, it was agreed that Bogle would become president and CEO of the merged firm. From the standpoint of his health, however, 1967 was not a very good year. He was frequently hospitalized, and at one point he was away from his desk for six weeks, one of the longest periods of time he had ever missed work.

Suffering from a condition known as heart arrhythmia, Bogle traveled to the Cleveland Clinic that spring to have a pacemaker installed. The clinic was the leader in cardiac catheterization and at the time was one of only a few hospitals in the country that installed pacemakers. Bogle was in such poor condition that a senior cardiologist in the Cleveland heart program gloomily predicted to him that he would never work again.

Bogle has retained a vivid, nightmarish image of the surgery required to implant the pacemaker: "They put the pacemaker in with a saw. They spread [my] ribs and cut a great big hole in my chest. Then they dropped the damn thing in. It almost killed me. Up to then, that was the closest

I'd ever been to death. I went into cardiac arrest. I got through that very luckily."[8]

Shortly after the pacemaker was installed, it became clear that his heart problems were not improving, so Bogle asked around for the names of the best cardiologists in the United States. The consensus was that he should turn to Dr. Bernard Lown at the Brigham & Women's Hospital in Boston. Lown was a pioneer in the emerging treatment of heart arrhythmia and had invented the defibrillator, which shocks irregular hearts into normal rhythm.

Putting Bogle through a motorized treadmill test, Lown expected that, like other heart attack victims, Bogle would fail the test after 7 minutes or so, but Bogle lasted 18 minutes, which would normally indicate that his heart was strong. Yet through careful observation, Lown detected a rare, potentially lethal condition in which the heart beats rapidly and becomes ineffective to function as a pump. Fortunately, Lown found that Bogle could identify the circumstances under which the arrhythmia occurred: when he arose early in the morning, and when he engaged in vigorous exercise. Knowing that enabled Lown to put Bogle on a regimen calling for high dosages of medication at those times. Bogle followed the doctor's instructions, which generally worked effectively for the next eight years.

After the merger, Wellington Management Company became more aggressive in its investment management strategies. By 1968, the bulk (70 percent) of its new sales came from Ivest Fund. From an asset level of about $1 million at the end of 1961, its first year of operation, Ivest had accumulated assets of almost $50 million by the end of 1966, and $340 million two years later. During the five-year period ending in 1966, Ivest Fund was the top-ranking fund in the country, ahead even of Edward Johnson III's Fidelity Trend Fund and Fidelity Capital Fund, managed by the legendary Gerald Tsai. (Tsai left Fidelity in 1965 to start the Manhattan Fund and his own fund organization. Manhattan Fund, like Ivest Fund, was to plummet in value as the go-go era ended in 1969.)

Reflecting Wellington Management Company's new aggressiveness, Wellington Fund's annual report dated November 30, 1967, had a different tone. In that report, Chairman Walter Morgan suggested that, while

Wellington Fund's investment objectives of "conservation of principal, reasonable current income, and profits without undue risk" still made sense, change was needed to bring the portfolio into line with modern concepts and opportunities. "We have chosen 'dynamic conservatism' as our philosophy," Morgan wrote. *Dynamic conservatism* was an odd phrase for the conservative Walter Morgan to use. Believing in a slow, steady, cautious approach to investing, he had always avoided go-go adjectives like *dynamic*. The new Walter Morgan was undoubtedly the product of a changing industry and the influence of Bob Doran, Nick Thorndike, and Walter Cabot; the words may have been attributed to Morgan, but the people behind the Ivest Fund seemed to have dictated those words.

Following the merger, the climate at Wellington Management Company had changed, seemingly for the good. Ivest Fund continued to fly high, its assets reaching $340 million by the end of 1968, a two-year record of growth that was remarkable in the burgeoning mutual fund industry, even among the go-go funds that had so attracted investors' attention. Trying to capitalize on the public's love affair with aggressive funds, Wellington Management added more funds. Explorer Fund (investing in stocks of emerging companies) was introduced in December 1967, followed in 1968 by Technivest Fund (investing on the basis of technical stock market indicators), and in 1969 by Trustees' Equity Fund (despite its name, trading on the basis of short-term trends in stock prices and engaging in rapid portfolio turnover). All of these new funds were highly aggressive and risk-oriented; all were run out of Boston; and all were greeted with enthusiasm by brokers and investors. Ultimately, all of them would fail to provide competitive returns, and all would tumble sharply in the ensuing bear market in 1972–1974. By 1977, only Explorer Fund survived.

Although conservative funds were anathema to the Boston group, in 1970 Bogle recommended that the firm launch a bond fund. Bogle had always had contrarian instincts, and he was inspired by an *Institutional Investor* cover illustration that depicted bonds as dinosaurs. Here was a chance for him to test his instincts by creating a bond fund, then almost universally considered an endangered species in the industry. (In 1970, there were just 10 bond funds; today there are 1,518.) The Boston group was shocked by the recommendation, and the Wellington Management Company directors would have none of it.

"The stupidest idea I've ever heard of," argued Stephen Paine, one of the four Boston partners and a particular thorn in Bogle's side. "Bonds are yesterday."

"No," replied an irate Jack Bogle. "Bonds are tomorrow." Bogle pressed on with the idea to the fund directors, who were more sympathetic. When Bogle offered a compromise by recommending an income fund comprising 60 percent bonds and 40 percent high-yielding stocks, both the Wellington Management Company directors and the fund directors approved it, and Wellesley Income Fund began operations in mid-1970. Nonetheless, Bogle persevered in his belief that an all-bond fund would be successful, and, early in 1973, both boards approved the formation of Westminster Bond Fund.

As 1973 began, Wellington Management was running 10 funds and had aggregate assets under management of $2.6 billion. Only three of the funds, however, were of any notable size. Although its assets were declining, Wellington Fund's $1.3 billion was one-half of the company's entire asset base. Windsor and Ivest, the other sizable funds, had grown to an aggregate of $900 million in assets.

With his health restored—at least for the time being—Bogle was hitting his stride, overcoming a sometimes cantankerous Wellington Management Company board, adding new funds, and building the company's narrow base into a broad-ranging fund family.

CHAPTER 5

Irreconcilable Differences

Throughout the late 1960s, Bogle was saying publicly that the merger was working better than anyone had expected and that it would be a boon to the company's stockholders, "even though," Bogle acknowledged later, "I was very skeptical that the merger would be good for me."[1]

Indeed, the merger slowly began to trouble Bogle, who started to question the rhetoric of the Boston partners and to doubt that they were as good at the investment management business as they claimed. He noticed, for example, that Ivest Fund's long-term performance record had been inflated by attaching to it the results of a predecessor private fund called Professional Investors, which was a private investment pool and not a mutual fund at all. He also questioned personnel decisions, including Doran's choice of Walter Cabot to handle the day-to-day management of the funds. Although Cabot was dubbed "Moses" because he was supposed to lead Wellington Fund to salvation, just as the biblical Moses was to lead the children of Israel to the Promised Land, his performance left a great deal to be desired relative to that of his biblical namesake. In fact, the fund's returns deteriorated alarmingly during the 1967–1974 period.

Bogle began to sense that the merger was fragile and vulnerable. Worse than that, he began to fear that the Boston partners' true intention was to seize control of Wellington Management Company, a fear that proved to be accurate. The Boston partners were troubled by Bogle's dominant personality. Doran and Thorndike claimed to believe in participative management, in which decisions are made only after all the pros and cons are debated. The only participant Bogle thought worthy of being included was himself. Barbara B. Hauptfuhrer, a member of the Wellington Fund board, asserted, "[Jack's] way is *the way*. Bob Doran was more of a consensus taker, a very thoughtful man, low-key in his approach." [2]

Geography played a role in the mounting tension as well. Boston focused its labors on the pension management business, a world driven by a select group of professionals who sold their wares to institutions. Philadelphia, in contrast, was actually running mutual funds, then a retail business aimed at consumers. Carrying out such different responsibilities, the Boston and Philadelphia executives had little empathy for one another. Compounding the problem, management of the funds was split between the two—Wellington Fund and Windsor Fund in Philadelphia; Ivest, Explorer, Morgan, Technivest, and Trustees' Equity in Boston. The Boston partners wanted to consolidate the entire operation in their city, which infuriated Bogle as a loyal Philadelphian.

Differences in investment policies added further fuel to the ire, particularly the issue of how to run Wellington Fund. As a balanced fund, it had typically invested about 60 to 65 percent of its assets in equities, with the remainder in fixed-income securities. The Boston group, which had the ultimate investment responsibility for Wellington Fund, wanted the fund to invest more heavily in equities—but with lower representation in traditional blue-chip stocks—and less heavily in fixed-income securities. The Philadelphia contingent, loyal to the fund's original objectives, thought that it should remain a conservative balanced fund, emphasizing high-grade securities. There were other differences in investment strategy. The Boston group adhered to a momentum strategy, hoping to ride the stocks currently favored by the market, while shunning whichever stocks were out of favor. In Philadelphia sat John Neff, manager of the

Windsor Fund and the closed-end Gemini Fund (established in 1967), a confirmed contrarian who seemed to want to buy any stock the Boston group wanted to sell.

As time went on, Bogle lost respect for the Boston group, believing that they knew less than he did about the business. He could have tolerated their aggressive investment strategies if those strategies had worked, but soon there was no disguising that the resentment had evolved into open, bitter hostilities. As the bitterness among the partners progressed, it began to spill over into Wellington Management's board of directors, in which the Boston group was heavily represented. As Bogle noted, "Wellington Management's board and I were in a real power struggle. I wanted to control everything, and so did they." [3]

Against this background, Walter Morgan, at the age of 72, decided to step down as chairman of the funds. The logical choice to succeed him was former Wellington Management Company president Joseph Welch, a fund director and a veteran Wellington executive. Yet Welch, also advanced in years, stepped aside quietly when Morgan suggested that Bogle was the better choice.

Even as he assumed this position of leadership in the organization, Bogle's relationship with the Boston group continued to deteriorate. Feeling that his back was against the wall in the feud, he thought about resigning. He even considered mounting a proxy fight against the Boston group, but it was by no means certain that he would win, and he was not sure he'd have the heart to put the company, in his words, through the wringer. [4]

Though Morgan's voting trust for Wellington terminated as planned on April 1, 1971, without notable event, the official transfer of power to the Boston Group meant that the handwriting was on the wall. For a while both sides did their best to keep the peace, but on September 26, 1973, one month after Wellington Management Company moved from Center City in Philadelphia to suburban Chesterbrook, near Valley Forge, the Boston Four met with Bogle. At the meeting, Doran informed Bogle that the four wanted more control over mutual fund activities. The dialogue was ominous, and Bogle felt that the die had been cast. Then, on November 14, 1973, Doran visited Bogle. "Things are just not working out," Doran said with more emotion in his voice than he usually betrayed. "I've talked to the others, and we think it would be best if you left the company." He added that there would be a financial settlement, suggesting a $20,000 annuity over 15 years; in return, Bogle would be required to relinquish his 4,000 shares of management company stock.

Although Bogle's heart stayed steady, his voice did not. "I've heard of few stupider things than that," he sneered. "I've done an effective job. I've gone the extra mile to assure communications and harmony with all of you. I am just tired and annoyed enough by all of this to say, 'Make me an offer in writing and have it signed by all four participants.'" Bogle's proposal, however, was little more than idle talk, for he had no interest in taking the money from the company as part of a deal that required his resignation and ceding control to the Boston partners, his opponents, who would pay nothing for the privilege.

Fifteen days later, Bogle and Doran met again. When Bogle made it clear that he had no intention of resigning, Doran presented Bogle with two options. One was to leave the Wellington organization completely; the other was to leave the management company, but to stay on at the funds solely in an administrative capacity, in essence as a chief clerk.

In an effort to discover whether there was a way to save the situation for himself, Bogle talked with some of the Wellington Management Company directors. But when the round of calls to the board members was over, he knew that the cause was lost. Doran had the votes, and he was going to be fired. Although the management company's board had all but made its decision, the Boston group wanted to keep the matter from going before the separate fund boards, so the group members pressured Bogle to agree to a financial settlement.

Within the Wellington Management Company organization, each fund was required by federal law to have its own separate board of directors, the majority of whom had to be considered independent of the management company. Yet, as at most fund companies, the same handpicked "independents" served on every fund's board to save on the expense of hiring different directors for each fund and to make it easier for management to retain its stranglehold over the funds. This one group came to be known as the fund board. Three members of Wellington Management—Bogle, Thorndike, and Doran—although not in the majority on the 11-member fund board, were also interested directors on it. With them overseeing every fund board meeting, the idea that their handpicked directors might stage some sort of revolt and go against the Wellington board's wishes was truly outlandish.

By law, contract negotiations between a management company and a fund's board are supposed to be at "arm's length," but in practice this is virtually impossible because of their incestuous relationship. If the management company decides to make changes in the officers who serve the fund, the fund as a practical matter has no real option other than to simply accept the designated individual. The only recourse the fund has is to terminate the contract with the management company. Yet for directors to do this would be like the employees of a machine shop firing the boss who hired them. It virtually never occurs. Wellington would be perhaps the one great exception, and this in part only because Bogle, as a former management executive, goaded the board in a specific direction.

By 1974, the funds' independent board members were beginning to sense that the feud was getting out of hand. Director Barbara Hauptfuhrer wrote to colleague Charles Root on January 3 of that year: "I am concerned about the possibility of reports of Wellington dissension causing damage to the shareholders. For example, such reports could conceivably trigger panic redemptions which would not permit orderly liquidations and therefore would be very harmful to the shareholders. Can this be avoided?" Apparently the answer was no, for four days later Bogle informed Doran that he would not accept the request for his resignation.

The formal effort to relieve Bogle of his posts as president and CEO would undoubtedly come at the next meetings of the Wellington Management Company board, scheduled for January 23, 1974, and the fund boards, scheduled for the following day. Bogle knew that the only weapon left in his arsenal was his brainpower, so he planned to use the board meetings to talk about what he had done for the company and to propose creative ideas for the future. To prepare for these meetings, he wrote a 20-page memo that he distributed to the independent directors of the fund boards.

In his memo, Bogle touched on an idea that had been in his mind for several years, an idea that he called mutualization. Starting in the early 1970s, he had begun to believe that Wellington's financial difficulties were partly the result of the company's organizational structure: the management company had all the power; the funds had none. In his view, the organizational structure was wrong because it permitted the management company to base its decisions on what was good for the company's executives and its shareholders rather than on what was necessarily good for the fund shareholders. Big profits for the management company did not always translate into strong returns for fund shareholders. In fact, the opposite was often the case, since the higher the management fees and profits were, the lower fund shareholder returns would be as a result.

Bogle believed that control and decision-making authority should be taken from the management company and turned over to the fund shareholders. Accordingly, he began to champion his proposed mutualized structure, which would transform Wellington Management Company from a publicly owned company into one that looked more like a mutual life insurance company. In essence, the fund boards would take over the management company, internalizing the various functions the management company originally handled. Bogle estimated that costs to the funds could be reduced by 40 percent, equal to the annual profits of $2 million then being earned by Wellington Management Company on its fund activities. Not surprisingly, none of his early discussions about this idea had met with much enthusiasm, particularly on the part of the Boston group.

Still, in his January 1974 memo, Bogle proposed that the Wellington group of mutual funds acquire Wellington Management Company and its business assets. Wellington Management would then become a wholly owned subsidiary of the funds and would serve as their investment adviser and distributor on an "at cost" basis. Bogle would remain as head of Wellington, which would retain the mutual fund assets, and the merger with Thorndike, Doran, Paine & Lewis would be dissolved, and they would go their separate ways. Bogle wrote: "This conversion from the traditional industry pattern in which the mutual funds are served by an external investment advisor is, I believe, unprecedented in the mutual fund industry."

Yet Bogle's proposal fell largely on deaf ears. On January 23 the board of Wellington Management voted 10 to 1 to request him to resign. (The one vote in Bogle's favor was John Neff's, while Bogle recused himself.) When he rejected this proposal, a second vote was taken, this time firing him outright, with 10 votes in favor and 2 abstentions (Bogle and Neff). Doran was then elected president of Wellington Management Company.

Although he was devastated by the Wellington Management board's decision, Bogle knew that the odds weren't so stacked against him at the funds board. Of its eight independent directors, there were five who had earlier served solely on the boards of funds managed out of the Philadelphia office, and three who had earlier served solely on the boards of the funds managed out of the Boston office. He suspected that directors might vote along geographic lines. Since Doran, Thorndike, and he were also on the fund board, Bogle figured that this might mean a 6 to 5 vote in his favor. His chances improved when board member Charles Root, noting the conflicts of interest, recommended that the three interested directors recuse themselves. The board agreed, and the potential favorable vote, in Bogle's opinion, moved to 5 to 3. His chance of winning had risen.

Before the official fund board meeting commenced on January 24, the fund directors met in an executive session and heard from Doran and Thorndike about Bogle's dismissal. Charles Root, who had never liked the Boston group, was convinced that Doran expected the boards to approve the dismissal without discussion, but he had no intention of being bullied by the Wellington Management board members. Like Bogle, he sensed what the rest of the industry up to that point had not— that the fund boards had power over the management company that as yet had not been exploited. The ace up their sleeve was the legal right to select for the funds not only their own chairman and president, but whatever management company they desired.

Once the official meeting began, the directors conducted a wide-ranging discussion. With Bogle's dismissal hanging in the air, the directors thought it legitimate to raise a whole set of issues, all revolving around the relationship between the fund boards and Wellington Management Company. Should the fund boards continue their relationship with Wellington Management? If so, who should be responsible for the investment advisory function? Should other investment managers be asked to handle some of the funds? Although there were no easy answers, what was significant was that the questions were being discussed at all. The most urgent question, however—whether Bogle should continue as president and chairman of the fund boards—had to be answered immediately.

Bogle weighed in with his own views. "You don't have to fire me," he insisted. "This is your corporation. You oversee these mutual funds on behalf of their shareholders. Wellington Management Company doesn't own the mutual funds. This is a great opportunity for us. The funds ought to have their own voice." Bogle must have sensed some support around the table, for he went on to argue for his mutualization proposal. It seemed unthinkable for the head of the funds to advocate so radical an idea, given the lock that management company boards had historically maintained over their fund boards.

The Boston partners were skeptical. They saw Bogle's mutualization proposal as nothing more than a clever, last-minute tactic designed to salvage his job. Bogle anticipated the attack and defended himself by pointing out that he had raised the issue several years earlier. In fact, in a July 1972 profile, *Institutional Investor* had reported that, "Bogle had explored the possibility of mutualizing all or part of Wellington Management Company . . . to have the management company largely owned by the funds," and that he had questioned whether "a business like ours should be publicly owned and try to make a lot of money."

After asking Doran, Thorndike, and Bogle to absent themselves, the independent directors returned to executive session to thrash out these issues. They concluded that Bogle should direct a major study—which would be called the Future Structure Study—that would examine whether and how the Wellington complex should be restructured. Bogle would be paid his regular salary and would examine the means by which the funds "might best obtain advisory, management and underwriting services in the future." Among the options to be studied by the fund board were:

1. Continuing the present relationship with Wellington Management Company.
2. Splitting up Wellington Management's institutional investment counseling and retail mutual fund management businesses.
3. Seeking one or more new investment advisers, managers, or underwriters.
4. Internalizing the funds' services by acquiring Wellington Management Company's mutual fund management assets.

Doran and Thorndike were shocked by the fund board's decision. They had remained convinced that the fund board would never take on the management company. All along they thought that they had solved the "Jack Bogle problem" and that Bogle would not fight back. Misreading him had cost them dearly, for now he appeared to be in a strong position to eviscerate Wellington Management Company. Mutualization was no longer pie in the sky; it had a chance to become a reality. The significance of Bogle's coup was that now he could get his hands on the management company's most precious assets—the funds themselves.

Bogle had no way of knowing whether the Future Structure Study would produce the kind of restructuring he advocated, but he was convinced that restructuring the mutual funds' relationship with Wellington Management Company would benefit fund shareholders. He pointed out, for example, that the CEO of the management company was also the CEO of the funds and that the management company directed the entire package of services—administration, investment advisory, and distribution. Together, these two critical factors created what he derisively called a "Gordian knot" that bound the funds to the management company. Only by cutting the knot and distancing the funds from Wellington Management could the funds negotiate lower investment counseling fees, either with Wellington or with other investment advisory firms. Costs could also be kept low by shifting ownership from the publicly held management company to the funds themselves, eliminating the need to generate profits and dividends for shareholders of the management company. In fact, the existing management structure was directly opposed to shareholder interests. The fees charged to generate profits for management company shareholders reduced the total return of fund shareholders.

Bogle began preparing the Future Structure Study a few weeks after the January 24 board meeting. The funds' independent directors held numerous meetings with the key personalities, including Bogle, Doran, and Richard Smith, special counsel to the independent directors. Smith played a significant role in shaping the outcome of the study by insisting that the final decision by the fund board's independent directors be unanimous. Smith knew that Wellington Management Company would do its utmost to block Bogle's mutualization proposal, which, if successful, would dismantle Wellington Management, but only after years of court battles. When Bogle learned of Smith's position, his heart sank. He knew that mutualization was now a long shot for the near future, since he was unlikely to get unanimous backing for it by the independent directors.

Proposals on other options flew back and forth, and the paperwork piled up. Bogle was relentless: he would prepare 50-page memos, outlining arguments the very least of which he knew the Wellington Management Company group would find outlandish. Wellington representatives would then write rebuttal memos; Bogle, in turn, would rebut the rebuttals.

As the study progressed, regular monthly meetings of the fund board, which might normally have lasted only seven hours—from 9 a.m. to 4 p.m.—often became day-and-a-half to two-day sessions, lasting long into the night. In addition, there were numerous special meetings and committee meetings. Thousands of pages of documents were presented to the fund board for analysis. But finally, at the March 20 board meeting, Bogle presented "The Future Structure of the Wellington Group of Investment Companies" study, in which he boiled down all the arguments into three options:

1. Wellington Management Company would continue to provide the funds with investment management and underwriting services, but the funds would provide for themselves all administrative services.
2. Wellington Management Company would continue to provide the funds with investment management services, but the funds would provide for themselves all administrative and underwriting services.
3. The funds would acquire all the investment company activities of Wellington Management Company, thus internalizing all investment management, administrative, and underwriting functions.

The independent directors' agreement that any decision on their part should be unanimous would, in Bogle's judgment, be likely to preclude option 3. Though he suspected that the radical step of mutualization was dead for the moment, he continued to press this proposal, hoping to negotiate down to what he regarded as the next best alternative— internalizing the administration and distribution functions. He was interested in controlling the investment management function, where the profits were earned, but at least control of the distribution function would give him the truly arm's-length advisory relationship with Wellington Management Company that he wanted.

This compromise would still represent a radical change, for Bogle knew that special counsel Richard Smith was concerned that the SEC might not allow the funds to pay for distribution directly out of shareholder assets. Bogle countered that the management company was already indirectly using shareholder assets to cover the cost of distribution, and it was charging higher advisory fees to cover those costs.

At the March 20 meeting, Wellington Management Company representatives opposed Bogle's mutualization plan on a number of grounds. They argued that Bogle was exaggerating the savings to be gained by the various options. They also noted that internalization would neither give the funds more independence nor diminish conflicts of interest between the funds and their management company. "It would," they argued, "only make the funds more dependent on their internal management and substitute new and novel conflicts of interest for the well-recognized and regulated ones posed by external management."

On June 20, 1974, the board finally made its decision by the unanimous vote that Smith had sought. The directors had, in the end, chosen the most conservative and least contentious option: investment advice and distribution would be left to Wellington Management, administration to the funds themselves.

Bogle was pleased that he had won something, even if it was a side of the business that was not very interesting to him. In retrospect, he realized that he had been thrown only a few crumbs. He would be, at least for the moment, little more than the "chief clerk," as Doran had earlier envisioned. But he was already planning to expand his responsibilities, even if some of them had not been formally agreed on.

An immediate problem was to define what constituted administrative functions. Wellington had been administering the funds for years, so the question had never arisen. Now, however, the fund board had to be specific about who was going to do what. What became known as the "belly-up theory" became the guiding principle: the funds would be responsible for any function that, if left unfulfilled, would force the company to go belly up—to cease operations. Accordingly, all tasks that had to do with legal compliance, financial accounting, shareholder records, ensuring that the funds' prices reached the newspapers on a daily basis, and balancing and auditing the books were to be handled by the funds.

While such responsibilities may have seemed insignificant, Bogle's partial victory was a remarkable achievement for someone who only six months earlier had been fired from his job, and he knew that he now had something to build on. "Everyone must have known I was going to try to make something more out of this," he said.

Everybody except perhaps Wellington Management. At the end of the summer, George Lewis, one of the Boston group, asked Bogle, "Aren't you going to be bored in your new job?"

With a smile on his face Bogle thought to himself, "Little does he know what's coming."

CHAPTER 6

From the Deck of
HMS Vanguard

On Friday, August 1, 1974, Bogle was driving north on the New York Thruway with his 14-year-old son, John, Jr., to their summer home in Lake Placid. At the same moment, back in Philadelphia, the fund directors were debating whether to retain the Wellington name. The informal title of the 11 funds, the Wellington Group of Investment Companies, had been used to identify them as the property of Wellington Management Company. At issue was whether Wellington Management Company would continue to use its corporate name or whether the funds could use it as their group identification.

The issue was not a trivial one to either Bogle, Wellington Management Company, or the fund board members. Certain members of the fund board, still bitter over the struggles earlier in the year, wanted to deprive Bogle of the Wellington name's goodwill. Others, however, were concerned that if the group had to take a new name, the funds would in essence be starting from scratch as a mutual fund company; all of the name recognition that had been built up over the years would evaporate.

For its part, Wellington Management Company saw the Wellington compromise as the start of Bogle's attempt to take control of all the funds' activities. For him to demand use of the Wellington name seemed presumptuous.

Bogle stopped at a rest area on the thruway and put in a call to Charles Root and Richard Smith, who gave him the bad news: the directors had agreed that Wellington Management Company should not be required to change its name. The funds could not continue (even if they wished to) their use of the Wellington Group name, though the name Wellington Fund would remain. Livid, Bogle told them: "This is the last straw. That is such a stupid decision. I'm out of here. I'm going to resign. Leave the whole business."

"We've come all this way," Root said. "Forget the name. The name isn't important. You can call the new firm any name you want. Then go out and make it the best name in the mutual fund industry."

Bogle quickly reconsidered the matter and relented. He chose, however grudgingly, to take the sensible course and search for another name. Most of the names he thought of reflected the historical tradition of the Duke of Wellington. And the ones he liked best began with the letters W or V. At one point he considered the name Victory in honor of Admiral Horatio Nelson's flagship HMS *Victory*, on which Nelson had died at the Battle of Trafalgar in 1805. Bogle concluded, though, that under the circumstances the name seemed a little too much.[1]

He finally came upon a name by accident. The fund directors had pressured the management company to allow him to keep his old office, but the prints on his walls, which were the property of Wellington Management Company, had been removed. He needed to replace them. An art dealer happened to call on Bogle in September to show him some Napoleonic War prints. Bogle bought a dozen, including six that depicted the Duke of Wellington's land campaigns and six, taken from a book published in 1825, that depicted Lord Nelson's naval battles. In appreciation, the dealer gave him the book, which had several pages that explained each battle. Browsing through it, Bogle came upon some stirring words that Nelson had penned nearly 200 years earlier: "Nothing could withstand the squadron under my command. The judgment of the captains, together with the valor and high state of discipline of the officers and men of every description, was absolutely irresistible." Nelson wrote these words from the deck of his flagship, fresh from an over-whelming victory over the French fleet at the historic Battle of the Nile in 1798; the flagship was the HMS *Vanguard*.

Feeling that he, too, had been through a battle and had let nothing stand in his way, Bogle wanted to command a modern-day Vanguard, a name that to him resonated with themes of leadership and progress—of being "in the vanguard." He was proud of his selection of The Vanguard Group as the new collective identifier for the funds. His decision was ultimately, if reluctantly, endorsed by the directors, who were apprehensive about the name. Thinking back, Bogle said, "The name Vanguard was almost too good to be true. It's as if it jumped off the page."[2]

Bogle thought it was imperative to create a new core corporate entity, which made more sense than having each fund handle its own administrative chores independently. Accordingly, he created a new corporation, formally named The Vanguard Group, Inc., which would be owned jointly by the 11 funds and, in keeping with the Wellington compromise, would provide administrative services to them. The company's expenses, including the salaries of its employees, were to be charged to the funds at cost, and the company would make no profit. No SEC approval was needed to create the new company, though the company did have to apply to the SEC for the right of the funds to share administrative costs. Pending SEC approval, The Vanguard Group of Investment Companies was incorporated on September 24, 1974. The 380,000 shareholders of the funds—Wellington, Windsor, Ivest, Explorer, Gemini, Trustees' Equity, Exeter, Wellesley Income, Morgan Growth, Westminster Bond, and Fund for Federal Securities—would be served by the new company.

With a staff of 59—of which 19 were in the executive and administrative groups, and 40 in the fund accounting group—Bogle continued as president of each of the funds, earning the same salary that Wellington Management Company had been paying him, that is, $100,000 annually. The portfolios of the funds continued to be supervised by Wellington

Management Company, which also continued to distribute the shares to the public through stockbrokers. Vanguard was responsible for keeping the funds' books and records, filing tax returns and official reports to government agencies, and handling other administrative functions that Wellington Management Company had previously performed. Typical of the administrative functions that the company took on were shareholder record keeping and share transfers, which an outside vendor had handled for Wellington, but which Vanguard decided, soon after its charter was approved by the boards, to internalize.

In a sense, when he started Vanguard, Bogle was starting from scratch, and he wanted others to judge him as a business leader based on his efforts at Vanguard. He talked of the Vanguard Funds as the only "mutual" mutual funds, a noble experiment, a test of whether a mutual fund complex could flourish under a new method of corporate governance, a new set of rules, and a new philosophy. Because The Vanguard Group was owned by its constituent funds, any profits it earned would be returned to the funds. While most mutual fund companies existed to make profits, Vanguard was unique in that it operated at cost, with only the interests of fund shareholders in mind.

When a senior executive from a Vanguard competitor said to him, doubtless in jest, "By giving the client a fair shake, you're going to destroy this industry," Bogle knew that he was on the right track—that too many mutual fund executives were putting the desire to earn profits for their management companies above the desire to earn profits for their fund shareholders. On another occasion, the same executive exclaimed, "Bogle, if you had to get into charity, why did you have to pick this fucking industry?" Bogle decided that in addition to launching a new firm, he was going to launch a crusade to transform the mutual fund industry.

Bogle would have preferred to start his new enterprise when the economy was flourishing, but unfortunately it was in the throes of a serious recession. Although the stock market was just starting to shake off the effects of the severe 1973–1974 bear market, the net cash flow of the Wellington—now Vanguard—funds had been negative for 40 consecutive months, a trend that would continue for 40 more long months, until January 1978. "The ghastly period of attrition," Bogle called those 80 months, when vastly reduced fund purchases by new investors were overpowered by huge redemptions from existing shareholders. In total, the net cash outflow was $930 million, equal to 36 percent of the funds' assets when the avalanche began. From its very creation, then, there were serious questions about whether Vanguard would survive and whether the fledgling company would have enough capital to keep the operation growing—in short, whether the Vanguard experiment would work. Though it was not an auspicious time to found a company, Bogle said he looked forward to getting "the fund shareholders out of the back seat and into the driver's seat."

The Vanguard Group immediately sought to establish a new, more independent relationship with Wellington Management Company. By diminishing Wellington Management's administrative responsibilities, the new arrangement quickly allowed Vanguard to reduce by $1 million—from $7.4 million to $6.4 million—the annual fees it had been paying Wellington. Beyond that, Bogle's goal was for Vanguard to be able to terminate part or all of Wellington's investment advisory services if required because of poor performance, high costs, or service quality. In fact, the funds already had that power, because their contracts with Wellington Management Company, like similar contracts in the industry, could be canceled with 60 days' notice. In reality, though, the management company held the funds hostage by retaining the distribution function it performed for the funds collectively. As long as Wellington Management Company distributed the funds' shares and absorbed the costs of doing so, the fund directors felt that they could not simply pull the plug on any individual fund's investment advisory contract.

Although Bogle wanted, as he said, "independence from our investment adviser and corporate and administrative self-sufficiency for the funds," he denied that the funds intended to abandon Wellington Management altogether. At the time he said, "Don't interpret [the Wellington compromise] as a halfway step in replacing Wellington Management Company. That's not been contemplated. We're trying to put our funds in the same posture as any pension fund, university, or foundation with money to invest, giving the funds the ability to deal with Wellington Management Company at arm's length. Under the new setup, our adviser will have greater incentive to perform because the contract is at stake." He added that Vanguard's eye would be solely on "the shareholders' interests in terms of the funds' expenses, the investment advisory fees they pay, and the funds' performance."[3]

On February 19, 1975, the company announced that the SEC had approved its proposal to reorganize itself as The Vanguard Group of Investment Companies. Proxies were soon distributed to shareholders, whose approval came at meetings held on April 22. Vanguard began operating on May 1, 1975, the newest player in an industry comprising 390 U.S. mutual funds, whose combined assets totaled $45.9 billion. The board of directors of the funds remained in place, becoming the new Vanguard board—an arrangement that troubled Bogle, for it meant that two of his adversaries, Doran and Thorndike, would still face him across the board table. With no intention of ceding to them any of his powers as president of the funds, Bogle developed a good rationale for removing them from the board: "If we're going to be independent," he told the board, asking for Thorndike's removal, "let's really be independent. Let's not have any Vanguard director associated with any fund's investment adviser." The board concurred: Thorndike left the board in 1976, Doran in 1977.

Early in its existence, Vanguard struggled with name recognition. Although many people recognized the name Wellington, few had any idea who or what Vanguard was. Because of the company's lack of identity, many of the staffers at Vanguard were afraid that the new arrangement would not work—and year after year of declining assets seemed to confirm those fears. At the same time, a sense of exhilaration somehow penetrated the gloom. The very fact that there was no real path or model to follow in their building of Vanguard created in the staffers a sense of camaraderie that helped them overcome the difficult days at the company's founding.

There was a lot of grunt work at the beginning, little of it terribly creative, but no one seemed to mind. One example: in the aftermath of the internalized administration, Ray Klapinsky had to prepare proxies for the shareholder meetings of the 11 funds, and revise and update all the funds' prospectuses. But even such nitty-gritty work was performed with enthusiasm. Said Karen West, who became vice president and controller at Vanguard, "We all thought it was very exciting, all this Wall Street activity. You'd listen to the news . . . and think that this could affect what I'm doing tomorrow. You felt a part of things. You were not just making widgets."[4]

The Vanguard Group needed this sense of excitement, for as a private company owned by the funds, it was not a candidate to go public. Given Bogle's aversion to company executives cashing in at the shareholders' expense, no one there was going to get rich quickly. Some were surprised. Ian MacKinnon, who would arrive at Vanguard in 1981, admitted, "I didn't realize until a year later that there wasn't a piece of the action to get, that I had signed up with a mutual fund company where there was no equity. I discovered, not to my dismay but to my surprise, that this was not a small investment company, but a small mutual company owned by the funds themselves, owned by the shareholders of the funds."[5] Word got around the mutual fund industry that one paid a financial penalty by going to work for Vanguard. Vanguard did little to dispel that reputation, but within a few years it would develop a unique plan that made every employee a partner, sharing in the firm's profits. Nonetheless, Bogle continued to believe that the members of his crew shared his idealism and worked toward a higher purpose: the welfare of fund shareholders. Bogle had gotten his way.

CHAPTER 7

Cutting the Gordian Knot

During the late 1970s, the only bright spot at Vanguard was its money market mutual fund. Introduced by Vanguard in 1975, it invested in very short-term (typically 30 to 90 days to maturity) high-quality debt securities such as certificates of deposit, high-grade commercial paper, and U.S. Treasury bills. With yields rising to as high as 16 percent and a net asset value of $1.00 per share that was expected to hold stable, money market funds had become an attractive alternative to low-interest bank accounts and even equity funds. They changed the face of a troubled mutual fund industry. By the end of 1981, the assets of Vanguard's money market funds had grown to $1.6 billion, representing 40 percent of the total assets of the company.

The rest of the mutual fund industry had also come to rely primarily on money market funds. Traditional long-term stock funds were in the doldrums, and Vanguard's stock funds were no exception. As the stock market recovered from the 1973–1974 crash, Vanguard fund assets grew nicely—from $1.45 billion in 1974, to $1.78 billion in 1975, to $2.05

billion in 1976. While cash outflow slowed—from minus $127 million in 1976 to minus $89 million in 1977—Vanguard's investors continued to redeem more shares than they purchased, and fund assets fell back to $1.85 billion by the end of 1977.

Early in 1976, only eight months after Vanguard had officially begun operations, Jack Bogle began to formulate a plan to reverse Vanguard's disappointing performance. Under the current arrangement, Vanguard was responsible only for the administration of the funds; distribution and investment advice were still in the hands of Wellington Management Company. Bogle's goal, no matter what he may have said publicly, was to make Vanguard fully independent of the management company by ultimately assuming control over these two functions. He decided to continue slashing at the Gordian knot that he had described earlier as binding the funds to the management company. He would do so by taking over the distribution function.

Vanguard—and the Wellington funds before its creation—had been content to allow Wellington Management to handle the distribution of its shares. While vital to the company, distribution was essentially a profitless task, and the management company had been willing to do it at cost, or even at a loss, because it helped to increase the company's assets under management, generating higher advisory fees. Furthermore, the management company knew that distribution was a valuable card. Bogle, however, knew that by taking the distribution function out of the hands of the management company, Vanguard would be free to negotiate advisory fees, terminate existing contracts, and hire any adviser it wanted to. And, because the largest profits in the mutual fund business arise from the fees paid to the investment adviser, Vanguard's freedom to choose its investment adviser would have a direct, adverse impact on Wellington Management's pocketbook.

"To confront that issue directly," said Bogle, "to say we're going to pay a distribution fee and a management fee separately so that we can deal with the manager at arm's length, was our goal. We were trapped because you can't really fire the investment manager. If you did, who would distribute the fund's shares? By taking over the distribution, we would basically shift the control over the operation to Vanguard. It would then be only a matter of time before we started to do our own investment management."[1]

The key to taking over distribution, Bogle believed, was converting the funds to a no-load distribution system. So Bogle began campaigning to eliminate the funds' sales loads and market their shares directly to investors, without a stockbroker acting as an intermediary. Wellington Management Company strongly opposed conversion to a no-load distribution system. Bogle, however, believed that the door had been opened for Vanguard to assume responsibility for this critical marketing area just as had been proposed in the 1974 Future Structure Study.

As is the case today, mutual funds then could be purchased either directly from the management company, which sold its funds through advertising, mail solicitation, and word of mouth, or from an intermediary such as a stockbroker, a financial planner, or a bank. Funds that were sold through these intermediaries charged a sales commission, or load. (A sales load is paid by the investor to an outside party, such as a broker, as distinct from the annual fees the funds paid to Vanguard directly for administrative services.) Generally, about 80 to 90 percent of the load went to the selling broker; the rest went to the management company to compensate it for distributing the funds. The companies that managed funds garnered large revenues from these sales loads, which, like Wellington's, started as high as 8.5 percent for purchases up to $10,000 and declined as the size of the purchase increased. Despite the revenues, sales loads placed an added burden on the management company: because the sales load reduced the size of the investor's return by the amount of the load, the load funds had to perform significantly better than the no-load funds just to stay competitive. As Bogle often noted, the sales load meant that an investor running a 100-yard race was starting on the 108th yard line.

Bogle believed that for Vanguard to survive, the investment performance of its funds had to become more competitive. The best way to do that, in his view, was to make Vanguard the lowest-cost provider in the industry. This required not only maintaining minimal operating expenses and negotiating rock-bottom investment advisory fees, but also offering the funds on a no-load basis. In the 1960s and early 1970s, though, when most mutual funds were equity funds, costs seemed to matter little to investors. Only when the money market segment of the industry began to burgeon in the 1970s did the issue of costs begin to command attention. Because there are fairly tight restrictions on the types of debt securities money market funds can own, most funds pay similar gross yields before deducting management fees and loads, and in this area of the market, investors can easily tell that low-cost no-load funds will almost always provide better returns. As a result, competition came to preclude most money market funds from charging sales commissions. The timing seemed right for Bogle to bring his idea to fruition.

By going no-load, Vanguard would no longer require the services of wholesalers, who for decades had been the link between the Wellington organization and the broker/dealer network. Employees at Wellington Management Company were used to the system, which had paid them enormous dividends over the years. The firm had relied on the broker/dealer network to distribute shares of the funds, and load funds had been the traditional distribution method since the industry's inception in 1924. Eliminating the wholesalers and having investors bypass the broker/dealers to deal directly with Vanguard would be a radical change from past practice, one that would be likely to cause immense anger among the broker/dealers, who had been entirely responsible for bringing in the assets of the funds.

Bogle believed that one of the powerful incentives for Vanguard to convert to no-load was the consumerism he had predicted in 1974: cost-conscious consumers were becoming less willing to pay the 8.5 percent sales load, so eliminating it could be a way to attract them back to the mutual funds they had been leaving. A second reason was that in the long run, it would become more and more difficult for fund organizations to get the broker/dealers to sell Vanguard funds, because the brokerage firms had a large and growing number of their own mutual funds to choose from and would soon begin to offer them through their broker/dealer networks. Third, and perhaps most important, Bogle thought that a major part of the future for mutual funds lay with institutional investors, which at the time represented only 20 percent of Vanguard's business, a figure he wanted to raise to 50 percent. Going no-load would encourage institutional investors to link up with Vanguard in larger numbers. Institutions were traditionally averse to paying a load; if Vanguard went no-load, its funds would automatically look more attractive to them.

Once again, Bogle had to face some old adversaries. Bob Doran and Nick Thorndike were still on the fund boards (though they would soon leave), and the two forcefully opposed Bogle's plan to take on distribution responsibilities. They understood its devastating implications for Wellington Management: a further erosion of its hold over the funds and, more significant, the decrease in advisory fees that would be in store for them, since advisory fees had been used to subsidize distribution expenses. They contended that the dealer distribution network was vital because dealers could do a better job of distributing and marketing shares than Vanguard's staff could. And by going no-load, they argued, Vanguard would automatically give up crucial sales volume. According to Bogle, Doran had described the likely result of a conversion to no-load as "the holocaust." (Doran would only say, "I might have used that term. I just don't remember.") Doran stated that he had been positioned as being against no-load, when in fact he had not been opposed to using the no-load approach as part of a broader "variable pricing strategy," which might have included a low load or even no load on fixed-income products and the highest loads on the most aggressive equity products.[2]

Whatever Wellington Management's stance on the proposal to convert to a no-load distribution system, Vanguard did not need Wellington's approval to implement either the separate pricing proposal or the internalized distribution proposal. Bogle, however, needed time to persuade the fund directors that the long-term rewards of this essentially irreversible strategy far outweighed the obviously substantial short-term risk of eliminating all sales through Wellington Management's network of broker/dealers before Vanguard could gain adequate distribution volume on its own. This problem was not trivial, because the funds would need an SEC exemption permitting them to bear the costs of distribution directly. Given the length of time required to secure such an exemption, unless the funds were permitted to put the plan into operation on an interim basis, they would be dependent on Wellington Management's willingness to continue to finance a distribution effort out of its advisory fees.

Emotions ran high at the Vanguard board meetings over the next several months. The Vanguard board was split into three groups: one that had wanted to go no-load when the company was first formed; a second that objected to all forms of internalization, even administration; and a third that favored absorbing the distribution function but was worried that the SEC might throw a roadblock in Vanguard's way. Ray Klapinsky, secretary of the funds, recalled: "You'd come into a meeting, Jack would present something, and Wellington Management would have an opposite presentation. Wellington Management opposed us the whole way."[3] Bogle argued that the wave of the future was no-load distribution, which would benefit shareholders and new investors. He further argued that the current distribution system was breaking down, that in fact it had been unprofitable to Wellington Management for a number of years, and that distribution had been subsidized by Wellington out of the advisory fees paid by the funds.

Despite the contentious environment, the fund board finally decided in Bogle's favor by a vote of 7 to 4 on February 8, 1977, after a lengthy discussion that concluded at 1:30 a.m. In the end, the chief reason for the board's decision was the majority's agreement with Bogle's conviction that no-load distribution was the wave of the future in terms of consumer preferences and successful marketing. Going no-load and choosing Vanguard as distributor also seemed a good way for the directors to address their concerns that Vanguard was too dependent on Wellington Management Company and too weak to force the management company to mend its ways. In effect, option 2 in the Future Structure Study had been approved just three years after it had been rejected. The second step along what would be a three-step path toward full mutualization had been taken.

Cynics in the industry scoffed at Bogle's steps. Dreyfus ran full-page ads with its lion roaring "No Load? No Way!" Brokers were incensed, and Bogle and his staff took numerous calls from brokers who loudly announced their dismay and anger with the new arrangement, and threatened to recommend that their clients redeem their Vanguard fund shares. The day after Vanguard announced that it was going no-load,

Jan Twardowski, one of Bogle's assistants, who went on to manage Vanguard's first index fund, took such a call from the head of a brokerage firm who was placing a $1 million order for the Windsor Fund, an enormous order at that time. Recalled Twardowski: "He went ballistic. He had convinced his client that Windsor was the best fund ever, and he wasn't going to get paid for his work. Who could blame him?"[4]

Vanguard's challenge was to find a whole new set of self-directed investors who could be lured into buying funds through direct mail and advertising, and eventually word of mouth. Bogle remained confident that, despite the interim peril, no-load was indeed the wave of the future and that he was going to ride that wave. Moreover, he was convinced that going no-load was simply the right thing to do for investors.

Aiding Vanguard significantly during the years following the conversion to no-load were the growing assets of the John Neff–managed Windsor Fund, which rose from $300 million at the end of 1974 to $600 million at the end of 1978. Bogle reasoned that Windsor's recent record, which had returned to top form in 1975 and 1976, along with Neff's growing reputation, would make brokers think twice about recommending redemption to their clients. Indeed, Neff's contribution to Vanguard's early survival was little short of immense, as Windsor would eventually grow larger than Wellington Fund in 1979 and pass the $1 billion mark early in 1982. This was not surprising, given that Windsor's 15-year returns from Neff's starting date in June 1964 to June 1979 were a cumulative 335 percent, compared to just 127 percent for the average growth and income stock fund during the same period, according to fund tracker Morningstar.

Accelerating Bogle's decision to go no-load was the company's impending plan to introduce Warwick Municipal Bond Fund, the first ever multi-series municipal bond fund. The fund would offer investors different bond maturities and various kinds of strategies. An investor could thus select a long-term municipal bond portfolio, an intermediate-term portfolio, or the equivalent of a tax-exempt short-term money market portfolio—the industry's first. Most directors agreed with Bogle that attaching even a 6 percent sales load to a portfolio of low-yielding municipal bonds would make it more difficult, even disabling, for the investment adviser to produce good net returns for fund shareholders.

Warwick began operations on September 13, 1977. In addition to the no-load distribution, Vanguard broke with tradition by hiring Citibank instead of Wellington as Warwick's investment adviser. "That decision was significant," recalled Vanguard attorney Phil Fina, "because it set in motion the possibility that Vanguard would be restructuring itself and making its own decisions."[5]

Adding momentum to the recovery of the assets of the Vanguard funds was the success of its new money market fund. For the investor who was accustomed to dealing directly with a bank, Vanguard's no-load money market fund—originally named Whitehall Money Market Trust—had large appeal. At the time Vanguard's money market fund was introduced, the interest rate that banks could pay on deposits was limited by federal regulation to 5.5 percent. As annual inflation rates soared into double digits, individual savers in bank accounts saw the purchasing power of their savings being quickly eroded. Money market funds gave individual investors a way to do what big corporations were doing—earn double-digit rates of interest on cash reserves invested in money market instruments such as commercial paper.

The growth of the money market segment at Vanguard was crucial to the overall company, for once investors were introduced to the money market funds, they were more inclined to try out Vanguard's other funds. The strategy appeared to be working: in 1977, some $80 million had flowed out of the company's coffers; by the next year, $52 million had come in, and $280 million the year after that. By the close of 1979, Vanguard's assets had reached $2.4 billion and were on their way to surpassing the previous high of $2.6 billion reached late in 1972. By the close of 1980, assets had crossed the $3 billion mark.

In the meantime, Vanguard was introducing other new funds. The company expanded its bond fund offerings by introducing a high-yield municipal bond fund and a high-yield corporate bond fund late in 1978. One year later, a GNMA ("Ginnie Mae") income fund was added, the first such fund available on a no-load basis. In 1981, an international growth portfolio was introduced as a distinct component of Ivest Fund—with a new manager, London-based Schroder Capital Management International. It was among the first mutual fund portfolios investing in foreign securities. (It would become a separate fund in 1985.)

Vanguard's marketing plan to build a comprehensive family of mutual funds was beginning to take shape.

Now that Vanguard had assumed the job of selling and distributing its own funds, it had to figure out how to pay for it. To Bogle, the answer was obvious: the money should come directly from shareholder assets. Indeed, there was now no other possible source. For many years, the funds had been paying an overly large investment management fee to Wellington Management Company that was sufficient to subsidize Wellington's distribution costs. Now that Wellington would no longer be paying the distribution costs, Bogle saw nothing wrong with overtly using shareholder assets to pay reasonable sums for distribution. After all, distribution was required if fund assets were to grow and economies of scale were to be achieved for fund shareholders.

Bogle's stance was directly opposed to the prevailing industry practice, in which distribution costs were covertly subsidized by large management fees, and the profits that were realized from economies of scale were salted away by management companies rather than benefiting fund investors. Bogle reasoned that the interests of full disclosure would be served by laying distribution expenses out in the open rather than burying them in the management fees paid by the funds.

The problem was that the SEC had concerns about Bogle's plan, and Vanguard had to receive SEC approval to use shareholder assets to pay for distribution. In the early 1970s, the SEC had made a number of public pronouncements to the effect that the Investment Company Act of 1940 made it improper for mutual funds to bear distribution costs. The SEC believed that the management company, rather than the funds, should bear the costs. Ironically, the SEC's own studies at the time revealed that industry-wide distribution revenues (i.e., sales charges) were not covering the distribution costs. Therefore, fund investors were already paying the costs of distribution out of their assets through higher management fees.

On September 13, 1977, the SEC issued a temporary exemption in response to Vanguard's application for distribution rights for Warwick

Municipal Bond Fund, but called for hearings on the issue. The hearings, under the aegis of SEC administrative law judge Max Regensteiner, were held in two stages. The first lasted from January 5 to February 3, 1978, five days a week, 8 to 10 hours a day. This was said to be the longest hearing ever on an application for an exemption under the Investment Company Act of 1940. Vanguard had proposed that each fund pay its share of distribution costs based on its relative net assets (each fund, then, would pay the same percentage fee), without regard to whether the distribution costs were incurred on its behalf. Judge Regensteiner, however, termed the arrangement inequitable because it placed an excessive burden on the funds that were not directly benefiting from the expenditures. He also decided not to allow Vanguard to refer to its funds as no-load.

When Bogle received the initial decision, he was so furious that he threw the document against the wall. The decision, however, was not a death blow. The temporary exemption remained in force, so Bogle and his staff moved quickly to meet the judge's demands, and on January 31, 1979, they submitted an amended application to the SEC. The new proposal, while it based the lion's share of the allocation of distribution costs on relative net assets, included a modest allocation based on distribution of shares. Thus, a slightly lower fee would be paid by funds that had lower sales volume, and vice versa. Although on October 4 the judge approved the application, he continued the ban on the use of the term no-load; however, three and a half weeks later, the SEC adopted Rule 12b-1, which for the first time expressly permitted an individual mutual fund to bear its own distribution expenses. (The rule did not deal with the critical issue of a complex-wide distribution fee, which was at issue in the Vanguard case.)

Whereas the SEC ruling allowed Vanguard to pass on the economies of scale that resulted from its future growth to shareholders in the form of lower operating costs, Rule 12b-1 had the opposite effect on the industry as a whole. In fact, the rule was later employed by other mutual fund companies to add a new layer of expenses to be borne by shareholders. While Vanguard's average expense ratio declined from 0.89 percent in 1975 to 0.20 percent in 2010, the industry's average expense ratio actually increased from 1.08 percent in 1974 to 1.19 percent in 2010. In a twist of irony, Bogle would later be tabbed as "the father of the 12b-1 fee," a moniker that infuriated him. As Bogle explained it, "It's sort of like Frankenstein's monster. I may have been Dr. Frankenstein, but the rest of the industry created the monster."

Finally, on February 25, 1981, the SEC ratified Regensteiner's verdict; it even allowed Vanguard to call its funds no-load. Bogle was ecstatic. It meant that Vanguard could now conduct genuinely arm's-length negotiations with its investment advisers. Following the ruling, Bogle's first objective was to reduce the fees paid to those advisers. When Vanguard began to distribute its own funds, Wellington Management no longer had a gun to the funds' head. By the end of 1978, Wellington's advisory fees were reduced by $2.9 million, or 39 percent.

Bogle's next objective was to internalize the critical investment advisory function. He had never envisioned Vanguard as a traditional equity money manager, but he could see great merit in running carefully defined, high-quality bond and money market funds. One motivation for this move was Citibank's poor performance as the investment manager for the Warwick Municipal Bond Fund. Another was Vanguard's ability to run both the municipal bond and money market funds at low cost. On August 15, 1981, Vanguard's board voted on internalizing advisory services for the money market and municipal bond funds: eight in favor, two opposed. "It is simply impossible to overstate the importance of this decision in the growth that followed," Bogle said years later.[6]

In effect, the board had now accepted option 3 from Bogle's proposal of March 1974, and the process of full mutualization was, in substance, complete. It had taken seven years—from 1974 to 1981—to bring Bogle's cherished goal to fruition. But it had finally happened.

Accordingly, in September 1981, Vanguard took the major step of internalizing the investment advisory function for its money market funds. At the same time, it took over the reins of the municipal bond fund portfolios that Citibank had managed since the fund's inception in 1977. Together, these fund portfolios had assets of $1.5 billion, roughly one-third of the company's total assets under management. From then on, Vanguard provided the investment advisory function for these funds at cost, gradually cutting annual portfolio advisory costs for each portfolio from about 0.20 percent of assets prior to the 1981 internalization to about 0.01 percent by 1995, when these assets had risen to $45 billion. The cost differential would amount to the staggering total of $85 million in annual savings to investors in the fund portfolios.

Yet Bogle knew that it was unrealistic to try to internalize the entire investment advisory function. Talented equity fund managers like John Neff were in short supply, and even Neff, though based in Philadelphia, was part of Wellington Management and served on its board. So Bogle's objective was to internalize the management of the bond and money market funds, but to continue to retain external advisers for equity funds. The major problem was that there was no one working at Vanguard at the time with the expertise to manage the bond and money market funds. So Bogle conducted a search for some new talent and soon hired Ian A. MacKinnon to be Vanguard's first internal investment manager.

Born in Niagara Falls, New York, MacKinnon graduated from Lafayette College in 1970 with a B.A. in economics. Later he earned a master's degree from Penn State. He worked for a year as an economist with Mathematica, Inc., in Princeton, New Jersey; then, beginning in 1975, MacKinnon spent six years with the Girard Bank of Philadelphia, where he was a portfolio manager and head of the bank's $3 billion fixed-income group. He was largely satisfied with his job at Girard and was less than enthusiastic when a headhunter approached him about the job at Vanguard. He finally took the job when Bogle agreed to hire him as the head of the new division and to let him hire his own staff.

"Embryonic" is the best way to describe the "division" that MacKinnon was about to head up. On his first day at work, he discovered that his "office" consisted of a table pushed against a wall. Behind him were rows of auditors going through reams of computer paper. On the wall was a rotary phone with a take-out pizza menu tacked up next to it. On November 16, 1981, $1.7 billion of fixed-income assets came into his "possession." Having handled twice that amount at Girard, MacKinnon was not overly impressed. Nonetheless, it was a hefty sum. "You kind of mentally lop off the zeros so you can sleep at night," he said. Vanguard was, as MacKinnon recalled, "dirt poor" in terms of revenues and therefore had a high expense ratio—by Vanguard standards, if well below industry norms—of some 0.60 percent (or $6 annually for each $1,000 in assets). But with each dollar that came in, the expense ratio dropped. "We were pinching pennies with pliers," said MacKinnon, who was turned down the first time he asked whether he could hire a municipal bond analyst.

Spartan, primitive, exciting, risky—it was all an experiment, and whether MacKinnon was trying to fix the air-conditioning or manage the money, he wondered whether the company was ever going to become a major force in the industry. Bogle's vision for Vanguard's foray into active portfolio management was to offer fixed-income and money market funds that maintained clearly defined investment policies, quality standards, and maturity standards. Their names would characterize their policies, as in Vanguard Long-Term Municipal Bond Portfolio, Vanguard Intermediate-Term U.S. Treasury Bond Portfolio, and Vanguard Short-Term Corporate Bond Portfolio. As Bogle noted, "The trick is to tell investors what the fund will do and describe the risks, and then just do it. And tell the truth to them in your annual reports."

Luckily for Bogle, in the fund industry, telling the truth to shareholders was a novel concept. When MacKinnon retired in 2003, Vanguard was running $225 billion in bond fund assets, more than any other fund company. Clearly, Bogle's decision to internalize the advisory functions had proven to be a complete success.

CHAPTER 8

The Vanguard Manual

The 1980s and 1990s were the golden age of Vanguard and the mutual fund industry in general. Under Bogle's conservative, fair-minded stewardship, Vanguard flourished, and the assets it gathered during those decades were, to use an odd industry term, "sticky." Shareholders came, and they never left, which was not the experience of some of Vanguard's trendier peers. Assets grew from $2.4 billion at the start of 1980 to $540 billion by the end of 1999, when Jack Bogle was forcibly "retired" from Vanguard's board of directors.

Bogle's philosophy began to come into sharper focus during the 1980s. For him, the shareholder always came first. He wanted the Vanguard experiment to make the words *focus solely on the interests of the shareholder* a reality. Others in the industry claimed a similar focus, but were actually pocketing considerable sums of money for themselves that rightfully belonged to fund shareholders.

Surely, one of the saddest dates in the history of the American worker was January 1, 1980, the birthday of the 401k. (The 401k was actually created by the Revenue Act of 1978, but the law didn't go into effect until 1980.) Prior to the 401k's existence, most employees at large corporations received traditional pension plans, or "defined benefit" plans. Such plans guaranteed workers a percentage of their salaries for life when they retired, and the burden of that guarantee was on their employers' shoulders. Pension plan trustees were paid respectable but not jaw-dropping salaries to run their plans and often hired external money managers for a modest fee.

Contrast that with the 401k, or "defined contribution" plan. Such plans shifted the burden of a secure retirement onto the employees' shoulders. Employees who didn't contribute a portion of their own salaries into their plans would have no safety net. So instead of a guaranteed income for life, they were forced to gamble in the securities markets and hope for the best. Most were ill equipped for this task, and study after study showed how poor "self-directed" individual investors were at self-directing. They tended to buy at the top and sell at the bottom, and they invested either too conservatively in all-cash portfolios or too aggressively in company stock. Many contributed too little to their 401k or not at all. About 60 percent of employees contributed to their 401k plans in 2009, but the median balance in those plans even before the crash of 2008 was only $18,942, according to the Employee Benefits Research Institute. By 2009, it was $12,655.[1]

But what was the employees' loss was the mutual fund industry's bonanza. Management fees for mutual funds were much higher than those for pension funds because instead of being negotiated in the free market, they were set by directors who were handpicked by management. According to a 2003 study titled "Mutual Fund Advisory Fees: The Cost of Conflicts of Interest," pension fund management fees were less than half those of comparable mutual funds, about 0.28 percent to mutual funds' 0.67 percent for funds of comparable size. And that number excluded administrative fees, which added an extra layer of fat to mutual funds, as they had to process trades for multiple employees and keep track of all the individual 401k account holders instead of just one pension plan.[2]

Once a fund was offered in a 401k with a limited number of choices, its management company had a captive audience of workers investing a continuous stream of assets into it that grew with every paycheck. In addition, some mutual fund companies that ran 401ks took a portion of the money they collected from investors and used it to pay consultants. These consultants, in turn, recommended which funds should be included in the 401k. Some consultants recommended only those fund companies that made such payments. This arrangement, officially known as "revenue sharing," but more commonly referred to as "pay to play," was really little more than a kickback. By one estimate, some 90 percent of 401ks are involved in such kickback schemes.[3]

But perhaps the greatest damage of the 401k era was psychological. The 1980s gave rise to our equity culture. According to the Investment Company Institute and the Securities Industry Association, in 1983, only 15.9 percent of American households owned stocks. By 2000, 50 percent did.[4] And most of that exposure came through 401k plans and specifically through stock mutual funds in those plans. This shift gave people the illusion that they were reaping all the benefits of our capitalist system, especially because the stock market continued to rise throughout this period. The so-called democratization of investing and the concomitant advances in online trading technology that came with it led John Q. Public to believe that he was a sophisticated investor when really all he was participating in was speculation and price/earnings ratio expansion. The amount of ownership may have been small, yet by 2001, nearly a third of Americans earning just $20,000 to $30,000 a year were trading stocks.[5]

Typical of the hype and irrational exuberance of the era was an article titled "A Nation of Traders" that appeared in the October 1999 issue of *Fortune* magazine. In it, the author boasts of the new era of democratized investing: "What we have here is nothing short of a revolution. Power that for generations lay with a few thousand white males on a small island in New York City is now being seized by Everyman and Everywoman. In fact, it's no overstatement to suggest that this movement from Wall Street to Main Street is one of the most significant socioeconomic trends of the past few decades. It's not only changing the way we invest, it's changing the way we work and live too." Later he would add, "Contrary to conventional wisdom, our new national fixation with investing can't be written off as simply a sign of a market top."[6] This was published only five months before the beginning of a bear market in which stocks would plummet by 44 percent, and many individual investors' portfolios were wiped out.

Even when employees owned stock directly in their 401ks, generally through shares of their employer's stock, their holdings were often so minuscule that the notion that they were enjoying some great equalization of corporate ownership was laughable. And yet the prevailing attitude was that all Americans were equal participants in the financial gravy train. Sure, maybe the janitors at Microsoft had fewer shares in their 401ks than Bill Gates, and maybe they ended up borrowing against their 401ks to pay their bills, but, hey, at least they were owners. When Microsoft went up, so did their piddling accounts. And since the markets kept rising nearly straight up for 18 years—from 1982 to 2000— no one seemed to notice that wages for Americans had been stagnant throughout the whole period, rarely rising more than 4 percent in any given year, a negligible amount when adjusted for inflation.[7] Couple that with a major housing bubble and access to cheap credit, and it's easy to understand how the once palpable American dream became a chimerical fantasy built on a whirlwind of debt and dot-com speculation.

The terrible irony was that while employees lost a great benefit in the shift from traditional pension plans to 401k plans, the excessive fees that most mutual funds charged were preventing investors from truly reaping the gains from being owners of America Inc. The concept of a democratized equity culture was being foisted upon them by a Herculean marketing effort, and yet they were never truly perceived as owners by their so-called fiduciaries in the fund industry. In fact, mutual fund management firms routinely rubber-stamped the most egregious executive compensation plans, leading to shortfalls in corporate revenue and excessive risk taking by those overpaid executives who ultimately cost thousands of fund shareholders their jobs. To the best fund companies, investors weren't owners; they were customers to be sold as much product as possible. To the worst, they were suckers plain and simple, getting clipped on one side by their employers who eliminated their pension plans and then getting clipped on the other by the fund companies that were eating away at the returns that were supposed to secure their retirement.

And yet despite these ethical lapses, from 1980 through 2000, assets in 401ks grew from $0 to $1.7 trillion. About half of those assets went to the mutual fund industry, while much of the remainder went into employers' company stock, both generally bad investments—the former because of the fund industry's high fees; the latter because it tied workers' investment capital to their human capital. In the subsequent two recessions, many investors lost both their jobs and their nest eggs. The most glaring example was Enron, in which employees, spurred on by management's blarney, piled into the stock and then lost everything when the company went bankrupt.

Given such a grim historical context, it's not hard to imagine John Bogle dressed like the Duke of Wellington riding into this ethical wasteland on a white horse. While Vanguard clearly benefited from the rise of the equity culture as much as any other fund company, it was the only one charging individual investors fees comparable to what pension plan managers were charged. In each investor who called Vanguard, Bogle may have seen something of his father and mother, caught in the turmoil of the Depression and hoping that someone would look after their savings. Or perhaps he understood that doing what's best for the shareholder was simply good business. Whatever his motivation, the invisible, faceless shareholder was at the center of Bogle's philosophy. He wanted to make shareholders come alive, often referring to them as "down-to-earth, honest-to-God human beings, with their own hopes, fears, and aspirations."

As Vanguard increasingly became independent from Wellington, Bogle felt more confident that his idea of a truly mutualized fund company was working. One way this confidence manifested itself was his decision to incorporate the Vanguard name into the company's funds. In mid-1980, Westminster Bond Fund, Warwick Municipal Bond Fund, and Whitehall Money Market Trust dropped their British "W" first names and, along with First Index Investment Trust, became the first Vanguard Funds. (By 1993, all the funds had incorporated Vanguard into their names, as Wellington Fund became Vanguard Wellington Fund, and so on.)

For the most part, Vanguard stood alone in its approach to the mutual fund industry. Rather than raise prices, Vanguard lowered them; rather than introduce speculative funds, it introduced conservative, relatively predictable funds; rather than trumpet yesterday's performance miracles, it committed itself to a modest advertising program that spoke common sense. As the Vanguard philosophy emerged, Bogle wrote its tenets down in what he titled *Vanguard's Manual for Officers and Crew.* These tenets included:

1. Above all, provide value, keeping operating costs paid by investors at the lowest levels in this industry and offering fund shares to investors without loads or hidden sales charges.
2. Hold to our course, concentrating our primary focus on the industry we know best: mutual funds.
3. Innovate soundly and sensibly, making intelligent bets on the future while never ignoring the lessons of history.
4. Generate rewards for our clients, consistent with the risks they expect, and generally surpass competitive norms.
5. Maintain a crew of dedicated people who have "signed on" to Vanguard's mission.

For each of these tenets, he gave a one-word summary description: value, concentration, innovation, performance, dedication.

One of the challenges for Bogle, given Vanguard's unique philosophy, was setting appropriate benchmarks for success. A traditional investment adviser used an array of measurements, from the profits it earned for its manager-owners, to the value it created for its private owners, to the price of its stock if it traded in the marketplace. In contrast, because it provided its services on an at-cost or nonprofit-making basis, Vanguard had goals that were more difficult to specify and quantify. Bogle recognized this in a memorandum he wrote in December 1987: "What the financial objective of our firm is, is very hard to say. Certainly we don't have financial objectives in the customary sense, where someone would say we've got to get a 12 percent or 100 percent return on capital. But I guess I'd say it is to be an enterprise that gives the customers—clients, as we call them—a fair shake. And that means high-quality funds with objectives that at least have the hope of being achieved—low costs, and a high service component. It sounds a bit like motherhood." Only Bogle, of course, would equate such measures with maternity.

Although keeping costs low was always a priority, in its first years, Vanguard had been at a distinct disadvantage compared to other mutual fund companies. While most fund companies had large sums of money to spend on advertising, Vanguard did not. Vanguard, though, turned this weakness into an advantage, suggesting that keeping costs low was not only good in and of itself but part of a sound investment policy. One of the primary concepts that Bogle would promulgate and champion throughout much of his career was that "strategy follows structure." Funds with high fee structures must by their very nature take on greater risks than lower-cost funds in order to beat their benchmarks, as the costs create a greater hurdle rate for them to cross.

Bogle conceded that actively managed equity funds may have needed higher-priced management talent, but the funds could absorb these higher costs only as long as they produced huge profits for fund shareholders. He argued, however, that costs were a critical issue in money market and bond funds, where investment managers had less ability to demonstrate their skills in selecting securities because these asset classes were less volatile and there were fewer opportunities for managers to assume extra risk to generate excess returns. Since much of the returns for high-quality bonds was determined by their yields alone, as opposed to security selection, any mutual fund company that could run these funds at a lower cost would enjoy a distinct yield advantage, and it was no coincidence that the funds in which Vanguard most excelled were the ones in which cost savings mattered the most.

With money market funds, for example, differences in yields among various funds were almost entirely the result of differences in expense ratios, which take into account the total cost of a fund's operations, including management fees and administrative expenses for a given year, expressed as a percentage of average fund assets. Expenses, Bogle argued, accounted for 95 percent of the differences in the performance of money market funds and 80 percent of the differences in the performance of fixed-income funds; for stock funds, he estimated the figure at about 65 percent of the differences in performance, at least over the long term.

Bogle boasted that the secret to Vanguard's low costs was shareholder ownership. Because the shareholders of the funds owned Vanguard, no profits had to be extracted from fund returns and paid to a parent company or management company. Vanguard also benefited from its ability to negotiate fees with investment advisers at arm's length, avoiding the conflicts of interests that are inevitable for traditionally structured fund companies. Bogle noted that, as Vanguard's funds began to grow in asset size, Vanguard was able to negotiate favorable fee rates and still pay the dollar level of advisory fees that was necessary to attract the most talented investment managers.

Indeed, examining Vanguard's relationship with the external money managers it hired as subadvisers easily exposed the flaws in other mutual funds' fee structures. Securities law professor John P. Freeman highlighted the power of Vanguard's arm's-length negotiations with money managers in his testimony before the U.S. Senate about excessive fund fees in 2004. In it he described how different fees could be for essentially the same product when negotiated in the free market: "Recently, Alliance Capital was charging 93 basis points (.93 percent) for managing the [then] $17.5 billion Alliance Premier Growth Fund. This is a fee paid by shareholders of $162.7 million per year. At the same time as it was charging 93 basis points to its own shareholders, Alliance was managing the Vanguard U.S. Growth Fund for 11 basis points (.11 percent)—less than 1/8 of what it was charging Alliance shareholders. Alliance was also managing a $672 million portfolio for the Kentucky Retirement System for 24 basis points . . . and a $975 million equity portfolio for the Wyoming Retirement System for 10 basis points."[8]

In addition to low costs, the other anchor of Vanguard's philosophy was candor, which meant, above all else, being straightforward about how a mutual fund was performing. Bogle sometimes referred, only partially in jest, to candor as an important Vanguard marketing strategy that differentiated the company from others in the industry. Candor became a critical part of Bogle's approach to the business. He disliked the marketing focus and guile that others used to get ahead in the industry, and he railed at those who profited from misleading advertising. At the same time, he suggested that it was far better to do business with a firm like Vanguard, which presented a full and accurate picture of each fund's performance results.

If a Vanguard fund had not done well during a particular period, perhaps because an entire market segment had underperformed, Bogle specifically mentioned this fact in the next report to shareholders and cautioned them that such performance might continue for a period of time. He was also careful to dampen expectations in hot sectors as well. In 1991, when health-care stocks were performing exceptionally well, Bogle wrote a letter to shareholders of Vanguard's Health Care Portfolio, cautioning them about the risks of sector funds and noting that, "It is highly unlikely that such absolute returns—or even the Portfolio's relative performance advantage—will be matched in the future. The Portfolio's performance resulted from the particularly favorable returns of health care companies as a group. Experience has shown that such periods of superior performance by an industry group do not continue indefinitely. Indeed, periods of outperformance are often followed by periods of underperformance."

The history of Vanguard is peppered with many similar examples during Bogle's tenure. In 1990, a booklet titled *Plain Talk about High Yield Bonds* was sent to all investors in Vanguard's High Yield Bond Fund. Among other things, the booklet warned that, "Clearly, given their risks, high yield bonds are not for (a) the faint hearted, (b) short-term investors, nor (c) income-oriented investors depending heavily on bonds as the source of their income." And in the 1995 annual report for Vanguard Index Trust 500—following a year in which index fund returns surpassed the returns of actively managed funds by a wide margin—Bogle stated emphatically, "I again caution you . . . stay off the indexing bandwagon if you seek short-term performance results. There *will* be years in which more funds outperform the Index than underperform it."

Some competitors doubtless saw Bogle's honesty as lunacy, but the financial press loved it, and, judging by their letters to Vanguard, shareholders seemed to appreciate his forthrightness. Vanguard board members, who supported Bogle's directness, even kidded him that the tougher and more candid his message, the more money poured into the funds. Indeed, Bogle had long realized that his candor was Vanguard's most effective marketing tool.

CHAPTER 9

Creating Loyalty and Respect

A s the founder of a new company, Bogle knew that attracting a loyal clientele wasn't enough to ensure that Vanguard would be successful. He also needed to engender the loyalty and respect of his employees, or "crew members," as he preferred to call them. He knew that if they failed to sign on to his and Vanguard's values, he would have no chance of widening his base of support beyond the company. One way he sought to do this was to create an environment that would foster a spirit of teamwork. This was challenging because the company was growing so rapidly that it would be easy for the whole operation to spiral out of control. Vanguard had leased corporate headquarters in an office park in Chesterbrook, a suburb of Philadelphia in Valley Forge, in 1983, when it had only 431 employees. But the company soon outgrew this locale, so in 1991 the board approved the purchase of a 200-acre parcel along Route 202 in Malvern called the Kilgore property. By August 1993, some of Vanguard's now 3,520 crew members had moved into the Victory building of the new Malvern campus.

To instill a sense of pride in the company, Bogle took the unique tack of making the headquarters look and feel like a 200-year-old British warship that was embarking on a crucial mission led by Commander Jack Bogle. Bogle admitted that the nautical theme may have seemed a little corny, but he believed that it was essential for "the captain" to give "the crew members" the sense that they were not working for just any mutual fund company.

There is a certain irony to the British naval imagery, given that Vanguard's headquarters are only a few miles from the spot where George Washington's army spent the icy winter of 1777–1778 in Valley Forge. Bogle, however, seemed oblivious to the heroic exploits of the founding father. Moreover, he had never skippered more than a sailboat and never longed for a naval career. His romance with things naval had more to do with a love of battle than with ships. Because he was enthralled by the symbols of Admiral Nelson's battle of the Nile and other naval battles, a visitor to Vanguard headquarters driving down Vanguard Boulevard soon crosses Admiral Nelson Drive, where a sign for the parking area says, "short-term crew parking." Walking into Vanguard's headquarters, the visitor might mistake it for a naval museum. Immediately to the left inside the main entrance is a scale model of the HMS *Vanguard* in a glass case. To the right are six circular medallions with anchors, ships, and flags. The main building is named Victory, after Nelson's last flagship. Other buildings bear the names of other Nelson ships that took part in the battle of the Nile: Zealous, Majestic, Audacious, Swiftsure, and Goliath.

Virtually every aspect of the company's headquarters is part of a modern-day HMS *Vanguard*—from the cafeteria (the Galley) to the fitness center (Ship Shape), from the company store (the Chandlery) to the telephone numbers Vanguard clients dial (1-800-662-CREW for client services and 1-800-662-SHIP for investor information). Antique prints of British naval battles adorn the walls throughout the sprawling complex.

Bogle used the naval imagery to craft what he hoped would be a family atmosphere at Vanguard. He seemed to think of each crew member as part of his extended family. In some cases, his assistants became almost as close to him as his six children, none of whom, incidentally, ever worked full time at Vanguard. He almost always hired people in their twenties without extensive business experience but with solid academic credentials from the nation's top schools.

Bogle liked to hire those who could be molded, learn on the job, and develop strong loyalty to him and to Vanguard without being sycophants. While he believed that he was usually right, he wanted young people around him who could think independently and speak up when they opposed his viewpoint. He wanted to hear what they had to say, to know all sides of an argument before making a decision. He threw a great deal of responsibility his assistants' way and then watched them sink or swim. They learned quickly. Three of his assistants—Jim Riepe, Duncan McFarland, and Jack Brennan—went on to head mutual fund companies themselves. Meanwhile, other former assistants such as Jim Norris and Jeremy Duffield now run some of Vanguard's most important divisions.

The veteran assistants have formed themselves into a more or less permanent club, having met with Bogle once a year since the early 1980s for squash, dinner at a Philadelphia restaurant, business talk, and mutual needling. The needling is said to approach the outrageous level, but is expected to be taken by the victim (often Bogle) in good humor. The yearly get-togethers, without wives, may run from three o'clock in the afternoon until near midnight. Bogle's traditional toast, sounded every year, begins, "You, sirs, are a tribute to my good judgment about the human character." Perhaps those words would later seem ironic in Brennan's case.

It was no secret that Vanguard's growth through the early 1980s had no substantial effect on the personal wealth of its employees. Had Vanguard been a publicly held company, employees would have had access to stock options and similar compensation programs. To head off discontent and to put Vanguard on more of an equal footing with other mutual fund companies, Bogle and his colleagues in 1983 instituted a yearly bonus program for senior executives, designed to provide an equity-like participation in Vanguard's success.

In every speech Bogle gave to the crew when a major milestone was reached, he emphasized how critical it was for Vanguard to drive its expense ratio even lower relative to the expenses of other complexes. The goal, he reminded each crew member, was to maintain and enhance the firm's standing as the lowest-cost provider of services in the entire mutual fund industry. Even as Bogle talked about the need to press for efficiency, he sensed that crew members were beginning to equate low cost for Vanguard clients with miserly compensation for them. As he became more concerned, he discussed the issue at length with Jack Brennan, who suggested that perhaps all crew members should have a chance to participate in the plan. Bogle immediately agreed and promptly developed a program in which crew members would be rewarded, in large part commensurate with Vanguard's asset growth and its ability to keep costs at the minimum level. So in 1984, the earnings participation provided in the executive plan was extended to include every member of the crew. It was called the Vanguard Partnership Plan.

Vanguard took a novel approach to calculating distributions under the plan. In publicly held companies, bonuses are paid from profits. Because it operates at cost, however, Vanguard disclaims having profits. Instead, it counts as profits the money it saves shareholders by keeping its costs well below those of its competitors. Put differently, Vanguard's savings are equivalent to the profits that a management company would have earned by reason of operating at a higher cost than Vanguard.

Because it is not a public company, Vanguard does not publish an earnings statement. Its "profits" are based on the extent to which its traditionally low expense ratios provide shareholder value relative to the expenses of its major competitors. This difference is then applied to Vanguard's average assets for the year—creating larger earnings as its cost position improves and as its asset base grows. This figure showed that in 2009, Vanguard served its shareholders at an overall cost ratio of 0.20 percent of assets, compared to 1.19 percent for the industry. As a result, the profits earned by Vanguard for fund shareholders totaled some $13.3 billion—its expense advantage of 0.99 of a percentage point, or 99 basis points, to use an industry term, multiplied by average assets of $1.34 trillion. (On an asset-weighted basis, this cost saving would be lower but still very significant.) A specified portion of this savings goes into the Partnership Plan pool and is adjusted for any value created by the Vanguard Funds' returns relative to the returns of other mutual funds with comparable investment policies.

Given Vanguard's increasing cost advantage and rapidly growing asset base, "profits" burgeoned, as did the Partnership Plan distributions. The company distributed $500,000 to the crew in 1985, $1.8 million in 1987, $3.9 million in 1989, $8 million in 1991, and $16 million in 1993—all through the Partnership Plan. Bogle estimated that "profits" would grow to over $1 billion in 1995 and that more than $25 million would be distributed to the crew. The remaining 98 percent of profits, of course, would go to the direct benefit of fund shareholders.

The Partnership Plan was, not surprisingly, an immediate success with the crew. As Bogle would later note, however, "money isn't everything." He felt strongly that too many companies demanded loyalty without giving loyalty in return. "Loyalty," he stressed, "must run both from the individual to the institution and from the institution to the individual." In message after message to the crew, he returned to the themes of mutual caring and respect between each individual member of the crew and Vanguard as an institution. "Caring," he noted in one speech, "is a mutual affair," calling attention to Vanguard's responsibility, as an institution, to provide each crew member with "respect as an individual; opportunity for career growth, participation, and innovation; an attractive environment in which to work, corporate information through a meaningful communications program, and fair compensation."

And yet the Partnership Plan remains one of the most controversial aspects of Vanguard's organizational structure from a fund shareholder's perspective. At one point early in the 1990s, Vanguard would disclose how much in partnership dividends it was distributing to its highest paid executives from its biggest funds, but it eventually stopped doing this because the SEC reporting guidelines requiring such disclosure changed. So at this point it is difficult to assess how much executives such as current CEO Bill McNabb or Jack Brennan or Jack Bogle himself have been paid. "Vanguard executives talk about the company like it's a nonprofit organization," says Daniel Wiener, editor of *The Independent Adviser for Vanguard Investors*, an investment newsletter devoted to Vanguard funds. "But it's only a nonprofit after they've determined these huge bonuses and salaries for themselves. Vanguard's board decides how much money goes into the Partnership Plan and says that's just a cost of doing business. Therefore, in Vanguard's view it runs 'at-cost' and is nonprofit. But that cost of doing business is a floating figure based on what the board determines."

The fundamental problem with Vanguard's compensation system is that it is undisclosed and no one really knows how efficiently or inefficiently the organization is run. The underlying Vanguard Group that manages the funds, yet is beholden to shareholders, is neither a publicly traded company nor a tax-exempt 501(c) nonprofit organization, both of which must, by law, disclose executive compensation. The one check shareholders have with respect to inefficiency, though, is the funds' expense ratios themselves, which, measured as a percentage of assets, are the lowest in the industry. But with Vanguard managing $1.4 trillion, who's to say that even greater efficiencies couldn't be realized? "Vanguard does operate very cheaply, but that doesn't mean it couldn't be cheaper," says Wiener. "Shareholders have no information on how much it costs to run the company we supposedly own. The cost of the Partnership Plan is a huge black hole. As shareholders, we ought to know what Vanguard is paying its people."

The compensation issue goes to the heart of whether or not Vanguard truly is a mutually owned fund company. One of Bogle's primary criticisms of the fund industry is that it "serves two masters," the shareholders of the funds and the fund management companies. Vanguard ostensibly eliminates that conflict of interest by operating at cost solely for its fund shareholders, who collectively own Vanguard Group much like a publicly traded company. And yet from a legal standpoint, the Vanguard Group is a private company that happens to be owned by the shareholders of its public funds. "Private companies do not have to disclose their executive compensation," says Ari Gabinet, a former principal of Vanguard's legal department. "Vanguard's shareholders are shareholders of its public mutual funds, not the private Vanguard Group. It is the funds as corporate entities that collectively own the Vanguard Group."

Since the shareholders own the funds, by default they own the Vanguard Group. And yet there is a legal veil between the Vanguard funds that shareholders invest in and the Vanguard Group that manages the funds. This allows the Vanguard Group to behave as a private company. "All you have to do is pierce that corporate veil to realize that Vanguard's shareholders collectively own the management company," says Bogle. And yet if the Vanguard Group were truly a public shareholder-owned company, it would be required by law to disclose its executive compensation just like every other public company. The fact that the Vanguard Group withholds this information from fund shareholders indicates that it, too, has the "second master" that Bogle is so critical of, even if the conflict is not as great as it is with Vanguard's competitors. Bogle's stance is correct though somewhat diplomatic on this issue. "I think all mutual funds should disclose their officers' compensation—Fidelity, Vanguard, the works," he says.

Aside from the disclosure issues, there is also the question of whether the Partnership Plan appropriately aligns the interests of Vanguard's employees with those of its shareholders. Although there is a performance component to the plan's calculation, as a matter of fact, it encourages asset gathering, which can be detrimental to fund shareholders and create conflicts of interest. Historically, the largest part of the equation in the partnership was the size of the savings for shareholders, which was based on expenses as a percentage of assets. (Although in 2009 there were rumors of changes to how the formula is calculated, Vanguard has not formally disclosed this information.) The bigger Vanguard is, the more the total savings for shareholders on the expense front as fixed costs are spread over a larger asset base.

For index funds, such economies of scale surely benefit shareholders. However, there are significant drawbacks for actively managed funds, which are forced to hold more securities as their assets grow, compelling money managers to buy lower-quality second-tier stocks instead of their favorites for liquidity purposes. Giant asset bases also make it harder for managers to buy and sell stocks, thus increasing the market impact costs to trade. So what Vanguard's Partnership Plan may not measure effectively is the opportunity cost of sacrificing potential outperformance in favor of asset gathering. It is in fact incentivizing Vanguard employees to let the funds get too big, tack on additional fund managers to existing funds, and create more and more fund products, some of which may not in fact be beneficial to fund shareholders.

Although the Partnership Plan is a superior bonus system to what exists at most other fund shops, there are means of eliminating the unique conflicts of interest it creates. For Vanguard's actively managed funds, this would mean getting rid of the expense-based bonus and replacing it with a bonus system based entirely on long-term risk-adjusted performance versus an appropriate benchmark. This way if a fund was getting too big and its performance was suffering as a result, Vanguard would be motivated to close it. Otherwise, executives would receive no bonus. As the system stands now, Vanguard executives can still receive sizable Partnership compensation for bloated funds that are underperforming.

Eliminating the problem of product proliferation with index funds and ETFs is a more tricky endeavor. Surely, having an incentive for low costs at index funds makes sense and low-cost ones will likely beat their actively managed peers. But just because a low-cost technology sector ETF beats high-cost actively managed technology funds doesn't mean it's a good product for investors to buy. Maybe every tech fund, including the ETF, will implode. And yet Vanguard executives are still incentivized to launch such a product as their bonuses are largely based on cost savings.

Here again increasing the importance of performance-based compensation while decreasing though not eliminating that of cost-based compensation might help prevent the creation of unnecessary or high-risk index products. But a more delicate balance and a better means of comparison are required. If for instance a larger portion of Vanguard bonuses were determined based on comparing all equity fund products to a total stock market index on a risk adjusted basis, then the incentive to create inferior high-risk products would be reduced. That's because the total stock market as Bogle rightly points out is the gold standard for indexing. By default the average fund must lag the market after deducting its fees. So also by default a bonus system that rewards executives only for beating the total stock market without taking on more risk would incentivize them to create only those products they deemed to be "above average." There would be no reward for an inferior high-risk product even if it was low cost.

Interestingly enough, Bogle has changed his mind somewhat about the subject of compensation disclosure since he abdicated the CEO post to Brennan in 1996. In the past, he was thin-skinned when it came to what he considered an invasion of his privacy. The problem came to a head in 1992 when Wiener told *Forbes* magazine his estimate of Bogle's salary for 1991: $2.6 million including the Partnership Plan. "When the story came out," Wiener recalled, "Bogle apparently hit the ceiling. Here was a guy who had made his reputation on being cheap, pushing low expenses, and saying we don't waste shareholders' money. How does it look that he makes $2.6 million a year?" The lion's share of his compensation was represented by incentives based on Vanguard's profits returned to fund shareholders and the relative performance of the Vanguard Funds. In any event, the *Forbes* story emphasized that Bogle's pay was in fact subpar, headlining the article "In the Vanguard, Except in Pay." In reference to Wiener's estimate, the article stated that "in today's boom in this industry, that's pretty small stuff."

Shortly thereafter, Vanguard sued Wiener's publishing company, insisting that it stop using *The Vanguard Adviser* as the title of its newsletter. Bogle claimed that angry letters and phone calls had come in from shareholders who had received solicitations from Wiener and assumed that Vanguard had sold their names and addresses to the newsletter. Wiener, in response, accused Vanguard of trying to put him out of business. He argued that Bogle was upset not by his use of the Vanguard name but by the *Forbes* report. "If the name was a problem, where were they for two years—were they asleep at the switch?" He issued a news release giving his version of events, and the press latched onto the story. In time, the matter was settled when Wiener agreed to change the name of the newsletter to *The Independent Adviser for Vanguard Investors*.

At the time, Bogle reported that his salary was only a fraction of Wiener's estimate—about 20 percent of the reported figure. But he has since acknowledged that Wiener's figures were close to being accurate. According to an article that appeared in the *Boston Globe* in 2006: "Bogle now talks numbers and said Wiener's previous estimates were about right. He was paid roughly $200,000 in salary and a $300,000 bonus in 1991, he said, plus around $2 million under a 'partnership plan' that gave employees a percentage of Vanguard's profits. His salary and bonus went up around 7 percent annually in following years, he said, but in the early 1990s he gave back about 40 percent of his partnership shares to Vanguard. He did so 'because I thought it was getting out of hand,' he said. 'I didn't want to be greedy, or appear to be greedy.'"[1]

Bogle now believes that all senior mutual fund executives should disclose their compensation. And he does not feel that he's behaving hypocritically by changing his mind, since, at the time that Wiener exposed his paycheck, other executives were not disclosing their salaries. "The issue I had with Wiener and the world was why should I be subject to disclosure that no one else was and we were the only firm that was trying to do things right?" Bogle says. "And that seems to me today to be grotesquely unfair. Let's disclose everybody's instead. Last I heard, Ned Johnson of Fidelity hasn't taken any vows of poverty." Indeed, Fidelity funds founder Ned Johnson and his daughter Abigail are collectively worth $19.5 billion, according to *Forbes*—far exceeding anything Bogle or anyone at Vanguard ever earned.

And yet Bogle's belief is at odds with Vanguard's management. In the same *Boston Globe* article in which he advocated increased disclosure, Vanguard spokesman John Woerth said: "Vanguard continues to hold that a fund's overall operating expenses—not the compensation paid to any one crew member—is far more relevant and meaningful."[2] It's not a subject most Vanguard executives obviously want to discuss, but when pressed, current CEO Bill McNabb echoes Woerth's sentiments regarding compensation disclosure: "I don't think it's helpful to the investor. What matters to the investor is what the investor pays. So to me, the number people need to focus on is the expense ratio."

Most other executives at Vanguard wouldn't speak on the record about the subject, but the company's stance on disclosure can be summed up by an article titled "'Yes, Virginia': The Compensation Question" written by Vanguard Principal Craig Stock on Vanguard's blog: "So how do you know Vanguard's executives aren't enriching themselves at your expense? You have to rely on your elected representatives: The eight independent directors of Vanguard's board, who together comprise the board's compensation committee. One key part of their job is to review and determine each year the compensation of senior officers to ensure that compensation levels are fair, competitive, and most importantly, designed with the best interests of fund shareholders in mind. These board members all are Vanguard investors, too, and they take their responsibility to fellow shareholders quite seriously." [3]

Wiener scoffs at the notion that shareholders should just trust the board to paternalistically do the right thing. "These board members are now being paid two hundred grand a year," he says. "That's not a bad gig, particularly as there is hardly any disclosure as to what's going on. It's very easy for the board to say, 'We're keeping up within industry standards with regard to executive compensation,' because the mutual fund industry is the best paid industry in the world." As for directors' ownership in Vanguard funds aligning their interests with shareholders, there is little evidence as to whether they're heavily invested in Vanguard funds or not, as the disclosure rules on director investments are lax too.

Ultimately, the Partnership Plan has proven more profitable to Vanguard executives than Vanguard's funds have been to shareholders. Although Wiener has been unable to uncover the total payouts to the plan, he's tracked the dividends for each individual unit or share of the plan and how they've grown over time. In a withering article titled "Partnership Still Beats Indexing" in the July 2009 issues of his newsletter, he revealed some of the privileges of partnership: "Over the past 25 years, the dividend has compounded at a 14.7 percent rate, which is a heck of a lot better than the 9.7 percent annualized gain for 500 Index. As I've often said in the past, it's a heck of a lot better to work for Vanguard than to invest in its flagship index fund." [4] In fact, such a record beats all of Vanguard Funds with the exception of Vanguard Health Care, a specialized sector fund.

And yet it's important to put the Partnership Plan in context. Although it is impossible to ascertain exactly how much Vanguard's top people are making, based on his previous calculations, Wiener estimated Brennan's 2008 compensation as chairman of Vanguard to be in excess of $7 million, while Bogle's he believed to be in excess of $11 million [5] if he was still holding all his partnership units, which Bogle says he isn't. Before he stepped down as CEO, Brennan's 2007 compensation, by Wiener's estimate, was between $6.5 million and $11 million. At publicly traded fund management companies, Gregory E. Johnson, CEO of Franklin Resources, made $7.6 million in fiscal year 2008 and $6.3 million in 2009, while CEO James Kennedy of T. Rowe Price Group made $5.7 million and $4.7 million in 2008 and 2009, respectively. At the high end, Laurence Fink of BlackRock, the world's largest asset manager, made $26 million in 2009, and Mario Gabelli of the much smaller Gamco Investors walked away with $43.6 million. As one can tell from this analysis, Wiener's estimates aren't exorbitant from the fund industry's perspective, yet they are by no means on a par with salaries found at the typical nonprofit organization, the chief executives of which earn an average of $160,000.[6]

In some respects, it's worth considering whether Bogle had any other choice but to offer the Partnership Plan. Given the outrageous salaries fund executives normally receive, to recruit top talent, he would have to be able to offer comparable pay. Executive compensation thus becomes an unavoidable arms race if one wants to engender loyalty, but with one key provision in this case. Vanguard runs index funds that do not need high-priced managers. The question then becomes whether Vanguard mistakenly expanded into areas it didn't need to be in and ended up spending more on recruiting top executive talent as a result. Unfortunately, it is a question shareholders can't currently answer because compensation is not disclosed.

If there was one battle for loyalty where Bogle triumphed unequivocally, it was with the press. Given the adversarial role he played in the fund industry, he faced a hard task in winning the respect of the members of the financial community. But he knew that Vanguard's unique structure and mission, if handled with complete candor, could generate favorable media attention. Essentially his own spokesman, he enjoyed talking to the press and, perhaps because of his own experience as a newspaper stringer in the summer of 1949, seemed to understand the needs of reporters better than most. He was brimming with controversial ideas, yet he spoke in simple, easy-to-understand sentences, providing numerous quotes that would add color to a story. He was always happy to take a call from a reporter, whether Vanguard was involved in the story or not. Even if the topic of the story was benign, Bogle, always the contrarian, found a way to make it controversial, not by design, but because of Vanguard's unique perspective. At the very least, he provided background that enabled the reporter to grasp the story's true relevance.

Bogle's candor was appealing to journalists, who had long found the mutual fund industry arcane and confusing and hence of little interest. Bogle prodded them to begin asking probing questions of industry leaders and to write stories on subjects that had long been taboo, such as the need for accurate disclosure of fund performance or for highly paid board directors to exert their influence on behalf of the mutual fund shareholders, whose sole interests they were supposed to serve. To the members of the media, who had long taken the industry's secretive behavior patterns for granted, he was a breath of fresh air. It was no coincidence that the same reporters who found Bogle such a good source of quotes began writing favorably about the news topic closest to Bogle's heart—The Vanguard Group.

Bogle's accessibility to the press was a pleasant contrast to the doors that were frequently slammed in the faces of journalists trying to talk to other industry leaders. The media found it so easy to reach Bogle that Vanguard's public relations department had little reason to call press conferences. Bogle preferred going one-on-one with a reporter; he enjoyed the give and take and saw the occasion as a chance to educate the writer, particularly about Bogle's own likes and dislikes.

High on his list of dislikes was advertising, a practice that the preacher found practically sinful. Bogle genuinely believed that if someone built a better mousetrap, customers would beat a path to his door. (One of his speeches was titled, "If You Build It, They Will Come," drawing on the theme of the movie *Field of Dreams*.) Bogle felt that mutual fund companies should have a trustee relationship with their clients, and he wanted to distinguish mutual fund distribution from the way products like beer or toothpaste were typically sold. "Bringing out new funds because the public wants new things is fine for Bloomingdale's," he said. "But supposing the public wants a fund that's a lousy investment? Does that mean we have to go out and sell it to them? I don't think so."

Given Bogle's strong views on advertising, it's not surprising that Vanguard spent relatively small sums—and those begrudgingly—on getting word of its funds out to investors, while its rivals, principally Fidelity, were outspending Vanguard many times over. In 1991, Vanguard spent $6 million on advertising; Fidelity was said to have spent some $50 million. By 1995, Fidelity had upped its advertising budget to an estimated $100 million; Vanguard, in contrast, was still spending its same $6 million. For Bogle, advertising was not just expensive, but often tainted as well. "Most advertising," he said, "takes the thrust that a particular fund is 'first in performance' and is therefore a good investment. The fund sponsors know . . . that today's 'first' may be tomorrow's 'last' and that the odds strongly favor a future return that is more or less average."

If Bogle was going to stake out the high moral ground on advertising, however, he knew that he still had to find some way to attract the attention of potential investors, if only to let them know that a better mousetrap had been built. One way to do so was to ensure that the message Vanguard communicated to investors was clear, sharply focused, and attractive. Beyond that, however, giving good quotes, supplying reporters with useful background information, and in general being contentious all became part of a conscious business strategy to win Vanguard continuing media attention. Jack Brennan, Bogle's successor as CEO of Vanguard, confessed: "Bogle's relationship with the press, being the first to be called on a lot of subjects, is a tremendous asset. It's worth millions of marketing dollars every year to us."

When it came to negative press reports about Vanguard, Bogle was so wedded to his company's values that if the reports were not solidly grounded in fact, they could infuriate him. For example, in its May 1, 1975, issue, *Forbes* magazine ran an article titled "A Plague on Both Houses" about the events leading to the birth of Vanguard. Enraged, Bogle grabbed a yellow pad and scribbled a six-page letter to editor James W. Michaels. "I hardly know where to begin in evaluating an article which is so breathtaking in the scope of its unfairness and its inaccuracy." He assailed the magazine for becoming a "self-appointed antagonist to the mutual fund industry." One of his chief complaints was that *Forbes* had used faulty research and thus unfairly criticized the performance of Vanguard's funds. Beyond that, he wrote, "The real tragedy of your article is not that you distorted and slanted some facts and figures. It is that you failed to take advantage of an opportunity to say something positive about a forward step for mutual fund investors. There is no doubt in my mind that our new structure is the beginning of a substantial change in our industry."

Bogle prides himself, though, on not holding grudges. *Forbes* was in his line of sight again after a May 8, 1995, article titled "Vanguard's Achilles' Heel," criticizing the company's equity fund performance. Bogle called the article "grotesquely unfair and incorrect," but rather than writing a letter to the editor, he wrote a blistering rebuttal addressed to the Vanguard directors and sent copies to the writers of the *Forbes* article. A week later, *Forbes* was writing an article on the fees paid to mutual fund directors. A reporter called, and Bogle agreed to talk to her about the issue.

"I'm surprised you're willing to talk to me," the reporter said to Bogle. "I saw the rebuttal letter you sent to your directors."

Bogle replied, "I would be willing to talk about anything. . . . We're not going to boycott the press no matter how awful the coverage is." Sounding Trumanesque, he concluded, "If you can't stand the heat, you ought to get out of the kitchen."

CHAPTER 10

The Great Bull Market

The greatest bull market in U.S. history began on August 12, 1982, and ended on March 24, 2000. During that period, the S&P 500 soared from 102 to 1,527, a cumulative price gain of 1,397 percent. The total return, which includes reinvested dividends, amounted to 2,033 percent, or about 18 percent annualized, almost double the long-term historical average of stocks.[1]

By just looking at these numbers, it's easy to see how people came to believe that, in the long run, stocks always go up and that the best thing to do was just let the market "work its magic" on your portfolio, if not the world. The mutual fund industry would capitalize on this naïveté. Investors, confident in a market that perpetually rose, wanted to maximize their exposure to it. There were two ways to do this—(1) buy high-cost aggressive growth funds that invest heavily in the riskiest, most overleveraged stocks, or (2) minimize the drag that fund expenses have on the market's returns and capture as much of the upside as possible. Vanguard, as the lowest-cost provider, had an immediate advantage in the latter case, while most other fund companies specialized in the former, but in the end it didn't matter. Every fund company triumphed as a rising tide lifted all boats. Fund assets soared from $297 billion in 1982 to $6.8 trillion by the year 2000; Vanguard's from $4.1 billion to $562 billion at the March 2000 peak.

Perhaps most surprising was that by the end of this speculative era, the Vanguard 500 Index, the company's most popular fund at the time, encapsulated both equity strategies, as outrageously overvalued tech stocks such as Cisco and EMC and fraudulent companies such as Enron and MCI WorldCom came to dominate the index. In the three years from the first quarter of 1997 through March 2000, the weighting of the tech sector in the S&P 500 increased from 13.5 percent to 33.9 percent.[2] If one included overhyped biotech, media, and telecom stocks in that number, no doubt the weighting in the most speculative stocks would have well exceeded 40 percent. At its peak, the average tech stock had an unheard of price/earnings (p/e) ratio of 135, while the index itself had a p/e of 30, more than double the historical average. The unintended consequences of this concentration was that even Vanguard's more conservative investor base was subject to undue risk.

Anyone who scrutinized the performance numbers from a historical standpoint should have been able to tell that they were suspect. Stocks had delivered an average return of 10 percent a year in the twentieth century. Half of that return (5 percent) could be attributed to earnings growth, while most of the remainder (4.5 percent) to dividend payments, and a small fraction (0.5 percent) to increases in valuation or the price/earnings ratio. But during the 1982–2000 bull market, 8 percentage points of stocks' 18 percent annual return stemmed from such valuation increases, or what is commonly referred to as p/e expansion.[3] There was no great earnings growth or dividend yields during the period to justify such returns. In short, speculation accounted for almost half the market's gain, and in the two bear markets to come, much of that speculative value would disappear.

Bogle, being more frank than most mutual fund executives, sounded a warning cry in his penultimate chairman's letter to shareholders of the S&P 500 index fund in March of 1999: "Just as the returns provided by stocks—particularly large-cap stocks—were well above average in 1998, so too were the returns over the past decade. That is sure to change. We are not forecasting a sharp pullback, though one may well occur. . . . That's why it's imperative for investors to build an investment program upon realistic expectations of future returns rather than an extrapolation of the extraordinary returns of the recent past. This is especially true when it comes to expectations for the S&P 500 Index. At year-end the index stood at a historically high price level relative to earnings and several other important measures. However, it cannot—and will not—continue to rise forever. Investors who ignore this truism of investing do so at their own peril."

What caused the market to go from frothy to completely rabid? Surely, to the free-market pundits or mutual fund hucksters, its surge must have seemed like providence or some form of financial manifest destiny—that as the earth revolved around the sun, so too must their beloved stock market rise year after year. Were the stars simply aligned? Or was there a concerted effort by those who stood to benefit the most from rising stock prices—Wall Street executives—to pump up prices as much as possible? The truth is a little bit of both.

The 1982 bull market emerged from the depths of what had been up until that point the worst recession since the Great Depression. Double-digit inflation during the Carter administration sparked by the oil crisis induced Fed Chairman Paul Volcker to "break the back of inflation" by raising interest rates to surreal heights. By 1981, short-term Treasury bills were paying unprecedented yields of 16 percent, while the prime rate to borrow for consumers was closer to 20 percent. Unemployment spiked as a result of the increased borrowing costs and the difficulty of funding any enterprise. But as more people found themselves out of work, the cost of labor declined, and inflation began to finally ease off. In the meanwhile, stocks, which had already been crushed in the 1973–1974 crash, continued to go nowhere.

Perhaps Nobel Prize–winning economist Paul Krugman explained the cause of the subsequent bull market best: "The secret of the long climb after 1982 was the economic plunge that preceded it. By the end of

1982 the U.S. economy was deeply depressed, with the worst unemployment rate since the Great Depression. So there was plenty of room to grow before the economy returned to anything like full employment."[4] All the stock market needed was some form of economic stimulus to light its fuse. The real spark for the explosion came, as Jack Bogle put it, on a hot Thursday afternoon in August 1982 when Wall Street economist Henry Kaufman predicted, among other things, that interest rates were about to drop. And so they did. The drop in interest rates, accompanied by a slowing of inflation, sent the stock and bond markets soaring.

Wall Street generally loves declining interest rates. As rates fall, bonds issued when rates were higher rise in price so that their yields are comparable to those on newer bonds. (Bond prices move inversely to their yields.) Stocks also begin to look more attractive as a source of return compared to bonds with falling yields. Meanwhile, investment bankers get to underwrite tons of debt for corporate borrowers that are seeking to leverage their balance sheets on the cheap. Consumers, of course, borrow more, too. Thus monetary policy stimulates the economy, but ultimately the extra leverage often proves destructive, as economies become overstimulated and inflation results. Or worse, companies and consumers who shouldn't have been borrowing become overextended and go bankrupt. The latter is precisely what was to happen in the wake of the greatest bull market in history. In fact, most Americans, who were supposedly making a mint off the stock market, were also becoming increasingly indebted. During that 1982–2000 bull market period, consumer credit, which doesn't even include mortgage debt, exploded from $383 billion to $1.6 trillion.

As is mentioned in Chapter 7, the high inflation of the 1970s changed the way Americans saved, since at the time there were federal caps of 5.5 percent on the amount of interest a bank savings account could pay. So for the first time, people became consumers of finance, shopping around for alternatives to passbook accounts and eventually stumbling upon money market mutual funds, which had no interest limits. Many became yield chasers, scouring the pages of the *Wall Street Journal* or *Donoghue's Money Fund Report* every week to find the funds with the biggest payouts. And this shift in mentality, from passively accepting their financial fate to aggressively pursuing the best returns, would have a dramatic impact on the stock market bubble to come, as the same pursuit of outperformance, of "beating the averages," would induce Americans later to chase after the hottest-performing stock funds.

While it's true that members of the middle class eventually became obsessed with the bull market, the impression in the financial media that they were huge beneficiaries of it is grossly misleading, as many didn't invest heavily in stocks until the rally was in its final innings. Although the mutual fund industry represents only a portion of total equity ownership, it is instructive to examine its asset numbers, as most middle-class investors achieve some of their stock exposure through it. And the evidence shows that it was the humble money market fund that most attracted individual investors' attention initially. At the start of 1982, only $41 billion of the $241 billion in mutual funds was in equity funds, while the remainder was in bond ($14 billion) and money market ($186 billion) funds. By the end of 1990, assets in bond ($291 billion) and money market ($498 billion) funds still outnumbered assets in stock ($239 billion) funds three to one. Only by the end of 1996 did assets in equity funds exceed that of their debt-oriented cousins.[5] From this it is fair to infer that many individual investors who did dive into the stock market did so near the height of what was then a bubble and probably enjoyed only a few years of solid returns before the 2000 crash.

So who did benefit? Corporate raiders, initially. As the middle class stampeded into money market funds in the 1980s, the low valuations in equities had sparked a leveraged buyout binge. By 1982, many stocks were so cheap that they were priced below the underlying value of their issuers' businesses. To exploit this phenomenon, corporate raiders would buy a public company and take it private. They would then sell off pieces of the enterprise to pay off the debt they had incurred to buy out the stock and try to prop up whatever was left of the remaining business. The trend, fostered by the likes of Carl Icahn and Michael Milken of Drexel Burnham Lambert, was terrible for the economy and caused unemployment to increase as companies were chopped up, dismantled, and sold, but it was great for the stock market, as share prices would rise in anticipation of the next takeover bid. No doubt fans of Joseph Schumpeter, an Austrian economist, would call thousands of employees losing their jobs because of one of these deals "creative destruction."

The mood of the 1980s was accurately captured by a speech Gregory Peck made in the 1991 film *Other People's Money* to shareholders of his company, New England Wire & Cable, about its imminent buyout by Danny Devito, aka Larry the Liquidator: "The Robber Barons of old at least left something tangible in their wake—a coal mine, a railroad, banks. This man leaves nothing. He creates nothing. He builds nothing. He runs nothing. And in his wake lies nothing but a blizzard of paper to cover the pain. Oh, if he said, 'I know how to run your business better than you,' that would be something worth talking about. But he's not saying that. He's saying, 'I'm going to kill you because at this particular moment in time, you're worth more dead than alive.'"[6] As a result of this kind of behavior, unemployment remained a high 7.5 percent on average throughout the 1980s even as the stock market gained 403 percent, or 17.6 percent annualized.

Whether most Americans benefited from it or not, the stage had been set for a monster bull market. During Reagan's presidency, he fired Paul Volcker, a Democrat, as Fed chairman in 1987 for not supporting banking deregulation and replaced him with libertarian Alan Greenspan, or "Easy Al," as he came to be known to his opponents. A personal friend of Ayn Rand and a believer in supply-side "trickle down" economics, Greenspan seemed to abandon his free-market ideology whenever it was necessary to bail out his friends on Wall Street by cutting interest rates and increasing the money supply, which he did several times during his tenure from 1987 until 2006, in particular during the savings and loan crisis of the late 1980s and early 1990s.

Specifically, in response to rising defaults in the consumer loan portfolios at S&Ls and most notably Citicorp in 1991, Greenspan cut rates by a full percentage point, to 3.5 percent. This increased the profit spread between Citi's short-term borrowing and long-term lending, thus enabling it to survive the write-downs. As financial columnist Jim Grant would later observe about Greenspan's responsiveness to the needs of the white-shoe class: "It was a short inferential hop to the conclusion that the Fed was now running monetary policy for the express purpose of bailing out Citi in particular, the banking system in general, and Wall Street in toto."[7] The same pattern of Greenspan coming to the rescue of Wall Street would recur again during the Long-Term Capital

Management hedge fund meltdown in 1998 and the dot-com implosion from 2000 through 2002.

Indeed, it's hard to look at Greenspan's behavior as not being the way Grant described it if one considers that the effective Fed funds interest rate went from a peak of 19 percent in 1981 to between 3 percent and 6 percent through much of the 1990s. Such low rates encouraged borrowing and consumption, but they also adversely affected savers, who earned less on their bank, money market, and bond fund accounts. By default, because the income payouts were so slim, those who were saving for retirement had two choices—save more or invest in stocks and hope for giant returns. To say that Americans simply "chose" the latter seemingly easier path ignores the fact that wages have been stagnant in real terms after adjusting for inflation since 1980, while the cost of housing, education, and medical care has soared. So the low rates and stagnant wages pretty much forced Americans to invest in stocks and resulted in their becoming increasingly mired in debt.

As a consequence, what began with a handful of corporate raiders far removed from mainstream America became a much broader trend in the 1990s. Some 76 million baby boomers born between 1946 and 1964 reached their peak earning and spending years during the 1990s. Aside from the increased level of general consumption they engendered, many were thrust into mutual fund investing as their employers switched from defined benefit pension plans to 401k plans. And as the bull market progressed, they began to invest increasingly in stocks. And yet, as previously noted, the account balances of all but the wealthiest 401k participants remained woefully inadequate to fund most people's retirements.

The real beneficiaries of the great 1990s bull run would always be the mutual fund companies and other financial product providers. They were the intermediaries between investors and their money, and they collected all those management fees regardless of whether the market went up or down. Bogle would observe in his book *The Battle for the Soul of Capitalism* that from 1985 through 2004, management fees consumed 43 percent of the average equity fund investor's return: "The investor put 100 percent of the capital and assumed 100 percent of the risk, but collected only 57 percent of the profit. The mutual fund management and distribution system put up zero percent of the capital and assumed zero percent of the risk, but collected 43 percent of the return."[8]

What was truly remarkable was that while assets in stock funds increased from $44 billion in 1980 to $4.0 trillion in 2004, the average equity fund's expense ratio rose from 0.94 percent to 1.56 percent. (Even asset-weighted, the expense ratio still increased from 0.64 percent to 0.92 percent.) The relationship between expense ratios and asset size is supposed to be an inverse one, since fixed costs are spread over larger asset bases as funds grow, but the opposite proved to be the case. So-called economies of scale should have been realized during this era of incredible growth, but if they were, management at most fund companies surely wasn't passing along those savings to shareholders. Instead, by 2004, the fund industry was collecting $37 billion a year in management fees.[9]

Sadly, as with any asset bubble, the most money flowed into stocks at the peak. Net new cash flow into stock mutual funds in the year 2000 was at an all-time record of $309 billion. Prior to 1990, stock fund investors had never put in more than $20 billion in a given year.[10] A similar pattern of the ignorant herd of investors stampeding into overvalued asset classes at the worst possible moment has recurred throughout history—from the eighteenth century's Dutch tulip bulb craze until today's housing bubble.

The advent of online trading at brokers and fund supermarkets such as Charles Schwab, E*Trade, and TD Ameritrade didn't help matters. Day trading in the 1990s became a fact of cultural life as commonplace as brokerage commercials with truck drivers who had purchased their own islands with their stock winnings. That the environment came to increasingly resemble a casino should come as no surprise to anyone familiar with the history of bubbles and manias. The online brokers and fund management companies were the lead croupiers at the roulette table. In the past, mutual fund shareholders would hold stock funds for years if not decades, but the online fund supermarket made it easy for them to buy and sell a fund with a click of a button. And increasingly the self-directed individual investors started chasing after the most speculative funds, investing in the most untried mirages of dot-com stocks.

Toward the end of the 1990s, as the bubble reached its frothiest, the economic theorists and academics stepped into the spotlight to justify the unjustifiable. Or rather, for the first time in their wonky lives, they got broadly noticed by the financial media. While the deregulate everything ideology of Milton Friedman had long been applied by his acolytes in government to sectors such as air travel, finance, telecommunication, and energy, for a number of decades some other members of the University of Chicago school of libertarianism were working in Friedman's shadow to prove that the capital markets were as efficient as those for telephones, accounting, and electricity, the deregulation of which fostered such smashing successes as MCI WorldCom, Arthur Andersen, and Enron. Their research was misinterpreted by the media as a legitimate rationale for why dot-com stocks with no prospects were somehow fairly priced, the solipsistic logic being that they were fairly priced because the market was always right.

In reality, many of the original efficient market academics were arguing that stock prices were random. So in their view the market wasn't always right; it was just that everybody who tried to figure it out was always wrong. Or as Keynes once quipped, "The market can stay irrational longer than you can stay solvent." So it might be possible for educated investors to realize that stocks were grossly overvalued or undervalued, but accurately timing the crash or comeback was virtually impossible. As a consequence, after deducting fees, money managers would lag the market. Although the theory failed to explain bubbles or busts, it proved a tremendous argument for indexing, with one major caveat: it never adequately explained whether it was worth owning stocks at all. It merely posited a relativistic argument that owning a low-cost index fund was better than owning a high-cost actively managed one. But was owning stocks better than not owning them at all? Only if you believed that taking on more risk always guaranteed more return.

Surely, if almost every stock was grossly overvalued, as most were in March 2000, owning stocks was a mistake altogether, even if you couldn't figure out when they would crash. But somehow the efficient market hypothesis added fuel to the notion that the market knew what it was doing and was accurately reflecting the underlying intrinsic value of the businesses it represented. The problem engendered by some of the hypothesis' proponents was extrapolating the market's past performance into the future and assuming that investors would be rewarded for taking on increasing amounts of risk. The public interpreted the theory as meaning that one must buy and hold stocks forever, no matter what the price. It was in retrospect a cruel irony of fate that the leading theory justifying the product Bogle developed to help investors get a fair shake was the same theory that helped exacerbate a stock bubble that would ultimately destroy much of their wealth. Over the next two and a half years, his beloved S&P 500 index would fall from its March 2000 peak of 1527 to a trough of 776 on October 9, 2002. It has yet to fully recover.

Bogle did his best to avoid much of the hype accompanying the bull market, although he certainly slipped once or twice. Every company was launching new mutual funds to capitalize on the investment craze. "Product proliferation" was the buzz phrase of the era. The number of individual funds rose from 665 at the start of 1982 to 8,155 by the end of 2000. In particular, funds with narrower, more speculative investment goals were rapidly supplanting more traditional funds, and funds with new investment strategies were copied just as fast as they attracted investor assets. In many cases, market demand replaced common sense. During different points in the era, Bogle spoke derisively about "government-plus" funds (creating phantom income by selling call options on their portfolio bonds), adjustable rate mortgage funds (purportedly offering higher yields than money market funds, but without added risk), and dot-com funds that sought to capitalize on the Internet craze. All the fad funds had their heyday before their investment promises proved illusory and assets plummeted.

Vanguard was as guilty of product proliferation as any other fund company, but with some crucial differences. The firm added some 82 new fund portfolios during the bull market, bringing the total number of funds it offered to 103 by March 2000, but instead of charging more for niche products, it charged less than everyone else. And instead of venturing into high-risk sectors of the market in an attempt to generate transitory, albeit eye-catching, returns that would attract assets, it generally stuck to the least risky sectors of that asset class. Of the 31 pure equity funds the company launched during the bull market, most were broadly diversified index funds such as Vanguard Total Stock Market Index or index-like—tax-managed and quant funds, which used computer algorithms to tweak the indexes slightly to get an edge but still held hundreds of stocks. Such funds generally courted much less sector-specific or stock concentration risk than their actively managed peers, with the 2000 tech bubble being one unfortunate and unavoidable exception. Even in the actively managed space, Vanguard tended to launch plain vanilla blue-chip funds such as Vanguard Equity Income that provided no thrills on the upside or chills on the down.

Although Bogle generally focused on funds with conservative strategies, there were a few he would later regret creating. "I made a lot of mistakes," he admits. "I allowed Vanguard to launch [closed-end] real estate funds. I also, in a moment of weakness—I was very ill at the time—started our sector funds. I thought we had created a system that was better than Fidelity's sector funds. But it was basically a marketing decision." Of the five sector funds launched in 1984, two—Vanguard Specialized Service Economy and Vanguard Specialized Technology—would ultimately be merged into other Vanguard funds in 1994. Although today Bogle hates volatile sector investing and counts these funds among his biggest regrets, as it turned out, the three remaining sector funds, investing in health care, energy, and precious metals, would go on to perform remarkably well relative to their peers. The two closed-end real estate funds, Vanguard Real Estate Funds I and II, would eventually be liquidated because of poor performance, although the company would subsequently launch a successful real estate stock index fund in 1996.

Yet the sector funds were the exception to Vanguard's overall strategy during Bogle's tenure, which was to offer funds invested in low-risk, high-quality securities and beat the competition on expenses. By the end of the bull market in March 2000, it had nine money market funds, which were unrivaled because their managers could buy debt issues of the highest credit quality and still generate superior yields to almost every other fund because of their low fees.

Vanguard also launched many bond funds, for a total of 27 by the end of 2000. Most of these invested in what Bogle called clearly "defined asset classes." Traditionally, bond fund managers at other shops practiced a "go anywhere" style that could sometimes get them in trouble if they chased after bonds with the highest yields but with shaky credit quality. Bogle believed in pursuing a strategy that targeted tightly defined slivers of the bond market so that investors knew exactly what they were getting when they purchased each fund. Typical for the period were the Vanguard Short-Term Federal and Vanguard Pennsylvania Long-Term Tax Exempt funds. The strategy was pleasing to shareholders for its simplicity, but it also gave Vanguard a competitive edge. By sticking to narrow sectors of the bond market, it made it impossible for competitors to make any great claims of beating Vanguard Short-Term Federal if they were investing in, say, long-term junk bonds. So the strategy forced them to compare their funds on an apples-to-apples basis, and inevitably, after deducting fees, they would lose in the comparison.

Fueling the engine of growth was the creativity that Bogle and his development team showed in devising new funds, including a Ginnie Mae fund, a short-term bond fund, a high-yield bond fund, a municipal money market fund, and state-specific municipal bond funds. Vanguard became the first mutual fund company to offer its shareholders the opportunity to choose from among three tax-exempt portfolios invested in short-term, intermediate-term, or long-term bonds rather than a single, vaguely described "managed municipal bond fund."

Did investors really need so many funds? Of course, in every burgeoning industry there is a tendency toward product proliferation as the field gets crowded with players and the original product becomes commoditized. Niche products with peculiar bells and whistles that no one actually needs become a way of increasing profit margins, since not every firm offers them. Companies can charge more because there is less competition in that particular sector of the market. This is the reason why when you go to the supermarket, you see 50 different kinds of yogurt and 100 brands of soap. One can tell that an industry has reached its saturation point by the length of the names of its products. When once there were funds with simple catchall names such as Wellington and Windsor, today there are funds such as AllianceBernstein Tax Managed Conservative Wealth Strategy and Vanguard Ohio Long-Term

Tax Exempt. Specialization becomes the name of the game in mature industries. The question is: how do we get people to buy more soap and/or pay more for it when soap is soap and everyone on earth has a bar?

In such commoditized markets, the low-cost provider always wins, and Vanguard was it. During the 1980s and 1990s, Vanguard essentially became the Wal-Mart of the fund industry. Perhaps the most pervasive trend in its favor was the growth of the direct marketing (usually no-load) segment of the industry. Since going no-load in 1977, Vanguard's assets grew at an astonishing annual rate of 25 percent through 2000. This phenomenon could not be explained away simply as a result of the bull market. Much of the growth from $1.8 billion in 1977 to $562 billion in March 2000 was a direct consequence of winning market share from people who had formerly invested in high-cost funds or load funds. Bogle would say as much in a 2001 speech: "The overwhelming portion of that huge increase has come from our rising share of market. Had our share held steady, our assets today would be $110 billion. The remaining $455 billion is accounted for by the increase of our share of total industry assets from 1.7 percent in 1981 to 8.3 percent today—without a single year of decline. This rise in market penetration has been accomplished with but a modest marketing budget, for I have always insisted: Market share must be earned and not be bought."[11]

Bogle had every right to feel vindicated after his battles with Wellington Management. Since going no-load in 1977, Vanguard grew from being the tenth largest fund company to second only to Fidelity, which it would subsequently surpass in 2008. Although Vanguard prospered from the mutual fund boom and from the direct marketing boom, it was Vanguard's other attributes that earned it the highest growth rate of any major mutual fund firm: the appeal of its low-cost funds in an era of consumerism, the performance of its funds relative to comparable competitors, its unique role in market index funds, and the public awareness of the Vanguard name, abetted by remarkably favorable press coverage. No matter how you looked at it, it was an era of incredible growth.

Above all else, it seemed to be Vanguard's low costs that caught the public's eye. Until Vanguard came along, no fund complex had staked a claim as the industry's lowest-cost provider. Ironically, when Vanguard started out on its own in 1974, its costs were slightly higher than competitive norms, with an expense ratio of 0.71 percent versus 0.70 percent for the average large fund complex. By 2000, Vanguard was by far the lowest-cost provider, having sliced its expense ratio to 0.27 percent, while that of the average large fund complex rose to 0.78 percent and the average fund charged 1.21 percent. Vanguard's huge cost advantage was a result of the combination of its unique "at-cost" corporate structure, its general operating efficiency, its economies of scale, its disciplined marketing and advertising expenditures, and its ability to bargain at arm's length in setting the fees paid to its external investment advisers.

While Vanguard easily won individual investors' hearts, it also made a successful foray into the institutional money management business during the great bull run. This posed a few problems that did not exist on the individual side. Vanguard had to continuously sell itself to institutional plan sponsors amid stiff competition. In the company's formal business proposal to prospective clients, senior officials at the institution had the chance to confront Vanguard executives and ask tough questions about the funds. They closely examined Vanguard's record-keeping service, its commitment to technology, and its ability to quickly and efficiently transmit information about a variety of investment plans to the institution's vast number of participants. Individual investors, in contrast, were more concerned with the funds' investment strategies and performance.

According to Vanguard executives, one reason the institutional side remained "the little sister" to the individual side of the business was that institutions were never one of Bogle's strong interests. His focus had always been on the little guy. Vanguard could woo individual investors one by one, through word of mouth. But "on the institutional side," said one staffer, "you had to use the S word, you had to sell. . . . The business doesn't walk in the door. And that's sort of anathema to Jack Bogle. He doesn't think investments should be sold." Nonetheless, Bogle enthusiastically endorsed the decision in 1984 to reach out for a larger piece of the institutional business. Vanguard's focus was on 401k thrift plans, already burgeoning in importance, and the firm began to put into place the complex systems required to administer them.

What little institutional business Vanguard initially had was largely the responsibility of Wellington Management, which continued to run money for various pension funds. As Vanguard grew rapidly on the retail side, the percentage of assets on the institutional side shrank throughout most of the 1980s, reaching a low of 22 percent of assets in 1991. But two new hires at Vanguard eventually turned the business around. James Gately, who ran Prudential Insurance's asset management subsidiary, was hired as senior vice president of the institutional division in 1989. "Jim Gately did a remarkable job in developing our business with institutional investors—especially in the 401k thrift plan arena," Bogle would later say. "He integrated our highly complex record-keeping activities with our marketing efforts and developed a first-class team around him." Under Gately's direction, Vanguard became one of the dominant firms in the institutional business, as its assets grew to nearly $70 billion by mid-1995.

In a reorganization of Vanguard's business lines in 1995, Gately left the institutional division to assume leadership of the individual division. His replacement in the institutional division was F. William McNabb III, who had worked closely with Gately since 1990 in developing the unit's strategic initiatives and had direct responsibility for all marketing, education, and sales activities. Leaving behind an assistant treasurer post at Chase Manhattan Bank, McNabb was hired at Vanguard in 1986 by Jeremy Duffield as a manager of insurance contracts.

By 1995, one-half of all corporate retirement plans were defined contribution plans, and in ever-increasing numbers, companies were trying to eliminate their defined benefit pension plans in favor of 401ks. For mutual fund firms like Vanguard, these plans were highly profitable, giving the company immediate access to millions of new investors.

Bill McNabb explained how the company won over a sizable chunk of the 401k business in the early 1980s: "It started out as a very entrepreneurial enterprise, and Vanguard was again a pioneer in the field. We took our retail computer system and modified it to do the administrative functions that were required in the 401k environment. The big thing we did differently . . . was to treat the participants in the 401k plan the same way as the other investors in our funds. This meant valuing their accounts every night, giving them an 800 phone number, and allowing them to switch from one fund to another." At that time, only a few mutual fund companies had matched Vanguard in pushing for 401k money, including T. Rowe Price and Fidelity. Vanguard's success was substantial, and its institutional business accounted for almost 42 percent of Vanguard's $562 billion in fund assets by the end of the bull market in March 2000.

As Vanguard gained strength and presence in both the individual and institutional markets, its asset growth began to compound. The first major milestone came on September 17, 1980, when the company reached $3 billion in assets under management, more than doubling the $1.4 billion initial asset base in 1974. Bogle threw a champagne party, and all 300 Vanguard employees squeezed into one room to hear him give a congratulatory speech while standing on a table. It had taken 31 years—from 1928 to 1959—for Wellington Fund, the Vanguard Funds' original flagship, to reach $1 billion. Total assets of all of the Vanguard (then Wellington Management) funds had first crossed $2 billion in 1965, a milestone that was long forgotten when the dark days of the early 1970s arrived and that Vanguard would not reach again until 1979. After that, the milestones were passed rapidly: $4 billion in 1981, $7 billion in 1983, $10 billion in 1985, $25 billion in 1987, $100 billion in 1993, $150 billion in May 1995, and $500 billion in June 1999.

While Bogle did not chase after growth, he accepted it as one of the best measurements of success. He appreciated the value of all those company milestones as employee morale boosters, and he made sure that there were celebrations and speeches to mark each occasion. He feared the consequences of growth, however, especially the development of a stultifying bureaucracy that would erode the flexibility and warmth that smaller funds could provide to clients. His dream for Vanguard was in some respects paradoxical. He wanted the company he founded to manage money for giant institutions yet avoid becoming like one, and one can sense the ambivalence in him about this subject to this day.

But he knew that growth was essential, citing in one speech to crew members the words of John Cardinal Newman: "Growth is the only evidence of life." Although Vanguard's conservative strategy and low fees were key to its success during the bull run, Bogle, ever the pragmatist, was candid about the role that luck played during this period. He acknowledged that even as the firm delivered on the mission it had sought for its clients, its growth was partly the result of events over which the company had no control—especially the emergence of money market funds and tax-favored retirement plans. Reminiscent of his comments about luck and a bull market, in a speech he delivered in June 1989, Bogle stressed: "Never underestimate the role of good fortune in our success." He could have been speaking for the entire fund industry when he uttered those words.

CHAPTER 11

"The Devil's Invention"

Vanguard launched the first index mutual fund, appropriately named First Index Investment Trust, in August 1976. Later, the name was changed to Vanguard 500 Index Fund. The company was not, however, the first money manager to track an index or even the S&P 500. But if you say to Jack Bogle that he created the first retail index fund, he'll holler, "No, no, no, no, don't use the word retail! This is the first index mutual fund period!" Although he readily admits that he wasn't the ur-indexer, he has, to put it mildly, a lot of pride in the invention, and certainly without him it's hard to imagine the index fund ever getting off the ground with the general public. The concept may have stayed within the rarefied field of academia or remained the exclusive province of institutional investors.

But the indexing idea had been kicked around for a long time before Vanguard launched its famous fund. Bogle himself had stated in his 1951 Princeton thesis that, "Funds can make no claim to superiority over the investment averages, which are in a sense investment trusts with fixed portfolios," although he would go on to explain the benefits of actively managed funds in the very same work. In fact, in 1960, when two University of Chicago finance wonks published an article titled "The Case for an Unmanaged Investment Company" in the *Financial Analysts Journal*, Bogle published a rebuttal titled "The Case for Mutual Fund Management" a few months later, using the pen name John B. Armstrong so as to avoid getting his employer, Wellington Management, in trouble with the SEC. In it he detailed how four unnamed funds—one of which was Wellington Fund—had beaten the Dow Jones Industrial Average for 30 years with less volatility than the market.[1]

The first indexed account was created by William Fouse and John McQuown at Wells Fargo Bank in 1971. Because at the time the Glass-Steagall Act prohibited banks from managing mutual funds, Wells Fargo could not launch an index fund for individual investors. So instead, Wells Fargo started to run institutional index money in a private $6 million account for Samsonite, the luggage manufacturer. Problems immediately resulted, though, because the benchmark Wells Fargo decided to track was the New York Stock Exchange, and McQuown and Fouse chose to equal-weight each of its 1,500 stocks. To maintain an equal position size in each stock required a great deal of turnover, and transaction costs consumed too much of the returns as a result. So in 1973 Wells Fargo switched to the S&P 500, a low-turnover market-cap-weighted index. Money manager Batterymarch Financial Management and the American National Bank in Chicago created similar indexed accounts for institutions at around the same time.

Although he always thought that most managers would lag the index, Bogle became a real convert in 1974 after reading an article called "Challenge to Judgment" by famed economist Paul Samuelson in the *Journal of Portfolio Management*. In the article, Samuelson pleaded for someone to start an index fund for retail investors. Bogle then read Charley Ellis's article "The Losers' Game" the following year, which outlined the basic argument for indexing: professional money managers now were the market in aggregate and would lag it after deducting their fees.[2] Ellis would later join Vanguard's board of directors.

As it happened, the timing to create an index fund couldn't have been better for Bogle. He had just launched Vanguard in May 1975 and was looking to internalize the advisory function of the mutual funds as the third step in "cutting the Gordian knot" that tied Vanguard to Wellington Management. "The biggest problem was selling it to Vanguard's board of directors because we had agreed not to get into investment management," says Bogle. "So I said, 'This fund didn't have a manager.' The directors bought that. Of course, technically, it's true. The fund is unmanaged." Former and present Vanguard index fund managers Jan Twardowski, George "Gus" Sauter, and Michael Buek might beg to differ, and Bogle himself would later say of his unmanaged fund pitch, "It was one of the greatest disingenuous acts of opportunism known to man."[3] Even index funds need a manager to make sure that the assets are invested appropriately.

Although he may have had some ulterior motives for starting the fund, certainly Bogle believed that indexing would produce the best results for investors. "We started operations in May of 1975 and I had the proposal for the index fund on the directors' desk in June of 1975—the first thing we did," he says. "Then the idea had to be sold to the directors, sold with data." Bogle crunched the numbers himself, calculating returns for the average mutual fund for the past 30 years versus the S&P 500 and proving that the index had an edge of 1.6 percentage points a year. "That was the evidence I needed to persuade the directors," he says. "I didn't need any persuasion myself." In May of 1976, Vanguard's board approved the filing of the First Index Investment Trust's prospectus.

But convincing the board was only the first step. Bogle also had to sell the index fund concept to investors and Wall Street itself. The reaction within the fund industry after the 1976 launch was decidedly negative: "the pursuit of mediocrity," one commentator called it; "un-American," said another; "the devil's invention," said a third; "a formula for a solid, consistent, long-term loser," said a fourth. Despite the naysayers, Bogle ultimately persuaded Dean Witter to lead an underwriting of the new fund. He'd hoped for $150 million, but it took three months to raise the $11 million that formed the initial base for the fund. By the end of 1976, the fund had grown to only $14 million. It was not going to be easy to convince investors to put their money into a fund that would merely match the market; investors wanted to *beat* the market.

Once the fund was launched, there were a number of technical challenges to running it. Computing technology was primitive in the 1970s compared to today, and instead of PCs, the fund's first manager, Jan Twardowski, had to dial in to a mainframe from a terminal via a slow acoustic coupler modem. Mainframes were big expensive devices that were shared with multiple users. Twardowski wrote the program to build the S&P 500 index portfolio using an antiquated computing language called APL. But at the time, the fund didn't have enough assets to buy all 500 stocks in the index, so Vanguard had to employ a sampling process of buying the larger stocks in the index and keeping sector weightings and other aspects of the fund similar to the index. Even though the turnover in a cap-weighted index is minimal, there were still significant challenges to buying and selling hundreds of stocks. Trading for most funds back then was usually in large blocks of single stocks, but the index fund needed to buy small blocks of hundreds of stocks. Vanguard had a special arrangement with an institutional broker to lower its transaction costs to a nickel a share, which, at the time, was a bargain.

Gradually, technology improved, transaction costs declined, and, most important, Vanguard began to win the ideological argument with investors and the rest of the fund industry about indexing. The traditional approach to equity portfolio management, and the one that remains the industry's modus operandi today, is to identify specific stocks that the fund manager believes will best achieve a fund's investment objectives and, most important, will perform better than "the market" itself. In this model, the adviser actively manages the portfolio by buying and selling stocks as perceived relative values change.

Vanguard's introduction of First Index Investment Trust represented a complete reversal of this active management approach—that is, a passive management approach, under which the manager, in effect, buys stocks in percentages representing the particular market to be emulated, essentially holding the securities on a permanent basis and hoping to replicate the performance of either the overall market or a predetermined, discrete sector of the market. Under the passive approach to investing, an index fund should perform about as well as the market it tracks. Active investors as a group—fund managers, individuals, pension managers, and so on—should also match the performance of the market; indeed, as a group, they *are* the market. But active fund managers as a group end up underperforming the market for their shareholders, largely because of their funds' advisory fees, operating expenses, and transaction costs, not to mention any sales loads paid by the investors who purchase the funds' shares.

Proponents of the passive school of investing argue that for the over-whelming majority of funds, active management works only in the short term, and then only for the gifted or the lucky. Ultimately, the returns on a mutual fund regress to the mean and then end up below the mean when expenses are taken into account. While this line of thinking had long been argued in academia, gradually the popular media began to take notice. In particular, the 1973 publication of Princeton professor Burton Malkiel's *A Random Walk Down Wall Street* marked a watershed moment in the history of finance, not because the ideas were new, but because the book explained the concept of efficient markets in lay terms and went on to be a bestseller, selling millions of copies. The book is currently in its ninth edition. Although he hadn't read the book prior to launching Vanguard's index fund, when he did, Bogle was amused by Malkiel's classic assertion that, "A blindfolded chimpanzee throwing darts at *The Wall Street Journal* can select a portfolio that can do just as well as the experts." Malkiel would go on to join Vanguard's board of directors, and he served from 1977 to 2005.

As it evolved, the efficient market hypothesis or EMH, as it is some-times called, splintered into three categories or "forms" of theory—weak, semistrong, and strong. Weak form EMH asserts that stock prices are random, and therefore most money managers cannot exploit the market to gain an edge. Although there is an acknowledgment that fundamental analysis might provide some excess return, whether or not money man-agers could exploit valuation inefficiencies in the market effectively over the long term is called into question. Semistrong form efficiency takes the argument a step further, claiming that the markets adapt so quickly to all publicly available information that even fundamental analysis doesn't add any value. Strong form efficiency arrogates that the market is so efficient that it already prices in all public and nonpublic information, and that even corporate insiders with private insights can't gain any legal advantage. According to both the semistrong and strong versions of the theory, the price of a company's share of stock immediately reflects all available information, as well as investor expectations, related to the company. In other words, the market is perfect and right all the time in its assessments of stocks' underlying intrinsic values.

Bogle never subscribed completely to the efficient market hypothesis, but rather to something he half-jokingly dubbed the "cost matters hypothesis." He examined the past performance records achieved by both the active and passive schools. He also examined the costs of each type of management. He concluded that a fund was far more likely to produce above-average returns under passive management than under active management. He based his conclusion on two factors:

1. All investors collectively own all of the stock market. Because passive investors—those who hold all stocks in the stock market—will match the gross return (before expenses) of the stock market, it follows that active investors as a group can perform no better: they must also match the gross return of the stock market.
2. The management fees and operating costs incurred by passive investors are substantially lower than the fees incurred by active investors. Additionally, actively managed funds have higher transaction costs because their managers' tactics drive them to buy and sell frequently, increasing portfolio turnover rates and therefore total costs. Since both active and passive investors achieve equal gross returns, it follows that passive investors, whose costs are lower, must earn higher net returns.

Putting numbers to this theory, the cost difference is dramatic. Vanguard was saving its index fund investors about 1.8 percent per year—the expense ratio of the 500 portfolio was 0.2 percent versus 2.0 percent for the average equity fund (expenses plus transaction costs). To put that amount into perspective, in a market with a 10 percent annual return, an index fund might provide an annual return of 9.8 percent, while a managed fund might earn an annual return of 8.0 percent. If this happens, over 20 years, a $10,000 initial investment in an index fund would grow to $64,900, while an identical investment in a managed fund would grow to $46,600, a difference of more than $18,000 in the accumulated account value.

IN THEORY. . .

As it turns out, the efficient market hypothesis was seriously flawed. Some of its proponents presumed that although market behavior was random, that randomness was controlled to a degree in that stock prices were expected to move according to a classic bell curve distribution around their intrinsic values, with many small price changes, a few larger ones, and no giant ones. But while such "controlled randomness" may occur to a degree in nature, human beings tend to be prone to fits of irrational exuberance and despair. As a result, the traditional bell curve, which flattened out at its extremities, actually possessed what became known as "fat tails" in the case of the stock market, meaning the occurrence of extreme price shifts was more common than originally thought. Such outrageous bubbles as we saw in 1999 and terrible panics as we saw in 1929, 1987, and 2008 meant that the semistrong and strong forms of the efficient market hypothesis were improbable at best, as stock prices so sharply diverged from any classical assessment of intrinsic value. This did not preclude the weak form EMH, however, which posited randomness but acknowledged that there were sometimes pricing inefficiencies in the market.

In many respects, the whole notion of "intrinsic value" seems absurd in the twenty-first century. Much of the academic research for efficient markets originated at the University of Chicago in the 1950s and 1960s. There's a reason why the ideological school of thought that the likes of Milton Friedman promulgated there was called "neoclassical economics." It espoused a belief in a rational, almost deistic universe in which men and women constantly seek to maximize their utility à la Adam Smith's invisible hand. And in this regard, the school really represented an intellectual backwater among both the social and hard sciences. The notion of any sort of eternal Platonic form of "value" went out the window the day Nietzsche uttered, "God is dead" in the nineteenth century. Values in the twentieth century became entirely subjective and earthbound. And the idea that people always behaved rationally in their own best interests was long gone by the time Freud and Dostoyevsky arrived, not to mention two world wars in which millions of people were exterminated needlessly. What was the rational utility of those? Even in the hard sciences, Einstein's quantum mechanics and the Heisenberg principle put the nail in the coffin of the idea that we live in an ordered universe with fixed values that are objectively measurable.

So if real scientists have trouble determining whether a unit of matter is a wave or a particle, where did these economists come off ascribing some sort of intrinsic numerical value to something as ephemeral and capricious as the stock market? Former Federal Reserve Chairman Paul Volcker recently expressed the problems of glomming neoclassical scientific methods onto the all too human realm of finance in an essay in the *New York Review of Books:* "One basic flaw running through much of the recent financial innovation is that thinking embedded in mathematics and physics could be directly adapted to markets. A search for repetitive patterns of behavior and computations of normal distribution curves are a big part of the physical sciences. However, financial markets are not driven by changes in natural forces but by human phenomena, with all their implications for herd behavior, for wide swings in emotion, and for political intervention and uncertainties."[4]

Even the founders of fundamental stock analysis, Ben Graham and David Dodd, who helped define concepts such as intrinsic value in their seminal 1934 book *Security Analysis,* understood how irrational human emotion constantly affected stock prices. In a section of the book titled "The Relationship of Intrinsic Value to Market Price," they write: "In other words, the market is not a weighing machine, on which the value of each issue is recorded by an exact and impersonal mechanism, in accordance with its specific qualities. Rather should we say that the market is a voting machine, whereon countless individuals register choices which are the product partly of reason and partly of emotion."[5] Ironically, this statement is often misquoted by money managers as "in the short run, the stock market is a voting machine, but in the long run it's a weighing machine." Not so. The stock market is always a voting machine determined by subjective ever-changing human assessments of values.

The only measurable values to be found in our relativistic age are within closed systems in which one thing is valued against another. So one may say that Microsoft is cheap relative to Amazon.com or the entire stock market or Treasury bonds or even to its own historical valuation, but one may not say that Microsoft is absolutely cheap. Our postmodern godless universe ascribes no specific intrinsic value to Microsoft as a business. (Even so-called discounted cash flow valuation models of Microsoft depend wholly on the relativistic vagaries of interest and tax rates set by irrational humans.) What's more, the field of semiotics, another 100-year-old area of inquiry that EMH supporters seem to have completely ignored, would argue that there is a persistent gap between the signifier of Microsoft as a stock and the "reality" or signified of Microsoft as a business. At the end of the day, Microsoft's ticker symbol "MSFT" is just letters signifying different things to different shareholders. "MSFT" is not Bill Gates and his software business. Moreover, the reality of Bill Gates and his software business is perpetually shifting, so there is no eternal Platonic form of Microsoft that can be measured as an intrinsic value. There is only Heraclitus's dictum: You can't step in the same river twice.

That said, within a closed system, any relative inefficiencies can potentially be exploited via arbitrage. The stock priced cheaply relative to the market can be bought while the stock priced expensively can be sold short or bet against. Eventually, if the market behaves rationally—a big IF—the valuation gap will close, and the arbitrageur makes a profit. Similarly, within the closed system of the stock market, the logic behind Bogle's cost matters hypothesis is also a kind of arbitrage and is, as a consequence, irrefutable. That's because one of the biggest inefficiencies in the stock market is the ridiculous fees money managers charge to invest in it. Within the closed system of all stock investors constituting the entire stock market, after deducting management and transaction fees, the average active manager will lag the market. So there is a relative 1.8 percentage point spread between the 0.20 percent expense ratio Vanguard charges for its index fund and the average fund's 2.0 percent in total management and transaction costs. And this spread has nothing to do with larger misguided concepts of efficient markets or intrinsic value. It is basic math within a closed system, and it is virtually guaranteed so long as management fees are contractually enforced by securities laws. In effect, Vanguard and Jack Bogle are practicing cost arbitrage.

Where the efficient market hypothesis and postmodernism meet is in the notion of randomness, but they diverge in the idea that the randomness is rational, that somehow the price movements of stocks are moving around some tangible anchor of intrinsic value on a bell curve. In this regard, the weak form of EMH was a real advance in finance, moving it ideologically into the twentieth century, but the strong form, which posits rationality, pushed it back into the eighteenth century.

Even though he was deeply committed to indexing, Bogle was willing to admit that some active investment managers could add value to the fund management process. In most cases, he argued, these managers either were lucky or were among a tiny group of true investment geniuses—market wizards such as Warren Buffett, Peter Lynch, Michael

Price, and Vanguard's own John Neff. In general, though, Bogle maintained that trying to outperform the market was a futile exercise. "Index funds," he said, "are a result of skepticism that any given financial manager can outperform the market. How can anyone possibly pick which stock funds are going to excel over the next 10 years?" In this context, the best strategy is to try simply to match the market in gross return and count on indexing's low costs to earn a higher net return than most competitors.

All of this, of course, was heresy to traditional active fund managers, who argued that the only reason to invest in mutual funds in the first place was to try to maximize returns, not simply match the market on the way up and the way down. But eventually, despite the ridicule of active fund managers, indexing began to catch on. The Vanguard 500 Index enjoyed positive net cash flow in each year of its existence and had grown to $500 million by the end of 1986—a decade after its launch. That same year, the Colonial Group introduced an index fund, the industry's second. (It would be out of business by 1990, however, because it carried a punitive load and a high expense ratio, thus eliminating any ability to match the index.) By 1988, Fidelity and Dreyfus had followed suit with their own index fund offerings.

Initially, Bogle spoke of the index fund as "an artistic, if not a commercial, success," but that changed during the 1990s, when investors started to notice that the fund was beating most of its peers. From 1985 through the end of 1999, Vanguard 500 earned a return of 1,204 percent, compared to the 886 percent average for the large-cap blend fund category, according to fund tracker Morningstar. Gradually, the fund's assets gathered steam, first topping the $1 billion mark in 1988 and beginning the 1990s with $1.8 billion. It then grew to $9.4 billion by 1995 and finally surged to $107 billion by the March 2000 peak, ultimately surpassing its archrival the Fidelity Magellan fund in the following month to become the largest mutual fund in the world.

Along the way, the technology for managing the "unmanaged" fund had improved dramatically. The fund's second manager, Gus Sauter, who today is Vanguard's CIO, took over the fund in 1987 and ran it through 2005. "When Gus first got here and looked at the software that was being used to manage the index funds, he said, 'You've got to be kidding me,'" says Vanguard CEO Bill McNabb. "The software was from the 1970s, a decade old. Gus came in, taught himself the old computer language, did diagnostics, and rewrote all the code in his spare time. You can see the difference in the index funds from the point Gus took over. There were two factors—one he rewrote the software, and two, he figured out how to use [index] futures. You can look at the tracking error in the early 1980s, and when Gus came in 1987, and you see this tremendous change in how tightly the funds began to track their benchmarks."

For Bogle, an index fund modeled on the S&P 500 was only the beginning. As the 500 fund grew in market acceptance and successfully operated at minimal cost, Bogle's confidence in the concept increased. The Standard & Poor's 500 represented roughly 70 percent of the market's capitalization. What about a portfolio that tracked the remaining 30 percent? Vanguard's Extended Market Index, formed in 1987, enabled investors to do exactly that, tracking the Wilshire 4500 Index.

Later, to simplify the process of holding both the 500 Index and the Extended Market Index, Vanguard offered the Total Stock Market Index, essentially owning the entire stock market by tracking the Wilshire 5000 Index, the most comprehensive market benchmark available. In 1989, the Small-Cap Index was introduced, using the Russell 2000 Index of small stocks, and a lower-cost 500 portfolio was designed for institutional investors with at least $10 million to invest. (Originally, most of the above index funds had slightly different names, often using the word "portfolio" instead of "index.") Today, assets in the Total Stock Market Index actually exceed those in the 500 Index, and Bogle himself prefers it as the best proxy for the U.S. stock market.

In a speech before the Financial Analysts of Philadelphia in 1990, Bogle said, "The introduction of index funds focusing on growth stocks and value stocks awaits only the development of a Growth Index and a Value Index." Standard & Poor's introduced these two new indexes in May 1992, and just two months later Vanguard launched portfolios with like objectives. Bogle was confident that the principles of indexing would also work in world markets—perhaps work even better, since the expense ratios and portfolio transaction costs of international mutual funds were far higher than they were for U.S. funds. Vanguard International Equity

Index Fund was introduced in 1990, with European and Pacific Rim portfolios; an Emerging Markets Index was added in mid-1994.

Nearly a decade after introducing the first equity index fund, Vanguard applied the indexing theory to the bond market, using the Lehman Aggregate Bond Index as a benchmark. (This index was renamed the Barclays Capital Aggregate Bond Index in 2008, after Lehman Brothers went bankrupt.) The Total Bond Market Index Fund, reflecting the market value of all taxable U.S. bonds, was founded in late 1986 to provide the same advantages of low cost, high quality, and broad diversification to bond fund investors that Vanguard 500 provided to equity fund investors. Early in 1994, without much enthusiasm from his associates, Bogle inaugurated three additional bond portfolios—short term, intermediate term, and long term—based on the appropriate Lehman indexes. The three new portfolios, like the original all-market bond portfolio, met with modest early acceptance but gradually became increasingly popular. As of October 2010, the Total Bond Market Index Fund had $89 billion in it, making it one of Vanguard's most popular funds.

Although Fidelity and Dreyfus funds joined the indexing fray in the 1980s, more out of expediency than out of desire, Vanguard faced no real competition from them in this area because they weren't really interested in selling such low-margin products. But gradually some other players that initially had flown beneath the radar emerged as a genuine threat to Vanguard's index fund dominance.

Perhaps it should come as no surprise that some of the same academics involved with the foundations of efficient market theory helped create Vanguard's first real competitors. One of the earliest was Dimensional Fund Advisors (DFA), which is based in Austin, Texas. Its founders, University of Chicago MBA graduates David Booth and Rex Sinquefield, were indexing even before Vanguard because Booth and Sinquefield worked, respectively, at Wells Fargo and American National Bank of Chicago on their institutional index accounts in the early 1970s. Together they launched DFA in 1981, providing index-like offerings with low expenses not to individual investors, but to financial advisers and institutions. Other efficient market "luminaries" such as Eugene Fama and Kenneth French soon joined DFA's board of directors.

DFA's approach to indexing differed from Vanguard's in that DFA wasn't afraid to venture into lesser-known, more risky areas of the securities markets such as micro-cap stocks and Japanese small-cap stocks. Its oldest fund, DFA U.S. Micro Cap, was launched in 1981. The firm was also not such a purist when it came to indexing, since it would sometimes tweak published benchmarks to gain an edge, tilting them more toward a valuation-driven model. Or it would create its own in-house indexes that it saw as superior to published ones. It also developed a proprietary trading system to minimize transaction costs. Although the value ($8.3 billion) of its largest fund, DFA Emerging Markets, is dwarfed by Vanguard's heavy hitters, its low-cost index philosophy was inspired by the same spirit of modern portfolio theory as Vanguard's, and many of its funds have proven highly competitive with Vanguard's best.

A far more significant threat emerged from State Street Global Advisors and Barclays Global Investors in the form of exchange traded funds (ETFs). These two money managers had already become fierce competitors in the institutional investor space for indexed assets in the 1980s and 1990s. For instance, total assets under management at State Street grew from $38 billion in 1988 to $142 billion by the end of 1993, and much of that institutional money was in passively managed indexed strategies. But then in 1993, State Street fired a broadside at Vanguard's retail business by launching the first ETF in the United States, the Standard & Poor's Depositary Receipt or the SPDR S&P 500 ETF, as it came to be called. The ETF followed the same benchmark as the Vanguard 500 fund, but it was tradable all day long like a stock and therefore was easily accessible to individual investors. What's more, the management fees were competitive with Vanguard's. In fact, by March 2000, State Street had reduced the SPDR S&P 500's expense ratio to 0.12 percent, which was less than Vanguard 500's 0.18 percent for individual investors at the time. By then the ETF had already attracted some $17.3 billion in assets.

It wasn't long before Barclays also entered the arena. The same division of wonky efficient market enthusiasts at Wells Fargo Bank that created the first institutional index account in 1971 was eventually acquired by Britain's Barclays Bank for $440 million in 1995 to become Barclays Global Investors. In the meantime, Barclays had already become an institutional indexing powerhouse. In 1996, it collaborated with Morgan Stanley to launch its World Equity Benchmark Shares or WEBS brand of index ETFs that tracked various international markets such as those of France, Italy, and Japan. These were later rebranded as iShares in May 2000, which was about the same time that Barclays started to aggressively launch other ETFs that tracked U.S. benchmarks similar to Vanguard's. By the market's peak in 2000, Barclays was already managing $800 billion worldwide, primarily in institutional assets, but the storm clouds were brewing.

At the time, Vanguard officially claimed that it didn't see ETFs as much of a threat. "To me it's effectively a product extension like instant coffee," said Vanguard spokesman Brian Mattes in March 2000, just as Barclays was preparing for a major rollout of new ETFs. "When instant coffee debuted, did it really hurt the sales of brewed coffee? No. People still liked brewed coffee. But it put coffee in the hands of people who couldn't wait for it to percolate."[6] But behind the scenes, the pressure was mounting. Indeed, although index funds had grown from 9 percent of total equity fund assets in 1999 to 17 percent by 2007, 7 percentage points of that number were from index ETFs. Without ETFs, the index mutual fund market share would have grown to only 10 percent.

Bogle, for his part, has always seemed ambivalent about ETFs. He thinks the low costs, broad diversification, and tax efficiency of the more conventional S&P 500 type of ETFs have the same advantages as traditional index funds, but he frets that excess speculation in them will eat into investors' returns via high transaction costs and thus cause investors to buy and sell them at inopportune times. "The ETF is a little bit like the famed Purdey shotgun that you buy over in London," he says. "It's the greatest shotgun ever made. It's great for killing big game in Africa, but it's also great for suicide." Needless to say, Vanguard launched no ETFs under Bogle's watch as CEO or chairman. And yet once he stepped down as chairman in 1999, it wouldn't be long before Vanguard, too, felt the need to enter the fray. Perhaps, despite Bogle's best intentions, his beloved index fund was on its way to becoming the devil's invention.

CHAPTER 12

The Two Jacks

Could two men be more different than John C. Bogle and John J. Brennan, or the two Jacks, as they were sometimes called? While Bogle had to struggle at an early age, with a difficult home life and the specter of the Great Depression at his doorstep, Brennan grew up during the 1950s and 1960s in the tony Boston suburb of Winchester, the son of well-connected parents whom a fellow financier called "the first couple of downtown Boston banking."[1] His father, Frank Brennan, ran the Union Warren Savings Bank and the Massachusetts Business Development Corp. and knew many of the local politicians and muckety-mucks.

What was truly remarkable was how far the Brennan family had come in so short a period of time. Brennan's grandparents John and Bridget were impoverished Irish immigrants who worked as janitors at Harvard. Yet, according to the *Globe*'s 2010 obituary of him, Frank Brennan's "resume over the years included being president of the Massachusetts Bankers Association; director of the Boston Mutual Life Insurance Company; director of the Mutual Savings Foundation of America; vice chairman of the board of Homeowners Savings Bank; and chairman of the board of Dreyfus/Laurel Mutual Fund."[2] And one can only imagine the strange heady elixir of pride yet also irony the entire Brennan clan must have felt when John J. graduated with an MBA from Harvard in 1980. To go from cleaning the grounds of America's preeminent university to graduating from it and running the largest mutual fund company in the world in three generations is no small feat.

The differences don't end there. With Bogle's legendary honesty and outspokenness, which have been a boon for an industry beset with conflicts of interest, there also comes a certain degree of hubris. Upon meeting him for the first time, Bogle will assail you with never-ending examples of his rhetorical brilliance, often citing passages from his own speeches verbatim off the top of his head. And yet he will intentionally undercut his flights of egomania with remarks like, "My brothers were both smarter than me," or, "I'm an extremely ordinary human being," or, "You could argue that the fact that I'm not brilliant is Vanguard's greatest asset." That said, many of those closest to Bogle don't quite buy the humble act. "He says he's not very smart all the time, and we all just roll our eyes," says his daughter Barbara. Perhaps his brother Bud put it best when he said, "Jack has an ego that's a mile high, but he handles it very well."

Brennan, by contrast, has always been modest, intensely private, and self-effacing. While Bogle remains a complete media hound, a 1997 *BusinessWeek* profile of Brennan published not long after he assumed the role of Vanguard's CEO was titled, "Vanguard's New Boss: 'Being Famous Was Never on My Agenda.'" The article's very first paragraph reveals how different he is from Bogle: "John J. Brennan has enjoyed his anonymity. But last November, after becoming chief executive of mutual-fund giant Vanguard Group, he discovered that privacy may be a thing of the past. While coaching his young son's soccer team, Brennan was approached by a player's mother who had seen him on a recent Wall Street Week with Louis Rukeyser, his first appearance there. 'She said: 'I didn't realize you were that Jack Brennan,' he recalls with a laugh. 'She thought I was a gym teacher or professional coach.'"[3]

Brennan rarely speaks to the press, especially nowadays since he officially retired from Vanguard at the tender age of 55. In fact, he declined to participate in this book. "Bogle will talk about himself till the end of time," says Jeremy Duffield, a former assistant of Bogle's who is today Vanguard's head of international planning and development. "Brennan won't talk about himself. He is much more modest and private. That is the challenge in getting the full correct story." Bogle has, in fact, mocked Brennan's occasional awkwardness with the media, calling Brennan's infrequent and, in Bogle's view, inarticulate television appearances an "embarrassment."

The desire for the spotlight and the complete avoidance of it may be the key distinguishing features between the two men. "I know that obviously Bogle has a large ego, and he obviously has a reason to have a large ego," says former Vanguard Windsor manager John Neff. "The thing that baffles me is why Brennan retired at 55. In other words, Jack Bogle wants to go on forever, and Brennan gave it up at 55. That's as sharp a contrast as you can experience, but I don't know how to expand on it. They are different people."

Even physically the men have striking differences. While both are avid sports fans and Bogle would sometimes risk his life to play his beloved squash, his heart condition on the negative side limited some of his physical activity but on the positive gave him a better sense of his own mortality and the fragility of human life at a very young age. If anything could inspire a philosophy of carpe diem, it would be such an ailment. Illness also can teach a degree of empathy with the less fortunate. It's hard not to suspect that Bogle's desire to keep working, even into his eighties, his charitable impulses, and his seemingly paradoxical combination of hubris and humility might in part stem from so many near-death experiences.

By contrast, as an undergraduate at Dartmouth, Brennan played varsity hockey, soccer, and lacrosse. Later, at Harvard, he took up rugby. An avid marathoner, he often skipped lunch at Vanguard in favor of a six-mile run through Vanguard's campus. Sports always served as a primary inspiration for him. When Brennan was Vanguard's CEO, hokey motivational books such as basketball coach Pat Riley's *The Winner Within* were displayed prominently in Vanguard's executive library.[4] So what did this man who always seemed to be the picture of health, who grew up with every opportunity, have to do with someone forged in the crucible of hardship like Bogle?

In the Venn diagram of their lives, the three key areas where the men's personalities overlap were in their shared sense of thrift, industriousness, and hyper-competiveness. Brennan, much like Bogle and Brennan's father, Frank, was never one for conspicuous consumption, mowing his own lawn, working in a small office, and driving a sensible Audi, which a friend described as his "only luxury."[5] In a rare Q&A Brennan conducted with *Money* magazine in July 1995, shortly after the succession plans were announced, he expressed his own vision of monkish austerity and frugality for Vanguard: "We don't have big shot executives. No one has company cars, parking spaces, or club memberships. I even feel a little bit guilty having an office with a window. We travel coach on planes, we eat in the company cafeteria, we don't play golf, we don't boondoggle." Referring to the enormous assets that Vanguard had accumulated, Brennan noted with pride, "I still look at every dollar that we spend as if it were coming out of my own pocket."[6]

Both men also liked to win and were willing to work themselves to death to do it, only their objectives seemed different. Bogle was more interested in the shareholders of the funds, while Brennan's interests were in the Vanguard Group as a business. And this, as we shall soon see, is part of an important philosophical divide between them. Their shared competitiveness, which worked so well when Bogle was Team Vanguard's manager, fell apart the moment Brennan assumed that role. "Jack believed in [Brennan] for so long," says Bogle's brother Bud. "He once told me, 'I used to get to work at 7:30 but then Brennan came to work at 7. So I started to come to work at 7. And then Brennan started to get there at 6:30, so I started being there at 6:30,' so Jack wasn't going to let Brennan outshine him."

This silent passive-aggressive battle of wills, whether intentional or not, seems cruel in retrospect, given Bogle's age and heart condition. That the über-competitive Bogle would take the bait despite his advanced age is no surprise. Brennan, who liked to put in 13-hour days and even came to work on Saturdays, probably should have known better. At the time prior to Brennan's succession as CEO in 1996, Bud, who had his own reservations about his brother's plans, questioned Jack about them: "To me, we had conversation after conversation about Brennan, and he was the greatest guy in the world: he was going to do everything, and all of a sudden, one day I asked, 'Jack, do you think it was a mistake that you chose Brennan to be your successor?' He said, 'Bud-ro,' in these words, 'it was the biggest mistake I've ever made.'"

Although Bogle himself would never publicly say those words, his animosity toward Brennan is palpable whenever the subject comes up. When I asked him whether now that Brennan has retired as Vanguard's CEO and Chairman, they could settle their differences and be friends again, Bogle replied, "I think that will happen when hell freezes over." Much of what he said to me about his falling out with Brennan he wanted off the record and instead kept referring me to a 2003 *Baltimore Sun* article by Paul Adams. In it Adams describes a chilly firsthand encounter between the two men:

> **Employees still greet [Bogle] reverentially as he strolls the halls, but he is no longer welcome in the executive offices upstairs. The unpleasant circumstances of Bogle's departure from the board have driven a wedge between him and his hand-picked successor, John J. Brennan. As they passed each other on the stairway one recent Friday, Bogle greeted his former protégé. Brennan, who was walking with a Vanguard attorney, never looked up. "I gave them their jobs," said Bogle, who was dressed comfortably in a green sweater and khaki pants. "I just don't understand."**[7]

According to Bogle, despite the fact that they worked in the same Victory building on Vanguard's campus for years, Brennan didn't speak to him during Brennan's entire tenure as chairman. Unfortunately, there is no "according to Brennan." As a consequence of this lack of communication, the greatest challenge in writing any sort of story about Vanguard is understanding what exactly transpired between Bogle and Brennan to ruin what seemed like a fairly close friendship. No one in the Vanguard organization really wants to talk about it. As one insider who declined to be named described their falling out: "It was like when you see two friends go through a divorce. You like both of them, and you can't understand why they can't get along." And because both men are so respected—and feared—in the Vanguard organization, no one wants to get caught taking sides in their dispute.

Part of the problem may stem from the fact that Brennan was not who Bogle originally intended to be his successor. His ideal replacement probably would have been Jim Riepe, his assistant and later Vanguard's executive vice president, who left in 1982 to accept a senior management position at competitor T. Rowe Price. "There were tears in Jack Bogle's eyes when Jim Riepe left that company," says Barbara Scudder, Vanguard's director of communications from 1974 through 1997. "Bogle thought the world of him." Riepe had been with Bogle since his Wellington days and was instrumental in the founding of Vanguard. He and Bogle were incredibly close. "We knew Brennan pretty well, and Jack picked him instead of someone I thought should have been the next head, one of Jack's best friends, Jim Riepe, who left finally, because he wasn't going to get to the top," says Bogle's brother Bud. "My brother wasn't going to assign the responsibility to someone else as long as he was able to do it."

In some respects, the issue of whether Riepe would have been a more appropriate choice or not was moot for precisely the reasons Bud Bogle raises. Riepe knew that Jack would never cede control as long as he was able to work and wisely made the right choice to move on. "Jack and I were very close. And, as I told him then, I thought that we would not be able to remain as close if I stayed," says Riepe. "Part of it was that Jack is a very strong guy, and he was still young when I left. Even though I knew he had all these heart troubles, I always assumed and still assume he will outlive me. I knew if I became his successor, he was still going to be there. This was his life."

Though he never really got over losing Riepe, Bogle knew that he had to develop an heir apparent, especially since his heart condition continued to deteriorate. Someone had to be next in line just in case the worst happened. In September 1982, he hired as Vanguard's president a former associate, Jerald L. Stevens, whom he hoped to groom as his replacement as chief executive officer. Stevens, who had proceeded from Yale to Harvard Business School, worked for Wellington Management Company after his graduation in 1967. He left Wellington Management Company in 1973 and ultimately became vice president for finance and administration at Yale University from 1977 until 1982, when he joined Vanguard. Bogle described Stevens as "brilliant," but the chemistry was bad between Stevens on the one hand and Bogle and the board of directors on the other, and Stevens left in January 1984.

With Stevens's departure, Bogle turned to Brennan, who had arrived at Vanguard two years earlier. When Riepe left, Bogle's assistant, Jeremy Duffield, moved up to become head of new fund development, and Bogle sought a new assistant. So in July of 1982 he recruited Brennan from Johnson Wax, the Racine, Wisconsin–based manufacturer of Pledge, Windex, Drano, Raid, and Toilet Duck. Before he joined the firm, Brennan had never even heard of Vanguard, having grown up in a Boston suburb where the mutual fund industry was synonymous with the name Fidelity. But his Harvard MBA caught Duffield's eye when he was searching a recruitment database. At the time, Brennan had most of his money invested in a Fidelity money market fund.

Too frugal to fly Brennan in, Bogle first had him interviewed by phone and then made him take a personality test. He was immediately impressed by Brennan's facility with numbers and financial data and hired him. Up until Bogle's heart transplant in 1996, the two seemed remarkably close, lunching together daily in the cafeteria and being in and out of each other's offices constantly. At one point, Brennan was even a trustee for Bogle's personal estate. The last thing anyone expected was for their relationship to hit the rocks. "I was his protégé running Blair and Brennan was his protégé running Vanguard," says Chandler Hardwick, the headmaster of Blair Academy. "He handpicked Jack Brennan, and he handpicked me. We were sort of peas in the same pod of Jack Bogle back then until suddenly the Jack Brennan thing fell apart."

While Bogle came to regard Brennan as his successor not long after he was hired in 1982, there was never any public announcement within the company that Brennan would someday take over for Bogle. Though he quickly rose to chief financial officer in 1985 and to executive vice president in 1986, the first clear indication that he would be Bogle's heir apparent came in 1987, when Brennan was elected to serve on the Vanguard board of directors. Then, in 1989, he was elected president.

If Bogle was reasonably sure about Brennan, the decision was never chiseled in stone. The closest Bogle ever came to a formal announcement was in a 1990 brochure called "The Vanguard Advantage," which described the virtues of the company. Included in the booklet was a photograph of Walter Morgan, Bogle, and Brennan; the caption read, "To clarify the line of succession, in mid-1989 John J. Brennan was elected President of The Vanguard Group and each of our investment companies." The picture told the entire story: here were Vanguard's leaders, past, present, and future. Nonetheless, in a December 1991 *Fortune* story, Bogle said, "Jack Brennan could still use a bit more seasoning."

Gradually, Brennan began to assume more responsibility for Vanguard's operations. He gave more speeches, his name appeared in print more often, he toured the country talking to groups of shareholders, and he began meeting with many of Vanguard's large institutional clients. Bogle made a point of consulting with Brennan on key strategic decisions, and Brennan began to place his mark on the company. This was both a gratifying and a frustrating time in his Vanguard career—gratifying because he knew that he would one day be captain of the ship, frustrating because he had to play a delicate game, remaining deferential to Bogle. Nonetheless, with the rest of the company and the entire industry watching, he was trying on the captain's uniform, occasionally even wearing it in public.

While Brennan would also face the difficult task of rallying the crew behind him, most staffers seemed to have the highest respect for him and thought that there would be some things to look forward to about the transition. Bogle had been so dominant and hard-driving that any of his personal weaknesses were dismissed as irrelevant. Some of his associates believed that, as the years went by, those weaknesses—some real, some perceived—were serving as an anchor that slowed the ship: Bogle had little interest in information technology; he was too inflexible in his disdain for riskier funds; he had no love for international funds, or international marketing of U.S. funds, or even for highly speculative funds. Brennan, in contrast, was a technophile, and he took a less rigid line on international expansion and more aggressive funds. To many staffers, he would be the ideal leader in the post-Bogle era.

What's more, while they admired Bogle and recognized that he was one of the giants in the field, Vanguard staffers knew that the company—indeed the entire industry—was changing, and they were dubious that Bogle would be able to change with it. Said Jim Norris, "I don't believe Jack Bogle is capable of being a facilitator, of doing 'the management thing.' He would probably say so himself. In fact, I remember him saying once, off the cuff, 'I've never managed someone in my life.' Jack Brennan, on the other hand is the consummate manager; he runs the day-to-day activities of this company. Jack Bogle's primary involvement has really been as the leader . . . his has been the vision."

By most accounts, Norris's assessment of the situation is an accurate one. For years before he donned the CEO's suit, Brennan handled much of Vanguard's daily operations while Bogle remained the visionary, the ethical and philosophical center of the organization who was less interested in the sometimes stultifying details of running a big institution. "Brennan's a Harvard Business School guy and could get into operational issues like are we spending enough on computers," says Burton Malkiel, who was a Vanguard board member from 1977 until 2005. "That kind of thing really wasn't Jack Bogle's forte. He was really the idea man who put the whole company together and its basic philosophy. Brennan probably couldn't have done and wouldn't have done the idea that started Vanguard, but he might be a better person to run Vanguard after it had become a big institution that needed to be managed."

Indeed, Bogle would always say a little derisively after he was ousted from Vanguard's board that Brennan was a "good manager." In one 1999 article about what would become an all-too-public flap over his retirement, he remarked, "The significant difference is, I created a strategy because I was on a mission. Now we have businessmen more than missionaries."[8] In another article published at around the same time, Bogle remarked about how he came to select Brennan as his successor: "The engine had been designed, created, and built. The tracks had been laid down. The real challenge was to make the trains run on time."[9] Behind the scenes, things may have gotten considerably uglier. "I remember a while back a friend of mine wrote a cover story for *Forbes* about Jack

Brennan, and Bogle called up my friend completely steamed and said, 'Why are you putting the picture of a caretaker on the cover?'" says Dan Wiener, editor of *The Independent Adviser for Vanguard Investors.*

And yet Bogle showed much more confidence in his decision when he first made it in 1995. At the May 19 board meeting, Bogle announced that he planned to step down as CEO effective January 31, 1996, but that he would, if the board approved, remain as chairman of the board. Bogle was ambiguous about what would change once the transition had taken effect. He told associates that he planned to come in to work four days a week, so little would change there, except that he would take more vacation time. He indicated that he planned to continue to watch over the interests of the shareholders and the crew, to write, to give speeches, and to try to keep the mutual fund industry moving in what he saw as the right direction. In short, he would continue to be Jack Bogle.

A May 25 press release confirmed these details. While the release appeared to convey the message that Bogle was stepping down, toward the end it quoted him as promising, "I will still be around." The press release also announced that he planned to nominate Brennan as his successor as CEO. In the release, Bogle called Brennan "the best person I could possibly have found . . . a man of extraordinary character, intelligence, diligence, and judgment." It should be noted that Bogle recommended, and the board agreed, to make Brennan's appointment effective seven months later because Bogle felt that Vanguard should give shareholders plenty of notice before the change actually occurred.

Though he may have lacked Bogle's creative vision, by any stretch of the imagination, Brennan was—everyone would agree—a fabulous manager. During his tenure, Vanguard's assets more than septupled from $180 billion at the start of 1996 to exceed $1.3 trillion when he stepped down in December 2009. (He abdicated his CEO post to Bill McNabb in 2008 but kept his board chairmanship till the end of 2009.) But if the only measure of Vanguard's success was its asset size, then Bogle's dream of running it solely for mutual fund shareholders would cease to be, because bigger is not always better when it comes to mutual funds. In fact, many fund companies pride themselves on remaining small and nimble so that their money managers can trade stocks more effectively. So while as a management company the Vanguard Group was utterly triumphant under Brennan, whether or not shareholders of Vanguard Funds benefited from the growth is not so clear.

Still, Bogle and Brennan's relationship seemed fine up until Bogle received his heart transplant. His cardiologists ultimately decided that his heart had deteriorated so much that he should have the operation. So on October 17, 1995, he was admitted to Hahnemann University Hospital in Philadelphia and stayed there a grueling four months until he received a transplant on February 21, 1996. Because there are long waiting lists for heart transplants and no favoritism is allowed, patients often have to wait many months and be near death before they receive one. Such was certainly the case with Bogle, who was "upgraded" from status B on the waiting list to status A in the summer of 1995 based solely on his terrible condition. "We usually list patients for transplants only when we think their one-year survival is in jeopardy," says Dr. Susan Brozena, Bogle's cardiologist. "In 1995 Mr. B.'s one-year survival was in jeopardy, and while some people have reversible heart disease, he did not. His condition was progressing, and it was only going to get worse."

Bogle would later remark that the heart transplant waiting process was as democratic as a traffic jam: "There's no saying that 'Bogle is an important guy,' or, 'Say, I'll give you some money and get a heart transplant.' That's not part of the game. It's extremely democratic, and it's extremely fair. So you wait your turn, and it comes gradually." Unfortunately, it became increasingly clear he was really at death's door. As the blood flow to the rest of his body slowed from his failing heart, his skin color turned grey, and his extremities—his hands and feet—swelled to strange proportions. He started to have difficulty breathing and moving, and he suffered from a terrible feeling of confinement during the final days before the operation. "At the time it was so clear the transplant was the only option," says his daughter Barbara. "He was in such poor health and so unable to participate in life as he wanted to. He could barely walk or climb stairs he was so restricted. And he had been such an active person. It was so clear it was the only option. But it was very very scary."

Anyone with the impression that Bogle might take it easy while he waited would be sorely mistaken. Despite his rapidly deteriorating condition, he continued to write Vanguard's annual reports, answer shareholder correspondence, and study Morningstar fund snapshot pages that were often strewn across his entire bed. "Oh, if you knew this man, you would never count him out," says Barbara Scudder. "His hospital room was like a small office. I will never forget it. He was wearing a red corduroy flannel shirt and maybe he had his pajama pants on, but he had a whole functioning office there, with a computer, pictures of his grandchildren on the wall, all kinds of paper and writing going on. Yes, he was very, very busy and stayed that way I'm sure until he walked back through the doors."

And Brennan by all appearances seemed to be right by Bogle's side every step of the way, visiting him in the hospital at least once a week, partially to discuss business, but also to check up on him. "I never quite understood their falling out," says Raymond Klapinsky, a retired Vanguard managing director. "It was really a shock to some of us old-timers there because Jack Brenann was like a son to him. I remember when Bogle was in the hospital over Christmas time, Jack Brennan was down there, Christmas eve, with his wife and kids, sitting with him, trying to cheer him up a bit. All of a sudden he gets a new heart and things certainly changed."

Although it took him some months to fully recover from the surgery, Bogle was soon back in his office and ready to work. And this is where his troubles with Brennan began. Although it is difficult to pinpoint exactly, the turn in their relationship may have occurred when Brennan and Vanguard's board of directors insisted that Bogle's title change to senior chairman so that Brennan could assume the role of chairman. "Within about a year after I returned, [Brennan] said the board looked—he said 'It's just not working. We have to get rid of Jack as chairman and [Brennan] will be both chairman and president,'" Bogle says. "During that whole period he never spoke to me. It was kind of messy. We were both at board meetings. As chairman I was running the meetings, and he was giving the management report. I would say I have questions about this or that—we have to declare a dividend or whatever the hell a chairman does—so that situation lasted I think until about 1997, when I was forced out of being chairman and became senior chairman, whatever that means, which is nothing."

The role of senior chairman seemed like too much of a figurehead to Bogle. To add insult to injury, Vanguard's board next insisted that he adhere to a long-standing rule of mandatory retirement for every member at age 70, so that he would have to completely vacate even his senior chairman post as of December 31, 1999. In some respects the uproar that ensued over this change was really like watching a train wreck in slow motion because Bogle knew very well about the policy and had long expressed a desire that the board make an exception in his case. In early 1995, before he made the decision to relinquish the position of CEO, an associate mentioned the age limit policy to him, and his reply appeared to suggest that he had no plans to step down voluntarily and that only his health would determine his future: "I don't know if I will make 66. If I make 70, I'm sure that the Vanguard directors will consider making an exception for the company's founder." (This was reported in the previous edition of this book.)

That's why it's somewhat surprising to hear Lawrence Wilson—an independent director on Vanguard's board from 1985 till 2008 and ultimately its "lead independent trustee"—say that up until news reports started hitting the airwaves about Bogle's dissatisfaction with the policy, the board had no idea that he really wanted to stay and was unhappy with its decision. "I don't recall any pressure at all from Jack to stay on the board," Wilson says. "Jack had reached retirement age. It was time for him to leave the board, in my mind." The board, according to Wilson, learned of Bogle's disapproval only after reports of its decision were published in the press in August 1999. "The thing is, Jack Bogle had created some discussions with the press about his leaving as chairman, and we thought, 'We don't want to have a public argument with Jack,'" Wilson says. "'If it's such a big deal to him, let him stay.'" So in September 1999 the board voted to extend his stay as senior chairman— a token gesture that Bogle ultimately refused.

In the meantime, many shareholders reached a near apoplectic state over the fact that their beloved icon, who, to them, was really the face of Vanguard, was now so rudely being shown the door of the company he founded. Some on the "Vanguard Diehards" forum at fund tracker

Web site Morningstar.com even talked of revolt. On the humble Internet chat board dedicated to Vanguard investors, diehard George Foster suggested "another course of action" to what Vanguard's board in its high tower dictated. In a September 1999 post titled, "If you don't like Bogle's departure . . .," he suggested shareholders start a proxy resolution to keep Bogle: "Since Vanguard is a 'mutual' mutual fund company, then theoretically shareholders of a fund could get a resolution to revoke (or waive) the 70 and out rule on a shareholder ballot." Another shareholder, "ntv1940," lamented in the same thread: "No matter how difficult it is to live with The Saint, Jack Brennan and Cie [sic] should realize that it is counter productive [sic] if not self destructive [sic] to make him a martyr in the house he founded, especially now that he has become a symbol of Integrity and Honesty in a world almost synonymous with fraudulence and backstabbing."

Even the press seemed incensed by the decision. In an open letter to the management of Vanguard titled, "Memo to Vanguard: You Need to Win Back My Confidence," TheStreet.com columnist Brenda Buttner wrote in August 1999: "Wait a minute, don't throw this letter in your 'Ignore: Diehard' pile. I don't fit that category. Yes, I find last week's unceremonious slap in the face to your Senior Chairman Jack Bogle more than offensive. Despite his obvious willingness to continue serving, you force him to leave the board of directors? Just because he turned 70? C'mon. In Bogle years that's far from retirement age. But the fact that you didn't extend basic courtesy to one of the industry's most legendary pioneers isn't my main issue as a shareholder. . . . Here's why you make me question my commitment to your fund firm: This was a bad business move. One of your biggest assets is walking—rather, being pushed—out the door."[10]

Adding salt to the wound was Vanguard's own PR spokesman, Brian Mattes, who, according to the *Philadelphia Inquirer,* posted at the Vanguard Diehards chat room at Morningstar in August 1999: "If you have been happy with Vanguard during the past three years, you have Jack Brennan to thank for that. Since becoming chief executive officer of Vanguard in 1996, Jack Brennan has presided over the best years in Vanguard's history, and, arguably, the best years any fund company has ever had in the history of the fund industry." The ultracompetitive

Bogle was so infuriated by this remark that he took his grievance public, responding to it in the *Inquirer*: "I think the company's success might have something to do with the bull market, index funds, the managers I chose, the structure of the company, my missionary work—all of which I take responsibility for. To credit that to someone else is extraordinary, unbelievable and irresponsible."

Truth be told, neither Bogle nor Mattes was right. Bogle surely provided the vision for Vanguard, but it was Brennan and a host of other Vanguard employees who faithfully executed that vision, brought it to fruition, and took it to the next level. The same is true for any successful company. For a chief executive or company founder, be it Bogle or Brennan or whoever, to try to claim full credit for a giant institution's triumph is the height of arrogance. For instance, although Bogle was the great innovator, surely one of Brennan's major contributions to Vanguard's success was his decision to invest heavily in technology. For a company that is marketed directly to shareholders instead of through commission-based brokers, the ability to reach investors via the Internet and enable them to buy and sell or check their account balances online became absolutely critical in the 1990s, and Brennan recognized this more than Bogle did.

Even before he moved into the executive suite, Brennan told *Money* magazine about his plans to beef up this aspect of Vanguard in 1995: "The home computer is becoming a new version of the 800 telephone number. Within a few years, people will be able to transfer money from their bank to buy a Vanguard fund through their home computers. I want to be sure we make the investment to stay competitive in the new technology."[11] And without all the necessary back-office IT Brennan built, surely it would have been harder to capture and manage the complex and sophisticated institutional investor/401k market—a business that grew dramatically during Brennan's tenure to be half of Vanguard's assets.

And yet Brennan was not one to toot his own horn. True to his reticent character, he was largely unavailable for public comment during most of the spat over Bogle's retirement, often recorded in the press as being holed up in his Cape Cod summer home. In one of the few cases where a journalist managed to speak with Brennan on the subject, *Institutional Investor*'s Hal Lux received the tersest of responses: "Still something is irking Bogle. Although he doesn't see signs of Vanguard losing its way, he says repeatedly that he would be just as happy if the firm didn't grow. 'I think Jack [Brennan] wants the measure of success, as well as the heart of success,' says Bogle. 'Whether the company can maintain its character, that is the only thing that is important to me.' When asked about Bogle's remarks, Brennan nods but says only, 'I didn't hear the conversation.' He won't acknowledge any rift and has only praise for Bogle. Pressed as to whether Bogle's statements more likely reflect a real conflict over strategy or typical succession issues, Brennan says, 'I would think succession.'"[12]

Brennan had always stated that the differences between him and Bogle were more matters of personal style than ideological and that at root they shared the same ethical values and vision for Vanguard. Prior to the public blowout over the enforced retirement, he commented to TheStreet.com in April of 1999 about the contrasts in their character: "'We have a lot of common values, which is the most important thing. . . . We're different in sort of outward ways, in that I like mucking it up and being in the midst of the business, and Jack's more prone to create controversy and that kind of thing.' Told of Brennan's comments Thursday [August 12, 1999, or four months later], Bogle responded in kind. 'I created a company. I don't think I created controversy.'"[13]

Although Bogle says he can't understand why Brennan wouldn't speak to him, it does seem that if anything would cause the tight-lipped Brennan to clamp up permanently, it was the fact that Bogle aired the grievance publicly in the first place. It also of course would seem ironic later that Bogle would put up such a fight over the loss of his chairmanship and then become one of the fiercest advocates for having an independent chairman instead of an insider like himself and Brennan at all mutual funds. At the time, though, he seemed to be right about the issues from a philosophical standpoint—why shouldn't an exception be made for the founder of a company?—but completely wrong in the manner in which he expressed his complaint. Given Brennan's reserved nature, surely it must have hurt and angered him that Bogle took the disagreement to the court of public opinion, where "St. Jack" obviously had an unfair advantage.

One friend of Bogle's who, because of the touchy subject matter, prefers to remain anonymous felt that Bogle was behaving badly at the time toward Brennan: "I don't think that Jack behaved terribly well during that period, and I told him that. And as he says, I give him good advice, but he just never takes it. He plays to all the reporters, all the press. He made a big deal about leaving, and that put more and more pressure on him, and the board was seen as the bad guy. Jack Brennan didn't like all the publicity and being made into the villain. So it got very personal for Jack Bogle, and it shouldn't have. I don't just mean with Brennan but with the directors and everyone else."

Perhaps the hardest part for Brennan to digest may have been Bogle's rebirth after the transplant. "When Bogle gave up the CEO position to Brennan, he was very sick prior to the transplant," says Burton Malkiel, who was a Vanguard board member at the time of the dispute. "It was hard for him to walk across a room without getting winded. Then he got a 26-year-old heart and was reborn. It was absolutely amazing to see him play squash again. And it's very clear that if he'd known that he'd come out of the surgery and feel the way he did, he would never have given up the CEO position in the first place." And yet at the time heart transplant surgery was still a relatively new phenomenon, and the possibility of a patient's body rejecting the newly transplanted organ still loomed large on the horizon. "I remember him coming in, right before he got his heart, and he went around the office saying good-bye to everybody," recalls Raymond Kaplinsky. "He said, 'I'm leaving, I might need a heart,' and there were tears in his eyes, and basically he didn't know if he would ever be back. I remember that was a very sad day."

Bogle disputes this account and says that he always intended to come back, only as chairman. "Of course I was going to come back," he says. "The agreement was, Brennan would become president and chief executive, and I would remain the chairman. He would be clearly the boss, but I would be running the board. And that agreement didn't last very long." And yet given the risks of the operation, it was understandable that many Vanguard employees might have thought that this was his last good-bye. "I have a lot of thoughts on [Brennan and Bogle's relationship]," Jeremy Duffield said to me. "None I want to talk about. They are both extremely good friends of mine, and I wouldn't comment on it. But think about it one way, Lewis—the problem of an incoming CEO and the rebirth of his predecessor wanting to hang around. Where is there a precedent for something like this? I cannot think of one. We are in the annals of American business history with it."

Perhaps Bogle's colleagues shouldn't have been so surprised. "There was every reason to believe if the transplant worked, he would be invigorated," says one of Bogle's cardiologists, Dr. Bernard Lown. "That's what happens. He had a failing heart but could function otherwise, so it stood to reason when he had a new heart, he would come out like a boxer. It isn't unusual. I've seen people with a transplant who went full blast back to business like they hadn't in twenty years. And it's increasingly common for transplant patients to live a long time. I have one patient now who's lived for thirty years. In fact, Jack would brag afterwards that the youngest part of him was his heart."

Even if Brennan or the board members didn't fully understand the medical realities of heart transplantation, it probably would have been better for them and for Vanguard if they'd just let Bogle have his way in the first place and allowed him to stay on as chairman past the age of 70. Bogle notes with much bitterness that exceptions to the age rule were later made for other Vanguard board members. Burton Malkiel, for instance, stayed on till he was 72. And Lawrence Wilson and Charles Ellis stayed past the 70 limit as well. "Some directors are in great shape at age 70, and some have contributed nothing at age 60 and are still contributing nothing at age 70," says Bogle. "[The age limit] was a way to get around the unpleasantness of having to say, 'You know, your time with this board is over.'" Malkiel, for his part, agrees that age is just a number. "I'm not sure I like the idea of mandatory retirement," he says. "We really make a mistake thinking people in their 70s are all washed up. Certainly, Jack Bogle is a perfect example of someone who isn't." And yet, according to board member accounts, no one dissented when the decision was made to enforce the retirement mandate. "[The age limit] was only a policy," Bogle says. "Policies can be changed, but [the board] decided. And it got to be quite unpleasant. The people to whom I was a hero a few years before I was suddenly not so much of one to anymore. And to an extent, [the board's argument] was perfectly understandable: 'Let's go with the future and not the past. These two guys disagree, and I want to bet on the future and forget the past.' All those things enter into it."

Perhaps some less savory elements entered into the board's decision to remove Bogle as well. "I don't know if it's useful in the book or not, but you should know this, as this is the kind of thing that happened which may explain what happened on the board," Bogle tells me with some reservation. "And that is, [the board] wanted to have a pension plan for directors. And I said, 'Wait a minute, pension plans are for people who give their lives to their company. You come in here for 60 hours a year. Maybe, you have jobs [outside of Vanguard] where you are already well taken care of for your retirement. Independent directors should not have a pension plan.' They put one in anyway, and then they gave it up a few years later. That probably didn't make me popular with them. I cannot remember honestly whether I voted against it, but knowing me, I think I didn't vote against it yet abstained. But it was just plain wrong by any standard, and I don't see why they couldn't see that, but obviously that kind of bluntness—'here's something we have to do whether you like it or not'—isn't the right way to run a nice consensus. In any case, a few years later, the mandatory 70 retirement age was gone."[14]

Regardless of whether Bogle antagonized the board or not, members had an easy way out with the retirement rule and largely felt that the wheels for Bogle's departure had already been set in motion the moment Brennan accepted the CEO post in 1996. As one board member put it, the tension between Bogle and Brennan was an "uncomfortable distraction" to the business of running a company: "Jack Brennan had been groomed for this job as CEO and showed every sign he was up for it. It would be very hard to justify discontinuing that role given Bogle's new lease on life. It would've been reversing history without reason. So on what rationale would we want to continue an uncomfortable situation on the board which had a natural ending point in the age restriction rule?"

Yet there's no denying that the decision left a bitter taste in everyone's mouth and sparked severe criticism and perhaps unjustifiable animosity toward Brennan. Recalls Bud Bogle: "I can remember that after one of the weddings that we went to of one of the Bogles, my brilliant wife said, 'You know, I don't know how Jack can trust that man? He's a bad apple.' And I said, 'Florence, how the hell do you know?' And the point is he turned out to be really. He turned against my brother because of jealousy, because when he learned that Jack was coming back with a new heart, that killed it for him. Number one, they hardly spoke before that, but he must have thought, '[Bogle's] out of my way forever. He's never going to show up here again.' And then [Bogle] came back, and I mean I can imagine how Brennan felt, but that's not the way you do things. He wouldn't even speak to Jack. Jack would speak to him. Who the hell does he think he was? Jack made him everything he was."

So why, then, given all these headaches, did the board cave in to the public pressure to extend Bogle's stay and reverse its decision to retire Bogle in September of 1999? Although Bogle declines to discuss the reason he subsequently refused the board's offer, some have said that the board knew that Bogle would not accept the offer and that it was really just a token gesture to assuage Vanguard's investors, who had been rattled by the whole experience. At least, that was the reason according to a *New York Times* article published about the subject at the time: "Some industry commentators said it was obvious that the vote, at a meeting at Vanguard headquarters in Malvern, Pa., was a face-saving effort to end a month-long uproar." At the time Bogle denied that such was the case, stating, "The thing I like about it is that they made it my decision." But in retrospect, it's hard to see the offer and his refusal as anything but a public relations strategy. As Dan Wiener put it at the time: "They're finally putting a good gloss on what was a real bad P.R. situation for them. This sort of takes care of that and makes everybody look good and everybody look happy."[15]

And yet Bogle did not leave the board empty-handed. Part of the agreement for his stepping down as senior chairman was that the company would help fund his ongoing advocacy for shareholders through the Bogle Financial Markets Research Center, which would be on the Vanguard campus itself. Ultimately, Bogle received his first floor office in Vanguard's Victory building and a small budget to hire three employees—Kevin Laughlin, Emily Snyder, and Sara Hoffman—who would become his crack team of researchers and general helpers who enabled him to produce all the great books he's written and speeches he's given and arrange all the events he's been feted at or attended since abdicating his executive post.

According to Bogle, after he left the executive suite in 1999 and moved two floors down in the Victory building to his research center, communications between him and Brennan were conveyed via Vanguard's managing director Michael Miller. Although to the public everything may have seemed hunky-dory again, perhaps it was in the silent intervening years after the media storm had died down that Vanguard's senior executives who'd been humiliated by the whole affair tried to exact a quiet revenge. "Some of the orders that have come down through the pipeline from Vanguard executives have been shockingly mean-spirited," says one insider. "There's a guy in the mailroom who picks Jack up in the morning and takes him home at night. They tried to take that away from him. They also tried to move his office off campus to another building five or ten minutes away, but he so enjoys being able to see the crew and stop and chat with regular folks."

Still, in many respects, Bogle had once again been fired with enthusiasm. For it was from his tiny office on the same floor as Vanguard's legal department that he would become the greatest shareholder advocate for investors in the history of Wall Street. Now that he was no longer in the executive suite, Bogle was truly free to speak his mind, and the books he subsequently wrote in his new digs would help alter the consciousness of many investors in the post-dot-com era. "I believe Bogle became a much better advocate after he left Vanguard," says Dan Wiener. Having built the company during the greatest bull market in U.S. history, Bogle couldn't have timed his end-of-1999 exit as a mutual fund executive better had he been Nostradamus. The next 10 years would become known as the "lost decade" for investors, but for him it was the start of a whole new career.

CHAPTER 13

"Don't Call Me a Gadfly"

During the 1980s and 1990s, corporate culture and Wall Street's culture—if such a thing can be said to exist—changed in a way that Bogle would ultimately find revolting. Executive compensation exploded during this period and was largely based on producing short-term results instead of enduring value and using accounting gimmicks to boost the bottom line. He identified the era that produced the greatest stock market bubble in history as a "pathological mutation" from traditional owners' capitalism, in which shareholders came first, to managers' capitalism, in which executives took everything for themselves.

Bogle would lay much of the blame for the stock bubble's excesses and the subsequent collapse on the financial services industry in general and the mutual fund industry in particular. He felt that money managers had been asleep at the switch when it came to corporate abuses and instead cared only about gathering assets. He recommended a return to the ethos of an ownership society governed by shareholders and their fiduciaries. And it is toward achieving this end that much of his advocacy in the wake of retiring from Vanguard's board in 1999 has been directed. He believes that the ownership society goal could be accomplished through stronger regulation, improved stewardship, and an exercise of shareholder democracy. Indeed, one of the chapters in his 2005 book *The Battle for the Soul of Capitalism* is subtitled "Owners of the World Unite!" alluding to Marx's famous clarion call to workers. If investors held stocks only for the long term—behaving like business owners instead of short-term speculators—and started participating actively in the corporate governance process, abuses would decrease and shareholder returns improve.

Strictly speaking, the term "shareholder democracy" is an oxymoron. In a true democracy, each person is equally represented in the government. The rule is one person, one vote, and every adult citizen of voting age is supposed to have an equal say in government. But in the corporate world, the rule is one share, one vote. This means that the wealthiest investors who own the most shares have a greater say in corporate governance than everybody else. So in reality what exists— or what is supposed to exist according to current securities' laws—is a shareholder plutocracy.

In other words, in a democracy, if you don't like your local politician, you and a bunch of other like-minded citizens can vote that person out of office. But if you own 10 shares of Apple and don't like the new iPhone and want to fire Steve Jobs, he couldn't care less. He owns 5.5 million shares of Apple and thus has 550,000 times more say in Apple's corporate governance than you do with your measly 10. Such entrenched corporate power is not exactly what the founding fathers meant when they used the term "democracy."

Yet as Bogle has observed, for many years now, even the shareholder plutocrats have been disenfranchised by a new class of potentates. These are their agents—the investment bankers, mutual fund, hedge fund, and pension fund managers in the financial world; the CEOs and CFOs in the corporate world—most of whom rarely do what is considered to be in the best interest of their wealthy shareholders. It is for these disenfranchised plutocrats that Bogle speaks the most. Not that he doesn't care about the small mom-and-pop shareholders too. He cares a great deal about them. But the benefits of his vision of "owners' capitalism," if it were somehow brought to fruition, would disproportionately go to the largest shareholders.

What would occur if we became an ownership society would be a transfer of wealth from the agent CEOs and money managers, who do surprisingly little for the immense salaries and bonuses they're paid, to the largest shareholders, who do just as little for the capital gains and dividends they receive. (The truth is, if you're an outside investor, your money doesn't "work for you." Other people work to produce your dividends and capital gains.) In addition, smaller shareholders would also gain in the form of increased returns proportionate to their more meager investments. Whether or not those with no money to invest would benefit would henceforth be up to the wealthy shareholder plutocrats instead of the investment bankers and CEOs.

In reality, Bogle was an advocate for owners' capitalism and shareholder democracy long before he retired from his board position at Vanguard in 1999. Simply by creating the first low-cost index fund and Vanguard's mutualized structure, he offered shareholders a means to participate in his vision of an ownership society. The index fund effectively disintermediates the managers' capitalism structure of Wall Street because the index is "unmanaged," or, to be more accurate, very lightly managed, so that the costs of the manager largely disappear. There can be no excess compensation for money managers in a low-cost indexed world. Vanguard's mutualized structure further enhances this manager disintermediation because it has no outside shareholders seeking to siphon off profits from fund shareholders. Since The Vanguard Group is owned by fund shareholders and funds are run at cost, investors receive as much of the stock market's return as possible. So they are truly direct owners of America Inc.—with one glaring exception. They do not actually participate in the corporate governance aspect of the individual companies held in the funds. Vanguard executives decide how the different funds will vote on corporate proxies.

Bogle also advocates for shareholders in the many books and speeches he has written. He has a tremendous love for the written word. In fact, he writes so much that his pinky is disfigured by a bulbous callus from working in longhand on legal notepads. The best example of Bogle's "scriptophilia" was the publication of *Bogle on Mutual Funds* in 1993. He labored tirelessly to get the manuscript just right, repeatedly reworking his drafts, never satisfied that he had written something in precisely the right manner. His goal was to produce a book on mutual funds that could hold its own with Benjamin Graham's 1949 classic on investment strategy and security analysis, *The Intelligent Investor*, in Bogle's view the best book ever written on common stock investing. To remind potential readers that he was trying to equal, if not outdo, the Graham classic, Bogle subtitled his book *New Perspectives for the Intelligent Investor*. "I wanted to write a book that not only would help investors make sound decisions but would change the mutual fund industry," he said. "This industry can have lower costs for customers, create much better disclosure, have honest advertising, and be overseen by more responsible directors. There is so much room for improvement."

The publication proved to be one of the signal events in his career. It received critical acclaim from investors and the media, and it spent many months on some best-seller lists. It has already become one of the best-selling financial books of all time. Bogle points with pride to the fact that he has received hundreds of letters from Vanguard shareholders who have read the book and bought additional copies for their children and grandchildren as gifts. Since then, Bogle has written eight more books and updated his classic tome *Common Sense on Mutual Funds* for a tenth anniversary edition.

In *Common Sense*, which was published in 1999, readers could already see a significant change of course and focus in Bogle's writing, moving from simply investment advice to advocacy for industry-wide reform. Bogle says as much in the original preface to the book:

> In writing this book, my objective is to accomplish two goals: first, to help readers become more successful investors, and second to chart a course for change in the mutual fund industry. My first objective is familiar terrain. In *Bogle on Mutual Funds*, published in 1993, I set forth a commonsense approach to developing a sound investment program through mutual

funds. . . . My second objective marks new literary, if not professional terrain for me. In the past decade, as strong financial markets have made mutual funds the investment of choice for millions of shareholders, the industry has embraced practices that threaten to diminish seriously their chances of successful long-term investing. Amid the mutual fund industry's disorienting promotional din, *Common Sense on Mutual Funds* identifies these practices and presents simple principles for implementing a sound investment program. These investment principles also form the basis for my call for industry change. If mutual funds are to remain the investment of choice for America's families, change is imperative.[1]

The title of the book, of course, alludes to Thomas Paine's revolutionary pamphlet "Common Sense," and Bogle even cites Paine's initially unpopular opinions about overthrowing British rule as support for his own "revolutionary" ideas for the fund industry. Throughout the text, he strikes an optimistic tone on the possibility for genuine change, advocating for lower costs, more disclosure, responsible stewardship, and the mutualized structure of Vanguard. That optimism for a corrupt fund industry healing itself would soon diminish after two of the worst, most scandal-ridden bear markets in history.

In the updated 2010 edition of *Common Sense,* Bogle remarks on how many of his earlier, more hopeful predictions for the fund industry haven't come true:

> While a decade has now passed, my hopes for either a revision of the status quo that gives fund managers essentially absolute power over mutual fund governance or a radical restructuring (truly mutual mutual funds) that places the power in the hands of the fund shareholders have not been rewarded. I am aware of no cases in which independent directors have become ferocious advocates for the rights and interests of shareholders or have begun to "negotiate aggressively" to reduce fund fee rates. And despite my choosing as the firm's name a term that means "leader of a new trend," Vanguard continues to stand

alone with its mutual fund structure. The firm has yet to find
its first follower.[2]

Increasingly, Bogle's speeches were directed against the fund industry as he made the transition from being an industry insider who ran one
of its largest fund companies to a maverick outsider who could speak
his mind more easily. Even as early as 1991, he delivered a speech called
"Losing Our Way: Where Are the Independent Directors?" to the North
American Securities Administrators Association in San Diego. Already,
he was lashing out against persistent abuses that would become his raison
d'être in years to come:

> Let me present, in the brief time allowed this morning, some
> of the concerns I have: (1) diseconomies of scale that should
> have been economies of scale; (2) fee increases and fee struc-
> tures that are appalling; (3) the baneful effect of the notorious
> 12b-1 plans that encumber existing shareholders with the cost
> of attracting—for whatever reason—new fund shareholders;
> (4) disclosure in fund reports that, in some instances, verges
> on the outrageous; and, last but not least, (5) advertising that
> hawks "reward" and ignores the two other determinants of
> investment return—*risk* and *cost*.[3]

In subsequent pre-2000 speeches such as, "The Silence of the
Funds: Mutual Fund Investment Policies and Corporate Governance,"
and, "Creating Shareholder Value: By Mutual Funds, . . . , or for
Mutual Fund Shareholders," Bogle would zero in on other issues of
management greed and poor corporate governance from funds' boards
of directors. Given Bogle's own unusually painful experiences with fund
boards, it is telling that they became a major hobbyhorse for him, even
when he advocated changes that contradicted his personal experiences
at Vanguard, such as suggesting that every fund have an independent
fund chairman.

In the press, Bogle was called an iconoclast; the *Washington Post*
affectionately described him as "the bad boy of the mutual fund business
. . . a man with an attitude." Before a large audience in open session at

a general membership meeting of the Investment Company Institute, Bogle heard himself described as a Communist and a Marxist. (When the speech was over, Bogle approached the speaker and, tongue-in-cheek, thanked him for his generous characterization. "In the office," Bogle said, "I am often called a fascist.") None of these kinds of comments deterred Bogle. "I don't think I would win any popularity contest," he said with an almost fierce pride.

Gradually, Bogle began to make the connection between poor corporate governance in the fund world and poor corporate governance in general. Hand-picked lavishly paid fund boards who worked maybe 60 or 70 hours a year would rubber-stamp every proposal for their lavishly paid fund management companies, and these lavishly paid fund management companies would rubber-stamp every proposal for the lavishly paid executives of the companies they invested in. In return for this tacit collusion, companies would hire money management companies to run their 401k and pension plans. And so the cycle of violence against shareholder rights continued. Bogle would observe in his 1999 "Silence of the Funds" speech that the commercial nature of the mutual fund business was now a primary obstacle to good corporate governance even outside the industry:

> **We've become a marketing business. Investment managers seek corporate clients, for that is where the big money is . . . and where the big profits lie for the managers. Corporate 401(k) thrift plans have been among the driving forces in generating new fund assets since the mid-1990s, and corporate pension funds—absent the need for all of that complex and costly subaccounting—are also considered plums by fund managers. Given the drive for corporate customers, the reluctance of fund managers to risk the opprobrium of potential clients by leaping enthusiastically into the controversial area of corporate governance is hardly astonishing, though it is discouraging.[4]**

Of course, no one paid much attention to Bogle's righteous indignation during the bull market. The rising tide of stock prices lifted all boats. Bogle's predictions of a coming shakeout were largely ignored until the dot-com crash began in 2000, and even then the fund industry hardly stood up and took notice. As first profitless dot-coms like Boo.com, Startups.com, and Pets.com went bankrupt, and then major scandals hit much larger companies such as Enron, WorldCom, and Wall Street's investment banks, leaders of the Investment Company Institute, the fund industry trade association, reflected smugly on what appeared to be their squeaky clean regulatory record. At a May 2003 general membership meeting—not long after the dust had settled on the WorldCom bankruptcy scandal—ICI president Matthew Fink boasted to an audience of industry leaders: "We have succeeded because the interests of those who manage funds are well-aligned with those who invest in mutual funds." His remarks echoed those of ICI chairman and keynote speaker Paul G. Haaga, Jr., who also took a swipe at the industry's detractors, including a veiled reference to Bogle himself: "Former SEC chairmen, members of Congress and their staffs, academics, Bards of Omaha, journalists, television talking heads, competitors—even a saint with his own statue—have all weighed in about our perceived failings. . . . It makes me wonder what life would be like if we'd actually done something wrong."[5]

Haaga would soon find out. On September 3, 2003, less than four months later, New York State Attorney General Eliot Spitzer announced that he had found evidence of "widespread illegal trading schemes" at several mutual fund companies that had cost shareholders billions of dollars.[6] Among those companies that were eventually implicated by Spitzer and the SEC were major industry players such as Alliance Capital, Invesco, Janus Funds, Strong Funds, and Putnam Funds. What became known as the market-timing or "late trading" scandal involved fund companies allowing preferred institutional investors such as hedge funds to trade their mutual funds after the U.S. stock market had closed at 4 p.m. Because many international stock markets in different time zones were still open at this time, the preferred investors would be able to lock in stale prices in their purchases and sales of foreign funds, knowing full well that values overseas had actually changed in the interim, and thus guaranteeing themselves profits at other shareholders' expense.

All of a sudden everyone wanted to talk to Bogle. Spitzer, for his part, had been talking to him for a long time, even prior to the investigations. "I first got to know Jack based on a recommendation from Warren Buffett," says Spitzer. "I called Buffett and raised some of the mutual fund issues that we were investigating, and he said the person you should really talk to is Jack Bogle. I picked up the phone and called Jack, and we chatted about mutual funds and all these shareholder issues that had become important to us. Jack also came by the office once or twice to help us. We talked about absolutely identical worlds in terms of what needed to be done with the capital markets to make them work properly. So a friendship arose out of that in terms of our having similar views. The fact that I had gone to Princeton didn't hurt either."

Bogle, for his part, already knew about the potential for unfair exploitation of foreign stock funds. He'd read an article in the July 2002 issue of the *Financial Analysts Journal* by four finance professors from New York University who demonstrated how to use time zone differences with foreign funds to game the system legally. Some of the funds mentioned in their article were Vanguard funds. At the time, Vanguard barely reacted to the article except to write a rather stern letter to the editor arguing that the journal shouldn't be publicizing such strategies—a tepid response that incensed Bogle. Several months later, the company quietly instituted redemption fees on its foreign funds to prevent excessive trading of them.

Bogle recalled the scandal and his meeting with Spitzer during one of our interviews. "Number one, everyone has known for a long time that there was something very odd going on with international mutual fund sales," he said. "And that is that they had a redemption rate of 80 percent per year. That means that 80 percent of investors were getting out and mostly coming back in later. The redemption rate was 7 percent or 8 percent when I came into this business. So 80 percent catches your attention. Yet I never could have imagined these deals that were made that Attorney General Spitzer discovered. At his request, I went down to visit him in his New York office. We talked about a whole lot of issues. He did not tell me he was filing these complaints, I can assure you of that, but we did discuss the problems of market timing, the problem with speculation with mutual funds, all of those things that were going on. The first time I knew the suits had been filed by the attorney general was when I read it in the paper. Though he didn't tip me off that it was coming, it did not surprise me a whit."

Bogle would soon testify before Congress about industry abuses on November 3, 2003. At a hearing before the U.S. Senate Governmental Affairs Subcommittee on Financial Management, the Budget, and International Security, Bogle attacked almost every industry offense he could think of, highlighting, of course, the inherent conflict of interest of fund management controlling fund boards to maximize their own profitability at the expense of fund shareholders:

> It can be little surprise that the mutual fund industry has not escaped the same kinds of scandals that have faced Wall Street and Corporate America. For in no other line of business endeavor is the conflict between owners capitalism and managers capitalism more institutionalized, and therefore more widely accepted. Yet by its very structure, this industry, for all its protestations about its dedication to Main Street investors, seems almost preordained to give the managers total control over the fund shareowners."[7]

Among the four areas of abuse that Bogle highlighted were management fees that were inversely correlated to fund performance, asset gathering until funds became bloated, aggressive and misleading marketing of high-risk specialized funds, and market timing itself. He also called out the ICI president, Matthew Fink, for his "self-aggrandizing comments" regarding the industry's interests being aligned with shareholders' and even issued a veiled attack of his own against Vanguard for waiting to institute redemption fees in its international funds until the *Financial Analysts Journal* article came out, revealing how easy they were for late traders to exploit:

> Yet the sole published response to the revelation [in the *FAJ* article on late trading] was a screed from a representative of the manager whose funds were mentioned in the article. He berated the Journal: "Publishing such a piece in a publication

that is aimed solely at financial professionals is a bad idea in the best of times, but is abhorrent when investor confidence is already shaken by corporate greed . . ." Nonetheless, just nine months later, the very firm that employed the respondent initiated a 2% redemption fee on its international funds. At long last![8]

For the most part, Vanguard executives and Bogle were on the same page during the market-timing investigations, since Vanguard hadn't been implicated in any criminal wrongdoing and was usually cited by Bogle as an example of the right way to run a fund company. In fact, Vanguard ultimately was an immense beneficiary of both the bear market and the scandal. Its low-cost, conservative, no-frills strategies became increasingly attractive to investors looking for someplace safe and reliable to invest their nest eggs.

And yet occasionally, as Bogle's congressional testimony illustrates, there would be a butting of heads with Vanguard management. In his statement, Bogle offered potential solutions to the industry's conflicts by increasing disclosure and further empowering boards:

> To seriously reform the industry, we must amend the Investment Company Act of 1940 to require an independent board chairman (presently, that post is usually filled by a director affiliated with the fund's manager); we must limit the fund's manager to a single board seat; and we must enable the board to retain its own staff to provide information that is independent and objective. Further, we must have full disclosure of all compensation, including each individual's share of the management company's profits paid to senior executives and portfolio managers. It is also high time that the Congress demands an economic study of the mutual fund industry, showing the sources of management company revenue and the uses of management company expenditures. "Follow the money" is a necessary rule if regulators and investors are to come to grips with solutions to the conflicts I've recounted.[9]

As it turned out, Vanguard was opposed to ceding control of the chairman's position of its board to an independent director. This would mean, of course, that John Brennan would have to step down from that position just as Bogle did. Irony, thy name is Vanguard. Ultimately, the SEC followed Bogle's advice and proposed a rule to require that funds have independent chairpeople, and early in 2004 it opened a public comment period, allowing industry players and investors to convey their support or concerns about the new rule to regulators. On January 7, Vanguard's lead independent trustee, J. Lawrence Wilson, wrote a letter to then SEC Chairman William Donaldson arguing that forcing fund boards to have independent chairmen would actually take away some of the independent directors' power to choose whatever chairman they saw fit.[10]

Wilson's letter was followed by two other letters on March 10, one signed by all six of Vanguard's independent directors and another from John Brennan himself. The directors wrote, "We seriously question the benefit of those proposals that would constrain the ability of independent boards to exercise their judgment on key governance matters. We strongly believe that once the Commission has assured the independence of fund boards, the Commission should leave to the independent directors those decisions that require the application of experience, expertise and judgment to the situation at hand. . . . Consistent with these concerns, we strongly believe that there is no need to dictate by regulation an independent chairman for all fund boards when the independent directors control the board by a substantial margin."[11]

Brennan's letter was considerably shorter and less detailed, mostly a statement of his support for the Vanguard board's letter on the subject: "Consistent with the comments of the Vanguard independent directors, we strongly urge the Commission to adopt rules that allow independent boards to determine the appropriate governance practices that will best serve the interests of fund shareholders."[12] Although it was widely known in the industry that Brennan opposed the independent chairman rule, in all likelihood he knew how touchy this subject was, given Bogle's own support for the rule, and wisely decided to let Vanguard's board do the talking for him. (Bogle, for his part, says that he was unaware that these letters from the board and Brennan had been written in the first place, so it wasn't a case of tit for tat but of basic philosophical differences.)

In essence, Vanguard was claiming that forcing the board to have an independent chairman would somehow limit the board's independence—a ludicrous argument on the face of things. To truly cut the Gordian knot that ties a fund to its management company, boards should be 100 percent independent, not just the 75 percent that the SEC ultimately required. At the time, Bogle himself didn't send a letter to the SEC, but rather sent a copy of one of his May 2004 speeches discussing the proposed regulatory reforms. In it he analyzes and refutes a study that Fidelity commissioned, ostensibly proving that funds run by independent chairmen underperformed those without, quipping, "If you accept uncritically that conclusion, I have, as the saying goes, 'a bridge I'd like to sell you.'"[13] Ultimately, the SEC passed the rule, only to have it challenged and defeated in federal court by the U.S. Chamber of Commerce. The Chamber of Commerce even used the Fidelity study that Bogle lambasted as evidence in its case. Later in 2006, as the issue was still being debated, Bogle would send a letter to the SEC advocating that 100 percent of a board's directors be independent.

Although Bogle was adamant that he was right at the time, he recognizes that he once thought differently on the subject and that it was easier for him to speak freely about it now that he was no longer a fund chairman himself. "I think we are allowed to change our minds," he says. "I was a very confident chief executive. I certainly wanted to be the chairman and president and chief executive. We were building a company from ground zero, and we needed to make decisions, and I thought I knew the decisions that had to be made. I was a very strong leader. You could argue too strong. And then the world changes. And I think Vanguard should have an outside chairman. I might not have said that ten years ago. I'm not sure what to make of that. You become a large financial institution, and it's not about individual leadership anymore. It's much more a collective kind of thing, and shareholders need more protection."

And yet to this day Vanguard is opposed to the concept of an independent chairman. "I don't think there is any evidence at all that you get better governance that way," says CEO and current board Chairman Bill McNabb. "You go back to, do you have an independent board, do you have a strong lead director, and to me those are more important principles. To me the most important thing is, do you have the right culture? If at the end of the day you can say yes to all of those questions, then I could argue that it's going to be more harmful with an independent chair because there is no way [the chair] is going to be plugged in to all the issues they need to be plugged into."

But it wasn't just Bogle's independent chairman idea that Vanguard disputed. The company didn't like his concept of disclosing fund executive compensation either. As the SEC considered a rule in 2006 requiring increased disclosure of hidden executive perks and benefits in publicly traded corporations, Bogle urged the commission to also force fund executives to reveal theirs. Because most fund companies are hired as outside contractors to manage publicly traded funds, they hadn't been required to disclose such compensation in the past. As Bogle would observe in his April 2006 letter to the SEC:

> When the Securities Acts of the early 1930s were drafted, investment companies (now generally referred to as "mutual funds") were but a tiny part of our nation's securities markets, and by 1938, when the Commission promulgated its first proxy rules for executive compensation disclosure, they were scarcely any larger. Given their relative unimportance, it is easy to see why no rules were set forth relating to the disclosure of compensation of their executives and of the executives of companies that managed them. . . . But today, with assets reaching nearly $10 trillion, mutual funds are our nation's largest financial institution and by far the largest owner of America's public corporations (holding some 28 percent of all shares). . . . The Commission's new proposals for compensation disclosure provide a timely opportunity to rectify the previous omission of compensation data for mutual fund executives. Perhaps the reason this compensation has been ignored for so long is that nearly all mutual funds are oper-

ated by separate management companies, and disclosure was limited to the aggregate amount of the contracted payments made by the funds to those management companies. Yet it must be apparent that there is no way for fund shareholders to appraise the compensation paid to the executives who serve them through the vehicle of the management company, even though they often serve at the same time as officers of the funds themselves (usually receiving no compensation directly from the fund). *It is high time that this corporate veil be pierced.*[14]

Vanguard opposed and continues to oppose such disclosure, even though, as is previously described, because it is a mutualized company owned by shareholders of its public funds, it is not a privately held corporation in the traditional sense. "Vanguard's shareholders really do own The Vanguard Group," Bogle says. "They have a right to know this information." But Vanguard CEO Bill McNabb sticks to the technical, legal definition of The Vanguard Group as a private company: "When we say we are shareholder owned, it's more metaphorically than technically from a legal standpoint. Because the shareholders actually own shares in the funds and then the funds own us. It's a great way to live."

Vanguard also opposed disclosure of fund managers' and executives' holdings in the funds they oversee. Once again there were dueling letters to the SEC about a proposed disclosure rule in 2004. Bogle wrote: "I would suggest that the Commission should also reexamine its rules on disclosure of mutual fund officers' and directors' holdings of fund shares. The extent to which fund directors, executives, and portfolio managers 'eat their own cooking' by investing in the shares of the funds they manage or oversee is a vital issue, with little solid information available. Management company officials and portfolio managers are not currently required to disclose either their holdings of fund shares or their fund share transactions."[15]

Vanguard counsel Heidi Stam stated the company's position: "A portfolio manager's personal holdings should not be considered an important indicator of how closely his interests are aligned with those of fund shareholders. Like anyone else, portfolio managers invest their personal assets based on any number of factors, some of which might have to do with age, family and financial situation, and others of which might have to do with investment strategy." Stam also said that that the rule would create "concerns that some professional money managers might avoid managing mutual funds in an effort to protect their financial privacy" and that the "dense array of new information required under the proposal would serve to obscure rather than illuminate the extent of a portfolio manager's faithfulness to fund investors."[16]

Although individual investors may sympathize with money managers' desire for financial privacy, the importance of a manager's fiduciary role that engages the public's trust requires a higher level of disclosure than ordinary citizens have. What's more, such disclosure has been required of executives of nonmutual fund corporations for decades. Why shouldn't the same rules apply to funds? Also, CEOs at publicly traded companies invest based on their age and financial situation just as money managers do, and yet analysts still feel that knowing that such executives invest in their company shares does influence how they manage, encouraging them not to take undue risks with their own money as opposed to "other people's money." Fund managers, if anything, should have more incentive to invest in their own funds, as the funds are diversified portfolios with less downside risk than individual companies.

Truth to be told, a manager's personal investment in his or her own funds cuts to the heart of Bogle's belief in owners' capitalism as opposed to managers' capitalism. If managers don't have their own money on the line in a fund, why should they care how well or poorly a fund performs so long as they get paid at the end of the day? They are literally just agents and employees, concerned more about their salary and bonus set by their employer—the management company—than about fund shareholders, which they are not. But prior to the SEC's rule change, shareholders had no knowledge of whether managers ate their own cooking or not, and disclosure is still quite limited. According to Morningstar, in 2010 the average Vanguard manager had $117,143 invested in Vanguard funds—an investment level that ranked 12th out of the 30 biggest fund companies. As Bogle said about compensation disclosure: "There is no rational reason for exempting fund executives from the spotlight of public disclosure applicable to their counterparts in regular corporations, indeed the very information demanded by the security analysts that fund managers employ. It is brazen hypocrisy for fund industry leaders to object to such even-handed treatment."[17]

If fund managers have no or little personal investments in their own funds, their primary goal becomes gathering assets rather than doing what is best for fund shareholders. Bogle would observe the real objectives of such managers in *The Battle for the Soul of Capitalism*: "For mutual funds are organized by managers who have only nominal, if any, ownership positions in the fund's shares. The rewards these managers seek rarely have any relationship to the amount of capital that they invest in the funds, which usually is modest to a fault. . . . Rather, the manager's prime focus is to earn an entrepreneurial reward, not from the returns earned by the fund itself, but from the profits the management company can make from the advisory fees paid to it by the fund, under a contract drawn by the manager, in which the manager—here a virtual dictator—represents both parties."[18]

Although most of these philosophical disagreements between Vanguard and Bogle were kept low key or outside the public eye, one made headlines in the most embarrassing way. On December 14, 2002, Bogle published an op-ed in the *New York Times* supporting a proposed SEC rule that would require mutual funds to disclose how they voted their shares in corporate proxy votes:

> **But whether structured like Vanguard or not, mutual fund directors, officers and managers are the agents; the fund shareholders are the principals. It is management's responsibility to act solely on their behalf. It would thus seem self-evident that each mutual fund shareholder has the right to know how the shares of the corporations in his or her portfolio are voted. Such shareholders are partial owners of these stocks, and to deny them that information would stand on its head the common understanding of the principal-agency relationship.**

> Given that relationship, the fiduciary principle underlying the
> SEC's proposal seems beyond controversy.[19]

Precisely one month later, in perhaps one of the strangest pairings
in mutual fund history, Vanguard's Brennan cowrote an op-ed with
arch-rival Fidelity's Ned Johnson in the *Wall Street Journal* titled "No
Disclosure: The Feeling Is Mutual." According to the two, the rationale
for Vanguard and Fidelity coming together to fight the proxy rule was
nothing short of histrionic: "The threat is so severe that we, the leaders
of the fund industry's two largest competitors, come together now, for
the first time ever, to speak out publicly against it."[20]

What were Brennan and Johnson so concerned about? Labor unions
and environmentalists, it appears. They go on to say: "Simply put, we
believe that requiring mutual-fund managers to disclose their votes on
corporate proxies would politicize proxy voting. In case after case, it
would open mutual-fund voting decisions to thinly veiled intimidation
from activist groups whose agendas may have nothing to do with maxi-
mizing our clients' returns."[21]

That the ultra-conservative Johnson would pen such hyperbole
should come as no surprise, but that Brennan would sign his name to it
must surely stand as one of the most embarrassing episodes in Vanguard's
history. To deny fund shareholders the basic right to see how shares of
stocks they own in their mutual funds are voted in proxies is to deny
their existence as shareholders altogether. And to say that somehow only
activist special interest groups would care how such shares are voted is
grossly misleading. It is in everyone's interest to care how proxies are
voted, especially since such votes have a dramatic impact on executive
compensation—ratifying options issuance and electing directors who
form companies' executive compensation committees. And Bogle cites
excessive and misguided executive compensation as being one of the
primary culprits behind the dot-com bubble and both crashes that followed it.

But a larger point would be, what business is it of Vanguard's or
Fidelity's to decide whether shareholder votes should be "politicized"
or not? The management companies of Vanguard and Fidelity are
stewards, not owners of the underlying corporate shares. In the cases of

shareholder proposals from unions and environmental groups seeking to change corporate behavior, those unions and environmental groups are also shareholders and have every right to have their voices heard by other shareholders. And if they wish to lobby shareholders of funds that own shares of the companies they are seeking to change via a proxy ballot, why shouldn't fund shareholders be allowed to know how their chosen stewards are voting their shares?

In fact, unions are significant activists in trying to limit and change the nature of executive compensation because they know that such compensation often is harmful not only to shareholders, but to the employees of those companies. Many CEOs, in order to get a short-term bump in stock prices and exercise their options, are willing to lay off thousands of workers, even if this does not produce any enduring value for shareholders. By contrast, the instances in which mutual fund companies have challenged such excessive executive compensation plans are rare indeed.

Given their desire to manage lucrative corporate pension and 401k plans, the drive by fund companies to win such accounts creates its own conflicts of interest that can unduly influence proxy votes and hurt long-term shareholder value more than union activists can do. Bogle writes of the incentive for fund managers to be passive and rubber-stamp corporate proposals that favor executives in *The Battle*:

> **One reason for the forbearance of these institutions from the governance process is the clear conflict of interest they face in managing the retirement plan assets of the very corporations whose shares they own, and collectively control. While industry leaders regularly deny that such a conflict exists, it is easy to imagine that a private institutional manager would be reluctant to vote against an entrenched corporate management that has hired it to supervise its multi-billion-dollar pension plan or 401(k) thrift plan, and was paying the manager huge fees to do so. Even when a governance or proxy issue involves a corporation that is not a client, the reluctance to speak out persists, giving credence to this perhaps apocryphal comment by a pension fund manager, "There are only two types of clients we don't want to offend: actual and potential."[22]**

More to the point, the argument that there would be some sort of union or "activist" takeover of a proxy vote seems absurd, given the fact that corporate governance has never been a democracy but a plutocracy, favoring those with the largest number of shares, and unions and their employee members of modest means are not majority shareholders. The only thing such disclosure of proxy votes has recently revealed is how indifferent or even hostile institutional shareholders are to such "special interest" groups. These institutional shareholders almost always vote against the proposals of such groups—a revelation that is a possible embarrassment to fund company management—but that shame perhaps should be the price of their indifference.

True to form, Vanguard's current CEO, Bill McNabb, denies that there are any such conflicts of interest in Vanguard's proxy voting policies. He says that the company's 401k business has "absolutely zero impact" on how it votes. "The 401k business is probably the most complicated, most capital intensive, most people intensive, and therefore the lowest margin business at Vanguard and in the fund industry in general," he says. "And I don't think anyone is going to bet the reputation of their firm on a 401k client. I just don't see it. When I ran Vanguard's retirement business as head of its institutional division, I was recused from all proxy discussions and not allowed to sit in. So we had a real Chinese wall there. I imagine that most firms do something similar." He also says that Vanguard's proxy policies are fairly inflexible, and companies know that: "We've taken some hard stands. I think that in my 20-plus years being in that side of the business, I think maybe one or two senior executives at client companies mentioned it kind of off-hand: 'We weren't too happy with the way you voted.' And I'd kind of say, 'We are really clear what our policies are, and we will always give you an opportunity to tell us why our policies don't make sense. But unless we are convinced that we've made incorrect assumptions or we are wrong, that's how we are going to vote.' When people hire us, I think they know that as well."

Bogle doesn't doubt that the compliance procedures at Vanguard and other fund companies are adequate to avoid explicit conflicts of interest and that proxy voting policies are uniformly applied. Rather, he believes that the industry's desire to attract institutional business could lead to a complete and uniform passivity in its proxy votes, and as a result investors will almost never see funds take an activist stance, even when such a stances would make a big difference in long-term returns for shareholders and benefit a company overall. "Do I think there's some secret agreement between Vanguard and IBM that Vanguard will always vote in its favor?" Bogle asks. "Obviously not. Does IBM know Vanguard will probably vote in its favor anyway? Absolutely." There is, as Bogle says, a "tacit agreement" not to rock the boat with shareholder activism.

McNabb says that Vanguard is actively engaged in corporate governance, although much of its activity is behind the scenes. "I sent out about 900 letters this year to major holdings reiterating our positions on various issues and encouraging dialogue," he says. "And it was very gratifying how many companies wrote back with specific questions or specific observations or invitations for discussions. Again, the world is certainly not perfect, but we think we can effect some change by taking that kind of approach. I think some of the activists out there that make these big public pronouncements and sort of pound the table—I don't think they get as much done all the time. There are certain issues that you perhaps need to do that, but it's amazing how much you can get done just by being very transparent with people and encouraging dialogue."

The stakes are particularly high. Mutual funds currently own 26 percent of the outstanding shares for all U.S. stocks, and institutional investors own about 70 percent in total. So how funds vote these proxies can be extremely influential. And Vanguard, as the largest mutual fund company in the world, is the gorilla shareholder with the most influence. Moreover, because the majority of Vanguard's assets are in indexed products, proxies assume a far greater significance because index funds must hold all the companies in their benchmark, whether those companies are well governed or not. If a company has poor corporate governance, unless Vanguard votes against that governance in proxies, it becomes a captive audience to management's corruption and incompetence in its index funds. Meanwhile, actively managed funds can simply dump the shares of the poorly run company.

Obviously, this is a sensitive issue to Vanguard, which is why it is ironic that Bogle played a role in getting the SEC proxy disclosure rule passed in 2003. Bogle says that his *New York Times* op-ed actually had an impact on the SEC's decision to ultimately pass the rule: "I wrote about classic agency theory [in the article]. The agent is supposed to put the interest of the principal first. The mutual fund manager is the agent, and the principal is our shareholders. I didn't use this language in the *Times,* but who the hell do we think we are saying that we don't have to tell our shareholders how we vote their shares? The arrogance of that. One of my friends at the division of investment management in the SEC, who I knew pretty well, called me up and said that the *New York Times* op-ed really made a huge difference to the commission—to see it in the *New York Times,* to get a whole column out there about it."

Thanks to the proxy vote disclosure rule, investors can now get a much better understanding of the role that mutual funds play in corporate governance procedures. So far, despite McNabb's previous statements to the contrary, the picture isn't a particularly inspiring one at Vanguard or in the mutual fund industry in general. In July of 2010, two corporate governance watchdog organizations, the Corporate Library and Shareowners.org, and a union, American Federation of State, County and Municipal Employees (AFSCME), collaborated to publish a report titled, "Compensation Complicity: Mutual Fund Proxy Voting and the Overpaid American CEO." In it they examined the voting records of the 25 largest mutual fund companies on proxies related to executive compensation and ranked them based on the results. Those that rated highest were labeled "pay constrainers," while the lowest were called "pay enablers." Vanguard ranked 22nd and was labeled a pay enabler.[23] "I found that very discouraging," Bogle says of Vanguard's ranking.

The study analyzed proxy votes on compensation-related proposals dating from July 1, 2008, to June 30, 2009. As in the 2008 version of the same study, in 2009 the 25 largest firms voted 84 percent of the time in favor of management-sponsored proposals regarding executive compensation, most of which were deemed harmful to shareholders. Vanguard voted 89 percent in favor of such management proposals. Meanwhile, for proposals put forth by shareholders to constrain executive pay, Vanguard voted only 3 percent in favor of them, compared to the 56 percent average favorable vote for the 25 fund companies studied.

The report also cited a number of studies indicating that high executive compensation was linked to poor shareholder performance, increased likelihood of default, and excessive risk taking by management—all validation for Bogle's thesis that paying outrageous salaries for short-term stock price performance is generally a bad idea.

Interestingly enough, most of the lowest-rated firms were major indexing shops, such as Vanguard, State Street, and Barclays Global Investors. Barclays was analyzed separately from its 2009 acquirer, BlackRock. Meanwhile, firms specializing in active management, such as Fidelity, rated higher. This seems illogical from a shareholder perspective. Passive index investors should actually be the most active in corporate governance because they have no choice but to be invested in these stocks and thus should care more about how they're governed. "I was profoundly disappointed that the big indexers are standing back from the fray on these pay issues," Bogle says. Perhaps an explanation for this phenomenon lies in the conflict of interest Bogle identified in the first place. The report's three bottom-ranked firms—Barclays, 25th; State Street, 24th; and Northern Trust, 23rd—actually have the lion's share of their asset management business on the institutional side, especially Barclays, which was ranked the worst pay enabler. It is quite possible that such firms are passively rubber-stamping every management proposal for executive compensation to avoid making any waves and retain their lucrative institutional accounts.

Yet the battle for good governance isn't just about proxy votes or writing letters to the editor. Bogle has also gotten involved in the courts. "Good words, good deeds, good talk doesn't cook any rice at all," says John P. Freeman, a mutual fund activist and securities law professor at the University of South Carolina. "If you want to get people's attention, you sue them." Freeman has worked with Bogle for many years on research he's conducted to expose the inequitable fees money management companies charge to run mutual funds compared to pension funds, which they also run in the same style for much less. Freeman was an adviser to the attorneys who brought a case against Harris Associates, the manager of the Oakmark family of mutual funds, which wended its way through the court system until it reached the U.S. Supreme Court in March 2009. When Freeman told Bogle about the case, Bogle decided to file an amicus brief for the plaintiffs. He was the only one in the mutual fund industry that filed such a pro-shareholder brief. Meanwhile, Fidelity and industry trade association ICI filed briefs for the defendants. "There were 12 to 14 amicus curiae briefs filed," says Freeman. "Jack's brief was the only brief talked about from that group. I don't think there's any doubt it had an impact."

At stake was a legal precedent called the Gartenberg standard, which stated that for an investment adviser to be in breach of its fiduciary duty regarding fees, it "must charge a fee that is so disproportionately large that it bears no reasonable relationship to the services rendered and could not have been the product of arm's-length bargaining" by the fund's board of directors. The attorneys for Jerry N. Jones et al., the plaintiffs, argued that Harris Associates had breached its duty because fees in its Oakmark Funds were more than twice as high as those of institutional accounts that it ran in a similar style. In reality, the fee was only twice as much on an expense ratio or percentage basis. Bogle revealed in his brief that on a total dollar basis, Oakmark's fees were 42 times as much as its institutional clients' because the mutual funds were much bigger than the institutional accounts, and shareholders should have benefited from economies of scale. His was the only brief to observe that investors in the Oakmark Equity & Income mutual fund paid $56.2 million in advisory fees compared to $1.3 million for an institutional account for essentially the same services. Meanwhile, when looking just at the fund's advisory expense ratio of 0.73 percent compared to the institutional account's 0.31 percent, the differences did not appear nearly so great.

Prior to the Supreme Court hearing, Chief Judge Frank Easterbrook of the Seventh Circuit Court of Appeals had ruled against the plaintiffs by asserting that fees were determined by the free market and therefore were subject to the necessary competition to allow investors to avoid being overcharged. This would have essentially nullified the admittedly meager protection offered by the Gartenberg standard. But Bogle argued in his brief that Gartenberg imposed a fiduciary standard on advisers to compare their fees to those negotiated in an arms-length transaction for similar advisory services, and said nothing about fees being determined by "free-market" competition. He concluded:

> In any event, the court's view is mistaken. The explosive growth in mutual fund assets has only exacerbated the problems about which Congress was most concerned [when it codified the Gartenberg standard]—conflicting loyalties of investment advisers, the failure of the advisers who are paid on a percentage of assets to share the enormous economies of scale that exist in fund management with fund shareholders, and advisers that charge captive mutual funds much higher fees for the same services than are charged to independent clients.[24]

The Supreme Court ultimately rejected Easterbrook's ruling and reaffirmed Gartenberg, with an additional bonus of saying that plaintiffs could compare fund fees to those of institutional accounts such as pension funds. In previous cases involving Gartenberg, fund industry defendants would always argue that comparing a mutual fund to a pension fund was comparing apples to oranges and an unfair comparison. Such is no longer the case. Since pension fund fees are invariably much lower than mutual fund fees, this was a small victory. But Bogle and other observers would note that the Gartenberg standard places a very high burden of proof on plaintiffs—so high, in fact, that, since the standard was established in 1982, no plaintiff has ever won a case.

Obviously, Bogle's advocacy is a point of pride for him and a perennial obsession. "Jack really is an iconoclast," says Vanguard's McNabb. "Does his advocacy help or hurt us? I'm not even sure, as I haven't thought that through. He's going to do it no matter what. So for me it just is. He generally does a very good job saying that these are my views, not Vanguard's necessarily. And there is a fair amount of overlap. I think we all agree on the basic principles, but sometimes we just differ on the policies to get there."

As the Harris case illustrates, despite opposition from an industry with entrenched philosophies and tremendous lobbying dollars, Bogle continues to push forward, refusing to stop goading his peers for not giving investors a fair shake. When I told him I considered naming my book *Birth of a Gadfly*, he said, "Don't call me a gadfly. That's a pest." Never mind that Socrates, probably the greatest philosopher and rhetorician in history, was also called a gadfly. Cliché-ridden, I asked him then if he still planned on tilting at windmills. He replied: "I don't tilt at them. I knock them down."

CHAPTER 14

St. Jack

Jack Bogle doesn't have colleagues anymore. He has followers. "He's sort of like Sigmund Freud to psychotherapy or Jesus Christ to Christianity or Einstein to relativity," says Gary Weinstein, a retired physician and avowed Boglehead in Pittsburgh. "That's where he stands relative to indexing. It would be like if Einstein created the theory of relativity and also built the atomic bomb."

The Bogleheads are a group of bloggers and investing enthusiasts who, according to cofounders Taylor Larimore and Mel Lindauer, "follow the beliefs of a remarkable man, John C. Bogle."[1] Instead of a cross or star of David, they have Bogle bobblehead dolls. And instead of the Ten Commandments, they subscribe to Bogle's Twelve Pillars of Wisdom, which range from such useful bromides as, "When all else fails, fall back on simplicity" to loftier verities such as, "Never forget that risk, return, and cost are the three sides of the eternal triangle of investing."

The Bogleheads were an outgrowth of a forum called Vanguard Diehards on fund tracker Morningstar.com's Web site. Retired insurance underwriter and former World War II paratrooper Taylor Larimore posted in Diehards' "Conversation #1" on March 19, 1998, and has since made more than 24,000 contributions to the forum. St. Jack, being the ministering spirit hovering over this enterprise, has dubbed Larimore "king of the Bogleheads," while retired graphic artist and former marine Mel Lindauer, who has posted 23,000 times himself, is "the prince." Laura Dogu, a State Department foreign service officer with 4,000 posts, is the queen.

Because the Diehards' Morningstar forum was so popular, eventually the group launched its own Web site called Bogleheads.org in 2007. Since then, the site has attracted some 16,000 members and has some 500 to 1,000 posts a day, for a total of about 600,000 since its launch. But the Bogleheads don't just write about investing online. They also religiously attend meetings at 38 local U.S. chapters of the group and one in Paris. And every year the most devout Boglehead acolytes make a pilgrimage to a modestly priced inn or resort somewhere within the nation's borders to meet the great man himself. These Boglehead conferences, or "reunions," as members call them, have all the celebratory redemptive air of revival meetings. Bogle will talk about the "sins" of the financial sector like a missionary, and his flock will testify to the eternal truth of "His" words: stay the course; the stock market is a giant distraction from the business of investing; any time you have a system that privatizes the rewards of an enterprise and socializes the risks, you're going to be in trouble.

In perhaps the best journalistic profile of Bogle ever written, Art Carey of the *Philadelphia Inquirer* described the churchy idolatrous atmosphere of the September 2008 Boglehead reunion in San Diego:

> **They stood in line for autographs. They posed for pictures with him. They thanked him for giving the small investor "a fair shake," for enabling them to retire early, to buy or build their dream houses, to finance their children's college education, to live in comfort and security.**
>
> **"We're an affirmation of his life's work," said Michael LeBoeuf, 66, of Paradise Valley, Ariz., a coauthor of *The Bogleheads' Guide to Investing*, who was wearing a "Jack Bogle for President" button. "Some mutual-fund managers chose to make millions. Jack Bogle chose to make a difference."**

"He has financially changed my life," said Jesse Payne, 66, a real estate investor and retired New York City police officer. "There's God," he said, placing his hand over his head to indicate the Almighty's lofty position, before dropping it slightly, "and there's Bogle." [2]

Although the Bogleheads don't call Bogle St. Jack or even claim to have coined the name, "Many of us feel that way about him," Larimore wrote me in an e-mail. No one seems to know who first nicknamed Bogle St. Jack, but almost everyone agrees that the moniker was originally meant derisively by his industry peers. Now it is taken more literally by Bogle's thousands of fans.

So what exactly is it about Bogle's character that people find so appealing that they think him akin to divinity? On a personal level, it's his outspokenness, his honesty, and his genuine concern with ethics and integrity. But Bogle also has something else, a much larger Weltanschauung that seems out of place in an age of cultural and moral relativism. One way Bogle characterizes himself is as an "eighteenth-century man." He is a lover of the Enlightenment period in history, the leading lights of which stressed a belief in reason and empirical science over passion, superstition, and intuition. It also was a period of great social reform and revolutionary ideals, fostered by such men as Thomas Paine and Thomas Jefferson in the United States and John Locke and Jean-Jacques Rousseau in Europe. And finally, and perhaps most important to Bogle's character, there is a belief in an absolute moral authority that springs implicitly from heaven above and, much like divine providence, is supposed to inform our actions on the material plane via an individual sense of personal responsibility for the greater good and an inviolate social contract.

"Jack likes the 18th century," notes Chandler Hardwick, headmaster of Blair Academy. "And what's true of the 18th century is that anything that is important has a moral authority [that] extends beyond a church or school . . . into every aspect of life, whether it's literature, music, or finance."

Arguably, the most philosophical and personal book Bogle has written is *Enough*, which was published in 2009. In it he describes what he feels is a decay of professional standards and conduct on Wall Street and in society at large. Although he believes that business principles still exist, he thinks that too many of his peers aren't following the principles they ostensibly espouse:

> **It wasn't so many decades ago that the standards in the conduct of business were close to absolute:**
> *There are some things that one simply doesn't do.*
> **But today we place our reliance on relative standards:**
> *Everyone else is doing it, so I can do it, too.*
> **Our society cannot and should not tolerate the substitution of moral relativism for a certain form of moral absolutism, and its debasement in the ethical standards of commerce.**[3]

Even the great Enlightenment thinkers' belief in reason and the scientific method had a tinge of morality to it in that not only did they prioritize truth as the greatest good, but, more important, they posited that finding the "eternal" truth was in fact both possible and preferable to accepting life as one of God's mysteries. At the root of this truth worship was a belief in Plato's eternal forms—that if we could extract all of life's variable qualities, we could get at a basic understanding of what, say, a lion is, what characteristics every lion throughout history has possessed. The notion of applying the scientific method to achieve repeatability in results became sacrosanct in the physical sciences and would eventually be attached to the much murkier dismal science of economics. But even in the realm of physics and chemistry, the "eternal truth" has become suspect today because although a scientist can, say, distill two distinct molecules of pure copper in a lab, each molecule would occupy a distinct place in the space-time continuum, and the scientist's own subjective observations would affect the results—hence the Heisenberg principle.

So if eternal, objective truth cannot be achieved even in the hard sciences, what can be said of Bogle's Chapter 5 of *The Battle* being subtitled "The Momentary Precision of Stock Prices versus the Eternal Importance of Intrinsic Values"? Like so many in the money management business, Bogle says that he believes in market fundamentals, that ultimately the stock market's total returns will equal its dividend payouts plus earnings growth adjusted upward or downward to meet the long-term average historical valuation. Unlike so many others, he actually does believe what he says. As passionate and fanatical as any Baptist missionary, he is a market "fundamentalist." And his sureness, his confidence, and his missionary zeal are part of what is so enchanting to his fans. Underlying all his bromides, such as, "Stay the course," is a basic faith in capitalism's inexorable progress, that in the long run stocks will go up, and that if investors just squirrel away enough in their 401ks week after week, they will be rewarded, provided they don't let the croupiers of Wall Street rip them off. Such a philosophy is immensely comforting to middle-class investors who often see the value of their entire life savings bounce around like a yo-yo during one of the market's rougher weeks.

Of course, moral relativism is the hallmark of the postmodern age and of democracies in general. Notions of absolute moral authority are actually the residue of kings and religion in the Reformation that was gradually transformed during the Enlightenment into a social contract ostensibly approved of and administered by the governed. In democracies, ethics that are not codified into laws by citizens or their elected representatives are personal and private, not moral absolutes. Even Protestantism itself shifted the locus of morality and spiritual feeling from an outside objective authority—the Catholic Church in Rome—to a personal, more subjective relationship with God during the Reformation. Yet much of what Bogle laments in *Enough* is the loss of what he thinks of as traditional values and a decline in Western civilization (which was never really all that civilized to begin with).

It often seems in his writing that Bogle is clear-eyed about the present but wears rose-colored glasses about the past, believing in some lost golden age of idealistic capitalism that never truly existed, or perhaps existed only for a brief time during his youth. Although he writes about the sense of fiduciary duty that imbued the fund industry in the 1950s when he started in the business, the truth is that the industry back then was still smarting from all of the financial scandals that had occurred in the wake of the Great Depression, scandals that inspired the government to pass the Securities Acts of 1933 and 1934 and the Investment Company Act of 1940.

In fact, many of the financial follies of the 1920s and 1930s seem eerily similar to those that occurred in the current generation, with the only difference being that the scale and complexity of the shenanigans are even greater today. Esteemed economist John Kenneth Galbraith devoted an entire chapter of his book *The Great Crash, 1929* to describing the tangled web of leverage, front running, and self-dealing employed by closed-end funds—the predecessors to today's open-end mutual funds—during that era. In the chapter titled "In Goldman, Sachs We Trust," he described how one of the most popular funds of that day, the Goldman Sachs Trading Corporation, applied increasing amounts of leverage via a weird sort of shell game in which one leveraged closed-end fund bought shares of another leveraged closed-end fund, which bought shares of another leveraged closed-end fund. The public had no idea ultimately how much leverage was used and what exactly these funds were invested in, since disclosure rules were virtually nonexistent back then. This sounds an awful lot like the shadow banking system in largely unregulated credit default swaps that exacerbated the 2008 crisis.

Nor were the scandals of the Great Crash the first time the financial services industry showed itself utterly lacking in any sense of fiduciary duty. In another classic by Galbraith called *A Short History of Financial Euphoria*, he described how scandals and financial fraud precipitated and/or exacerbated almost every crash in history. Invariably, each collapse had to do with the financial euphoria associated with bubbles, lax or nonexistent regulatory standards that allowed crooks to game the system, and finally, and most important, the application of new and increasingly complicated forms of leverage. Boom times inevitably encourage financial engineering via leverage so that investors can get "more bang for their buck" when buying outrageously overpriced securities. And rare is it in financial history that a fiduciary turns away the would-be speculator and says, "No, no, I can't take your cash. That's too risky." On the contrary, it is often such putative fiduciaries who created the leveraged product that destroys investors' wealth in the first place.

Leverage is an essential ingredient of every bubble and every crash because it is not only what allows prices to be inflated but also what forces borrowers to liquidate their positions quickly in a decline, as their margin balance is called and their creditors refuse to lend to them any more. This causes a snowball effect that makes crashes both rapid and severe. As Galbraith would remark, "All crises have involved debt that, in one fashion or another, has become dangerously out of scale in relation to the underlying means of payment."⁴ The only question to ask with each bubble is what new form of financial engineering will create the leverage that causes the system to implode.

So when precisely was this golden age of capitalism where honest fiduciaries were good stewards of capital? In *Enough,* Bogle cites his own formative years and the Enlightenment period as examples of periods when greed wasn't good. But even the Enlightenment's great Isaac Newton famously lost a chunk of his fortune in the South Sea Bubble, remarking, "I can calculate the movement of the stars, but not the madness of men." Bogle, for his part, says that he is specifically referring to the fund industry in the 1940s and 1950s when he speaks of money managers seeing themselves as true fiduciaries: "Let me say that I found the investment business in 1949, when I first looked into it in college, to be a strong business in terms of ethics and values. The mutual fund business was run by small firms where the trustees were money managers, often partners in the firm, and even if they didn't have an express fiduciary duty to the funds, they knew what the heck their duty was. They were sitting there with the directors every month or so. It started to fall apart in the late 1960s, the go-go era when all this trading volume jumped up."

Although he does acknowledge that regulators and the Investment Company Act of 1940 played an important part in the positive change in attitude that occurred in the fund industry, Bogle believes that the industry in many ways corrected itself in the wake of the 1929 crash. "I'm not starting [my analysis] at 1929," he says. "I agree with you, the abuses were terrible. They got corrected, by an enormous bear market and by an enlightened sense of self-interest. That's what happens! You want to make something out of this business, you better clean it up. It would take a pretty obtuse mutual fund manager not to figure that out. Congress didn't go far enough [with the Investment Company Act]."

But would the industry have healed itself on its own without the passage of new regulations? It seems doubtful. Whenever the regulators don't keep up with the financial engineers, disaster is sure to be lurking around the corner, and it doesn't seem, as Bogle sometimes claims in his writing, that it was just a philosophy unique to our era—a shift from an ownership society to an agency one—that caused the dot-com bubble or the 2008 crash. Although Bogle is right to say that more agents than ever are controlling the market, even when they weren't nearly so prevalent, the market was prone to bubbles, corruption, and spectacular crashes. Owners as well as agents have been prone to speculation throughout history, and ne'er-do-wells have been prone to rip them off.

The thing about Bogle that I think people find so likable is not that he presents an accurate depiction of the way capitalism once was or is even today, but that he shows the way it should be if it functioned in his ethical universe. He is ultimately an idealist, not quite a pie-eyed one, but an idealist nonetheless. And his enthusiasm to build a better world is contagious. "It's called investors of the world unite in *The Battle for the Soul of Capitalism*," Bogle says. "And that is, we've got to get investors focused on long-term investing, less trading, less speculation. All of this [speculation] costs money, and that's why the index fund is ultimately the solution. You get the market return less a tiny cost, and everybody else together shares the market return less substantial cost. So you've got to wake up people. You've also got to get the money managers to work as fiduciaries. How can you be a fiduciary when your owner is the Bank of America or whoever it might be? The directors have a fiduciary duty to those management companies as well as the fund shareholders, and that [conflict of interest] has to be done away with ultimately."

Being a utopian at heart, Bogle has figured out a plan of action to achieve his just ownership society in which enlightened investors refuse to be speculators and honest money managers behave as fiduciaries: "There are two ways of bringing this new and far better system into existence. One is by some sort of government fiat. Pass a fiduciary duty standard and apply it to everybody. Set up some broad gauge standards, don't try to write narrow rules and say this is the deal for money managers. And if the money managers behave as fiduciaries, they will vote their corporate stock actively because they are not trading all the time. They will say, 'I want to make sure GE, for example, is run in the interest of the stockholders and not in the interest of the management or in the interest of its momentary price.' So, you can have this government decree, and I would do that if I could, but you could also have an evolutionary strategy, an Adam Smith type strategy, and that is when investors figure out what their own best interests are and apply them. Buy index funds, buy low-cost funds, don't put any money with fund managers who aren't behaving as fiduciaries, and that will change the industry's 'selling proposition'—I hate that phrase—to one of 'we are your service provider and we are your fiduciary' rather than 'we are giving you the latest hot performance.'"

Bogle's vision of an ownership society rests squarely in the Enlightenment ideology and values of the eighteenth century—John Locke's "life, liberty, and property" and the Protestant work ethic of the Quakers—yet he sees this ideology reaching its apex during the technological innovation of the nineteenth century via the industrial revolution. In *The Battle for the Soul of Capitalism*, he cites the eighteenth-century Quakers who dominated the mercantile class as exemplifying the ideology of trust necessary for capitalism to function properly: "Their emphasis on reliability, absolute honesty, and rigorous record-keeping infused them with trust as they dealt with one another, and other observant merchants came to see that being trustworthy went hand in hand with business success. Self-interest demanded virtue."[5] And this "virtuous circle" of trust, as Bogle calls it, enables capitalist economies to grow.

As a consequence, it's hard not to see him as some sort of walking anachronism from a nobler era that exists more in books and in his own idealized version of history than in reality. (Largely absent from his account of capitalism's glorious rise is the existence of slavery, indentured servitude, imperialism, and the exploitation of labor in general.) He seems the epitome of what an ethical Quaker businessman should be. In fact, he almost perfectly embodies the hard-working Christian capitalists that sociologist Max Weber wrote about in his classic tome *The Protestant Ethic and the Spirit of Capitalism*.

Not that Bogle is fanatically religious, although he is certainly a churchgoer. Rather, work is his religion, and labor, instead of being a means to an end—money and sustenance—is an end to itself. One can see the residue of the Protestant ethic in Bogle's strict Scottish upbringing, in which his grandmother would routinely tell him, "Idle hands are the tools of the divil." This is a man, after all, who has been employed practically without interruption since he was a young child. Although he has long been wealthy enough to retire, Bogle says that his work—his showing up in an office four days a week in his eighties—isn't really work but "play for me." Moreover, Bogle's frugalness, his unwillingness to spend money, even though by most accounts he has a tidy fortune, is the hallmark of the Protestant asceticism Weber described:

> The complexity of this issue is above all apparent in the *summum bonum* [supreme good] of this "ethic": namely, the acquisition of money, and more and more money, takes place here simultaneously with the strictest avoidance of all spontaneous enjoyment of it. The pursuit of riches is fully stripped of all pleasurable (*eudamonistischen*), and surely all hedonistic aspects. Accordingly, this striving becomes understood completely as an end in itself—to such an extent that it appears as fully outside the normal course of affairs and simply irrational, at least when viewed from the perspective of the "happiness" or "utility" of the single individual. Here people are oriented to acquisition as the purpose of life; acquisition is no longer viewed as a means to the end of satisfying the substantive needs of life. Those people in possession of spontaneous fun-loving dispositions experience this situation as an absolutely meaningless "reversal" of a natural condition (as we would say today). Yet this reversal constitutes just as surely a guiding principle of [modern] capitalism as incomprehension of this new situation characterizes all who remained untouched by [modern] capitalism's tentacles.[6]

And so we have Bogle and perhaps the only other frugal superstar of post-modern capitalism—Warren Buffett—living in a modest house, driving a modest car, preferring simple "all American" foods, and shopping for discounts wherever he can find them. And at the end of their lives, after accumulating massive fortunes, Bogle and Buffett both plan to give most of their money to charity in true Christian form.

HOW FRUGAL IS HE?

Bogle has always eschewed the "good things" in life. Even when he traveled as Vanguard's CEO, he flew coach. His home in Bryn Mawr, Pennsylvania, is not ostentatious. According to his daughter Barbara, Bogle drove his 1987 Honda Acura for about 15 years until he was no longer able to and gave it away to his son Andrew. "I wouldn't dream of buying a Jaguar or a Mercedes," Bogle said. "It would seem like I was trying to show off." In fact, in a family of eight, the Bogles never had more than two cars. "There was at a time six drivers living in one house," Barbara says. "We had a Volkswagen bus for a while because we needed something to tote us around in." Perhaps with Bogle at the wheel, though, no one mistook them for the Partridge family.

Although some stories are perhaps apocryphal, the six Bogle children remember their parents' thrift very well. When they were growing up, the family lived in a big old drafty barn of a house in Haverford. "The [thermostat's] temperature was probably set at 58 degrees, and because we had drafty old windows, there would be mornings in the wintertime I would wake up and there would be frost on the inside of the glass," recalls Barbara. "And we would say we were cold, and my parents would say put on more clothes."

While styles changed, Bogle remained happily locked in the past. The crewcut he wore beginning at age 13 made him in the 1980s look like a boy playing hard-driving executive. (His hair grew long during an extended hospital stay in late 1993, and he decided to keep it at a more conventional, but short, length thereafter.) Blue or white button-down shirts were part of his dress code long after men's shirts turned sporty. "For him," says Jim Riepe, "it was a big departure sometime in the 1970s when he wore a yellow shirt. You'd think he was wearing a zoot suit." Ever frugal, he wore dark wool ties, not light-colored silk (wool lasted longer, and dark colors could be cleaned promptly and put right back in use), and off-the-rack (although Brooks Brothers) suits. He is said to have worn the same belt for something like 20 years.

One often retold incident perfectly illustrates Bogle's asceticism. He was checking into New York City's plush Plaza Hotel in 1984 and asked for the cheapest room in the house. The clerk informed him that the cheapest room was $230 a night (before a 20 percent corporate discount). "There is absolutely no way I'm going to pay that price for a room," Bogle said. "Whenever I've come to the Plaza, and I've been coming here for 15 years now, I've always had the cheapest room in the house, and it used to be less than $100. I'd like that now." The clerk offered a small room next to a noisy elevator shaft.

"How much?" Bogle asked.

"One hundred dollars."

"Do I get the corporate discount?'

"No," said the embarrassed clerk.

"I'll take the room anyway."

Meanwhile, a long line was forming behind Bogle. An impatient man behind him asked, "Aren't you John Bogle?"

"How on earth would you know that?"

"I'm a stockholder in Vanguard funds. I've seen your picture."

When Bogle apologized for creating a delay, the man replied, "Oh, no. Don't feel that way. At first I didn't understand what you were doing. Now that I see who you are, I understand completely. Vanguard—low costs, no loads, isn't that right?"

Bogle himself has told me that he doesn't particularly enjoy the money he's earned, and yet he will happily boast of the discipline he's shown saving it. Is not in fact Weber's description of the ascetic's postponement of spending the perfect characterization of almost every bourgeois saver and investor in her 401k plan who follows Bogle's advice to dollar cost average and slowly accumulate capital over time?

Moreover, almost everyone who knows Bogle thinks that he works too hard, including himself. One of his biggest regrets, he tells me, is that he didn't spend more time with his family. And yet he has remarked on more than one occasion that he feels that if he stopped working, he would die. "I was at Baylor College speaking years ago, and this nice young couple—married, graduate school—asked how did you handle the work-life balance, and I said, 'badly,'" he remarks. "There was no other way to do what I was doing in the business world. There's only 24 hours in a day. I think I did an adequate job as a husband and father and grandfather, and I think my kids might say I did better than that, but you know, it could have been better."

Bogle explains his attitude toward work and money in classic Weberian terms, seeing helping others as the end, while largely dismissing or downplaying the material rewards of labor: "Think about it this way. I'm not in any privation. I'm going to be warm tonight. I'm going to be dry tonight. I'm going to have a nice dinner, probably with a nice glass of wine, probably jug wine because I don't care for the expensive stuff, and I had a wonderful day working, which is like I've been in heaven all day. What more could anybody want? And I do think you end up—it's an awful self-centered thing to say—but you end up thinking if you've done the world a little bit of good, then you had a good day."

And yet Bogle's love of work clearly had some costs. He has six children and only one wife, Eve, who largely raised them by herself. Meanwhile, her husband, during his executive years at Vanguard, worked thirteen-hour days, six and sometimes even seven days a week—and often even needed nurturing himself because of his persistent heart condition. Eve is a private person who doesn't give interviews, but the general impression one gets from speaking to family members, friends, and Bogle himself is that she is the real saint of the family for sacrificing so much of herself so that her husband could become a great success.

"[My mother] truly was Herculean in her ability to manage the household with six kids," says Bogle's son John Bogle, Jr. "She literally had no domestic help. We had a babysitter if they had to go out. And I think as we got a little bit older, her mother would arrange for someone to come by once every couple of months and help straighten up the house. But that was it. She got us all up in the morning, had breakfast for us, got us to school. We came home and she was cooking dinner, helping us with homework. And it's six kids. The ages were spread out quite a bit, so there wasn't really a time when she had complete discretion over the kids, to use a financial term, because by the time Andrew [the youngest child] was born, my oldest sister was just about in college. So she had the older kids to help out a bit. That is not to belittle anything she did. It was just an extraordinary effort on her part; it is probably a little bit more interesting of a book than my Dad—I mean that tongue in cheek."

Although the Protestant work ethic is so ingrained in our culture that it's difficult not to see labor as ennobling, one wonders what the world would be like if every man wished to work as hard as Bogle. Surely, women would have no choice but to be homebound and perform their traditional roles as wives and mothers, like Eve. Our environment would be totally polluted because of the extra production from everyone working 13-hour days and never retiring. Or, alternatively, there would be massive unemployment because with all these Bogle Übermenschen toiling ceaselessly, there just wouldn't be enough jobs to go around. Consumption would decrease, and we'd enter a recession, as everyone would be frugal and think material ends are beside the point. And as Weber would write so eloquently, even if some heretics secretly disavowed this laborious ethos, they would be locked in "a steel cage" of the workaholic's mindset, forced to compete with ascetics who are unable to appreciate the more sensuous and, some would argue, finer side of life. That doesn't seem particularly pleasant to me—saintly perhaps in a self-flagellating way, but pleasant no.

A major drawback to excessive labor is the dehumanization of and alienation from the self that occurs. One literally becomes one's job and seems to have little or no life outside of it. Indeed, when I talk to Bogle, it often seems as though he eats, drinks, and sleeps mutual funds. Despite his volubility on the subject, he is actually a difficult person to get to know on any sort of personal level. He is friendly and polite to a fault, but whenever I've asked him about his private history as opposed to his public Vanguard one, he usually tries to change the subject. Interestingly enough, he has occasionally expressed regret at his chosen career path. In a telling aside near the end of *Enough,* he remarked that he does a lot of "lonely wondering about the worth of my own life and career,"[7] and when asked by the the *Philadelphia Inquirer*'s Art Carey to elaborate, he said: "At a certain stage in your life, you become more introspective, a quality that is so lacking in our society. . . . You begin asking yourself: Why am I doing this? What am I doing this for? I think I added huge value to the investment business, but I wonder if I could have added huger value doing something else."[8] Bogle tells me he might've liked to have been a lawyer or an architect or even something "useful" like a social worker, although when he took an aptitude test in the eighth grade, the results indicated, "The one thing you should never become is a social worker."

Central to the Protestant work ethic is the belief that having a vocation or calling is spiritually uplifting and more important than material desires. Bogle fits Weber's model of "Puritan vocational asceticism" to a T. He has given speeches and written whole chapters of books on the importance of devoting oneself to "professionalism" instead of just profit, of creating value for society instead of extracting it. At one point in *Enough,* he even cites an article by Roger Lowenstein "bemoaning the loss of the 'Calvinist' rectitude that had its roots in 'the very Old World notions of integrity, ethics and unyielding loyalty to the customer.'"[9] At another point, he literally describes the idea of a calling as the key to being a true professional, citing a "commitment to the interests of clients in particular and the welfare of society in general"[10] as being a defining characteristic of professionals.

Even Bogle's notion of being a good steward or fiduciary, of putting the client's interests before one's own, is grounded in a secularized version of Protestant theology. Consider the parallels in Weber's description of stewardship: "The idea of a person's *duty* to maintain possessions entrusted to him, to which he subordinates himself as a dutiful steward or even as a 'machine for producing wealth' lies upon his life with a chilling seriousness. And as one's possessions become more valuable, the more burdensome becomes the feeling of responsibility to maintain them intact for God's glory and to increase their value through relentless work—*if* the ascetic temper meets the challenge. . . . This spirit, however, first found its consistent ethical foundation in the ethic of the ascetic Protestantism. Its significance for the development of [modern] capitalism is obvious."[11] All Bogle has done to Weber's definition in this case is substitute the word "clients" for "God."

Such secularization of Judeo-Christian ideals is nothing new. Weber already observed in 1904 how the actual spiritual aspect was extracted from capitalist values when it was no longer needed. For himself, Bogle, though he goes to church every Sunday, takes religion with a grain of salt. "To be very clear, I consider myself a religious person," he says. "I happen to be an Episcopalian, although we go to the Presbyterian Church. On the other hand, we are all there together every Sunday, not everybody but at least one of our family, sometimes more. But I'm somewhat skeptical about a lot of that stuff. No, I don't believe the Bible is the word of God. If it is, how did He learn to write in Hebrew and then Greek? . . . I think Jesus is a remarkable historical figure, but you're pushing me when you tell me that the Virgin Mary is sent physically up to heaven. Up, there she goes! So long, Babe! How can anyone believe that?"

And yet when Bogle was in the hospital waiting for his heart transplant, he recited Psalm 23, "The Lord is my shepherd," and/or the Lord's Prayer every night. "It was a prayer for recognition. The not 'my will,' but 'thy will be done,'" says Bogle. "That's the way life is anyway—recognizing that there is something bigger than us out there and we're really not all that important." It is the same attitude of the dutiful servant of a greater cause that makes for the best financial stewards.

Perhaps the most important part of this sense of civic duty is doing charitable work, so that after we're gone, the wealth that we produced can continue to help society. Bogle has again fulfilled the Christian ideal by giving so much of what he's earned to good causes. And what could be more fitting for Vanguard's eighteenth-century man than to help found the National Constitution Center, the first museum dedicated to the U.S. Constitution, in his hometown of Philadelphia? The center, which is located in Philadelphia Independence National Park—where both the Constitution and the Declaration of Independence were written—is 160,000 square feet and includes several historical multimedia exhibits, a theater, and a Signers' Hall, containing 42 life-size bronze statues of the 39 men who signed the Constitution, as well as the three who dissented. One can just imagine Bogle hobnobbing at the Philadelphia Convention in 1787 with Ben Franklin, author of such utilitarian Bogelesque maxims as, "Time is money," and, "Money can beget more money, and its offspring can beget more." No doubt they'd have been fast friends.

Bogle's contribution to the Constitution Center's successful opening was immense, as he served as its chairman during its formative years from September of 1999 through 2006 and was one of the primary fund-raisers to help gather the $185 million necessary to build its facilities. When Pennsylvania Governor Ed Rendell stepped down from the chair position to be the head of the Democratic National Committee in 1999, the center's president, Joe Torsella, knew that Bogle, who was a trustee at the time, was the best man for the job. The timing, of course, couldn't have been more perfect, as Bogle was about to be retired from his chairman post at Vanguard. "We had to get Jack to do it," says Torsella. "We had not a lot of money at that point, maybe $40 million of the $185 million we needed. We hadn't done the bulk of the private fund-raising. So we had to take the fund-raising show on the road. And I couldn't think of anyone better to do it than Jack. The Jack Bogle brand meant so much to advance the project. He did it with a real passion for the cause."

Bogle also gave a significant undisclosed sum of his own money. "We were a bit short of our goal, so we created a challenge gift fundraising drive," Torsella says. "Bogle agreed to be the donor, but asked that his gift be anonymous. He has a bit of a Puritan streak in him that way." Ultimately, the secret that Bogle was the benefactor was leaked to the board, and his donation was henceforth jokingly referred to as the "Bogle anonymous gift."

The center's groundbreaking on September 17, 2000, exactly 213 years after the signing of the Constitution, and its official opening on July 4, 2003, were both crowning moments for Bogle, and he continues to relish taking guests on tours. "He loved taking people to the sculpture room where the framers are and talking about how the statues are life-sized and how that worked, and he always put his hand on Madison's shoulder, who was the giant of the making of the Constitution but the shortest guy of the conventioneers," says Rick Stengel, who was the center's president from 2004 to 2006.

Stengel agrees with the assessment that Bogle resembles the quintessential Enlightenment man: "I think the rationality of the Enlightenment appeals to him. Jack is a preeminently rational person. I think the kind of pragmatism of some of the founders, like Benjamin Franklin, definitely appeals to him. I think their patriotism and idealism also appeal to him. He's a mixture of a pragmatist and an idealist or an idealist and a realist. And I think the framers' mixture of those two things speaks to him." Bogle readily acknowledges the comparisons that are often made between him and the author of *Poor Richard's Almanac* but downplays them: "Several people have compared me favorably to Benjamin Franklin, nice—undeserved but nice." Franklin, as it turns out, was the focus of a considerable portion of Weber's text in the *Protestant Ethic.*

Of course, Bogle isn't involved only in the Constitution Center. He's also been a major donor to the Blair Academy and Princeton University and to medical research into arrhythmogenic right ventricular dysplasia—his and his daughter Nancy's heart ailment. (Although his total contributions remain undisclosed, the fact that Princeton and Blair Academy have both named buildings after him cannot but mean that the sums are significant.) In many ways, it was his charitable activities that filled the void in his life once he was no longer in the executive suite at Vanguard. "Whatever the peace he made with Vanguard, he had made already by the time he became chairman of the Constitution Center," says Stengel. "Again, since he wasn't working full time anymore and mainly speaking and writing, I think he was looking for other things to do." Simply the fact that Bogle gave 40 percent of his Partnership Plan dividends back to Vanguard's shareholders reveals how much he takes his ethos of stewardship and civic responsibility seriously.

If Bogle has any worldly sins, his pride would surely be counted among them. The seven-foot statue of him at the center of Vanguard's campus seems an oddly idolatrous display, given his Puritanical desire to keep his own vanity in check. Still, even such obvious ego trips must be taken in context. At the time that Bogle agreed to have the statue made, he appeared to be at death's door. "We had already commissioned a portrait of Mr. Bogle as well as a portrait of Mr. Morgan, Jack Brennan, and Jack Bogle together in the early 1990s," says Barbara Scudder, who helped commission the statue. "Mr. Bogle was failing in health, and it was obvious—and I wouldn't want to say it in front of him—but I'm sure he knew he was close to death. In fact I recall many times seeing him walking down the hall toward my office, and the tips of his ears would be black because there was so little oxygen flowing."

With some reservation, Bogle agreed to the project while he was in the hospital waiting for his heart transplant. But he insisted that the statue accurately depict his physical flaws. "His hands are very arthritic," Scudder observes. "They are kind of crippled. And he wanted them represented. If you went to the statue and looked at it a little bit more up close, you would see how gnarled his hands are. He felt that was really a part of him." So saying that the statue was simply a vanity project is not quite accurate. Yet the irony of the model's for the "John C. Bogle Monument," as the sculptor officially titled it, still being alive some 14 years after it was erected cannot be lost on anyone.

As for any sort of materialism in Bogle, the only trace of it might be found bobbing by his summer home in Lake Placid—a 22-foot-long, 1928 Chris Craft that once belonged to Marjorie Merriweather Post, heiress to the Post Cereal fortune. Her boat was called Post Haste, which Bogle's father-in-law rechristened the Sis Boom Bah after an old Princeton cheer. "I bought it for book value," Bogle boasts in classic skinflint fashion. "It was worth a bit more than that, and I had it restored, put an engine in it. And I say that if you really had to push me, it's my only indulgence. It's totally unnecessary, and I feel somewhat guilty about it, but I'll get over it." Even his huge rustic summerhouse Bogle inherited from his wife Eve's family, the provenance of which dates back to the 1950s. "Rustic makes it sound too charming," remarks his son John Bogle, Jr., adding that once the house's heater broke and his father didn't want to fix it: "You know in the Adirondacks it can get well into the thirties at night or even colder." Bogle no doubt would have preferred that everyone just wear sweaters all the time.

Unfortunately, not everyone can live up to Bogle's high ideals. Even as early as 1904, Weber observed the fundamental paradox that those Protestants who were the most successful at both working hard and suppressing their worldly desires would soon become wealthy and be tempted to give up their Protestant faith. Weber quotes liberally from John Wesley, one of the founders of the Methodist Church, regarding Wesley's concerns that religion produces frugality and industry, which as a consequence make people rich, but as wealth increases, so does "desire of the flesh" and worldly things. Wesley fretted that Methodism was doomed as a result unless the faithful remained charitable or, as Weber observes, "There follows the admonition that those who have 'acquired all they can' should also 'give all they can'—in order to grow in grace and to assemble a fortune in heaven." But, in Weber's view, this deterioration in ethical standards was inevitable in an increasingly secularized and rationalized world: "As the paroxysms of the search for God's kingdom gradually dissolved into the dispassionate virtues of the vocational calling and the religious roots of the movement slowly withered, a utilitarian orientation to the world took hold."[12]

Of course, this utilitarian orientation might well apply to almost every fund industry executive today other than Bogle—making money for themselves is their primary goal; making it for fund shareholders is secondary. "Everybody in the fund industry is partly in a profession and partly in a business," Bogle says. "Vanguard is 90 percent profession and 10 percent business. Everybody else is 10 percent profession and 90 percent business." That is utilitarian efficiency taken to the extreme in the wrong direction, extracting as much wealth from fund shareholders as possible and returning as little as is acceptable to them as possible. Bogle's Quaker forebears would no doubt be displeased.

CHAPTER 15

The Rise of the Speculator

Bogle has always believed that long-term buy-and-hold investing is the best means for fund shareholders to achieve their financial goals. And because an index fund that tracks the entire stock market is a passive investment that essentially buys and holds forever, Bogle thinks that investing in one is the optimal choice for implementing such a strategy. That's why it is a cruel irony that the index concept he helped champion has been exploited to create exchange traded funds (ETFs) for speculators whose holding period can often be just a matter of minutes.

Since 1993, when State Street Global Advisors launched the first S&P 500 ETF in the United States, the market has exploded to include more than 1,000 tradable funds, passively tracking every index or asset class imaginable—from Treasury bonds to Brazilian small caps to cotton futures to leveraged funds that promise to triple the inverse daily return of semiconductor stocks. The mind-boggling array of lunatic, specialized high-risk index investments is enough to infuriate someone like Bogle, who has always advised investors to "keep it simple" and to index as broad a basket of stocks and bonds as possible to achieve true diversification.

To make matters worse, investors aren't buying and holding these ETFs. They're trading them like wildfire, and not just the speculative specialized ones. Gradually, as the abuse of his beloved creation became more apparent, Bogle became more vocal in his concerns. In 2004 he gave a speech at Washington State University in which he singled out the S&P 500 and Nasdaq 100 ETFs, nicknamed "Spiders" and "Qubes," as being subject to terrible speculation:

> **Bought to be sold is hardly hyperbole. ETFs turn over at rates I could never have imagined. Each day, about $8 billion(!) of Spiders and Qubes change hands, an annualized portfolio turnover rate of 3000 percent, representing an average holding period of just 12 days! (Turnover of regular mutual funds by their shareholders now runs in the 40 percent range, itself an excessive rate that smacks of speculation.) The extraordinary ETF turnover should hardly be surprising, however. The sponsor of the Spiders regularly advertises this product with these words: "Now, you can trade the S&P 500 Index all day long, in real time." (To which I would ask, "What kind of a nut would do that?")[1]**

Not that Bogle's concerns about ETFs were anything new. When he was still CEO of Vanguard, Nathan Most, then a product developer with the American Stock Exchange, approached Bogle with the idea of launching an S&P 500 ETF in 1991. Bogle sent him packing, arguing that a tradable index fund would defeat the purpose of indexing, which was to buy and hold for as long as possible.[2] Then Most went to State Street with the idea, and the rest is history.

That's why it marked a pivotal moment in Vanguard's evolution when Jack Brennan approved the launch of the first Vanguard Total Stock Market ETF, which opened to new investors in 2001. "I was having a meeting with Jack Brennan," says Vanguard's CIO Gus Sauter, who first suggested the idea. "At the end of it, I gave him a very brief memo just describing what we should be doing in the ETF space, and his first reaction, after reading it for 30 seconds, was, 'This may be the dumbest idea I've ever seen.' The next morning he reread the memo, and came back and said, 'Well, it may not be the dumbest idea.' A month or so later the board of directors approved going forward with ETFs. Jack Bogle was not involved with that decision; at that point he was no longer on the board. I remember seeing him later. We announced [the ETF launch] when he was on vacation, and he came back and I saw him in the foyer of our cafeteria, and I remember him booming over at me, 'Gus, what the heck is going on here?' So, he wasn't too wild about launching the ETFs."

And yet Bogle doesn't disapprove of ETFs as an investment vehicle if used appropriately. What bothers him is when people abuse them. "I like ETFs if you are going to buy broadly diversified, classic index funds in ETF form: Vanguard 500, Vanguard Total Stock Market, Vanguard Total Bond Market, Total International Stock Market, and perhaps emerging markets," he says. "If you are going to buy them and hold them forever, it may even be a little bit better than buying the underlying mutual fund—it's not clear because you've got commissions but a slightly lower expense ratio. So for those purposes I have no problem with ETFs at all. I think they are fine. I've always said that."

The problem is that because ETFs were designed to be traded, there is a temptation for investors to do precisely that, and at the worst possible times—buying hot ETFs at the top and selling beaten-down ETFs at the bottom. In 2009 Bogle did some research using statistics from fund tracker Morningstar to analyze the "investor return" of the average dollar invested in Vanguard ETFs versus comparable Vanguard index mutual funds over the previous five years. This measure calculates not how the funds or ETFs performed but how investors fared inside the funds, thus revealing the intelligence of their buy and sell decisions. The results were pretty damning to ETF investors. Investor returns in ETFs consistently lagged not only the benchmarks the funds tracked by a wide margin, but also investors in comparable Vanguard mutual funds. The range in ETF-to-mutual-fund performance lag was anywhere from 0.06 percent for a large-cap value index ETF to 12.0 percent for a real estate investment trust (REIT) index. For the S&P 500, the lag was a wide 7.1 percent.[3]

When Bogle revealed the results of his ETF research at a Webinar hosted by the *Journal of Indexes* and IndexUniverse.com, he remarked: "Investor lag in the ETF category is large and significant. The . . . mutual funds have a lag here and there, but in general, come very close to the markets they are in. So we have evidence—strong evidence—that exchange-traded funds, because of the timing that goes on in them, are not acting in the best interest of investors. Or, that investors are not acting in their own best interests, which may be a better way to put it."[4] Because of investors' self-destructive tendencies, Bogle has called the ETF "a wolf in sheep's clothing," adding in *The Little Book of Common Sense Investing*, "Simply put, the ETF is a fund designed to facilitate trading in its shares, dressed in the guise of the traditional index fund."[5]

But if Bogle's initial concerns about speculation, voiced as early as 1991, have all proven to be correct, why is Vanguard aggressively moving into the ETF business? The decision to do so raises doubts about the company's shareholder-friendly ethos. Some industry critics have remarked that the ETF launch was more about trying to defend Vanguard's market share in the index fund space from increasingly aggressive competitors than about offering shareholders a superior investment option. "In the back of my mind I thought if we didn't offer ETFs, people would just go to Fidelity for them or someplace else," remarked Lawrence Wilson, a retired Vanguard director who was on the board when it approved the ETF launch.

Concerns about market share are what one expects to find more often in the executive suites of for-profit companies than at Vanguard. After all, if Vanguard is shareholder-owned, then the goal should be to maximize shareholder returns, not to gather assets and increase market share, right? "What is the responsibility of the trustee who creates products that are subject to misuse?" Bogle asks. "There are two attitudes to that: one, you cannot be the guardian of the investors' investment objectives, and two, probably in the long run it's not a good idea to give people dynamite so they can blow themselves up!"

Should the attitude at Vanguard be to just give the public what it wants, even if it's harmful? Bogle doesn't think so. "When you start down that path, it becomes a very slippery one," he says. "Suppose today that all our competitors are selling Greek bond funds. Money is pouring into them. Is that a good argument for us to start a Greek bond fund? I think that it is really the reverse. This [scenario] has happened a lot of times: 'Everyone is doing it, so we should do it too.' I refer again to my rules on market share. Market share is a measure and not an objective. If you lose market share because people are selling insane products, take that into account. Don't say, 'We are failing.' Say, 'We are just not going to jump onto that bandwagon.' The rule is that market share must be earned and not bought."

Thankfully, Vanguard hasn't launched any Greek bond ETFs. But should it be launching ETFs at all if investors tend to underperform in them? "Any investment vehicle, whether it is a traditionally structured fund, an ETF, or an individual security, can be used or misused," says CEO Bill McNabb. "The broad points that Jack makes about people being too speculative and not taking a longer-term perspective—no one disagrees with any of that. In fact, those principles are near and dear to all of our hearts. I happen to think that the ETF is an expansion of the use of indexing and low-cost investing more broadly among brand-new constituents. Are there speculative corners? Yeah. Do we like that? No. The good news is that [speculators] pay their own way in these vehicles because of the way they are structured, so they don't impact the longer-term holder. The bad news is they exist. We are not catering to that crowd."

One of the hallmarks of speculation is chasing the hot performance of a narrow sector of the market. Sector funds invariably are more volatile than broad market ones because of their lack of diversification and their focus on one specific industry. Speculators attempt to feed off sectors' volatile price movements regardless of underlying fundamentals, hoping to ride the temporary momentum of an upswing. Most such speculators fail because of poorly timed moves and excessive trading costs.

Although Bogle acknowledges the potential benefits of broadly diversified ETFs, he largely despises sector ones. In *The Little Book of Common Sense Investing*, he writes:

Yes, these specialized ETFs are diversified, but only in their narrow arenas. Owning the semiconductor industry is not diversification in any usual sense, nor is owning the South Korean stock market. And while sector ETFs frequently have the lowest expense ratios in their fields, they can run three to six times the level of the lowest-cost all-market index funds. What's more, sector ETFs not only carry brokerage and trading costs, but often are sold as part of actively managed fund portfolios with adviser fees of 1 percent or more, or in wrap accounts with annual fees of 1.5 percent to 2.0 percent or more. The net result of these differences is that sector ETFs as a group are virtually certain to earn returns that fall well short of the returns delivered by the stock market.[6]

Despite these relevant concerns, Vanguard launched 11 sector ETFs in 2004, including ones that track tech, health care, financial services, energy, and real estate stocks. Most of these ETFs have proven more volatile than the Vanguard Total Stock Market ETF, making them ripe for speculation. Bogle says that Vanguard's ETFs are more broadly diversified than the typical sector ETF, but he doesn't really approve: "I just don't think people should use them, and if they do, they shouldn't trade them."

Vanguard CEO McNabb says that the sector ETFs can serve a specific purpose for the right type of long-term investor who may want to reduce her exposure to a particular sector by holding all the sector ETFs in the market other than the one she wishes to exclude. So, for instance, if someone is working in the software industry and has a lot of her employer's company stock in her retirement plan, which must be held onto for several years because of the vesting or lock-up rules, that investor may want to have less exposure to the software industry elsewhere in her portfolio. "[Such investors] will come to us and say, 'we want to index everything else, but we want to go light on technology,'" McNabb says. "So we are giving them the broad building blocks to do that." Bogle has heard this rationale for sector ETFs before but doesn't quite buy it: "The argument was always made to me, if a guy works for Microsoft, he can buy the S&P 500 without technology. My response to that was, 'Yes, but has anyone actually done that?' I don't believe anybody has ever done it."

One thing is certain: the explosion of ETFs has made it more confusing for investors to choose among them. The array of 46 Vanguard ETFs virtually ensures that the unschooled individual investor will need some sort of financial advice to choose wisely. And the financial adviser community is one of the main targets for ETFs in general and those at Vanguard in particular. "[Vanguard] claims that we are working with advisers and we are basically using the ETFs in an intelligent way to allocate assets," Bogle remarks. "Why do they need these ETFs? That's a damn good question. Or to put it another way, they don't need the ETFs, but ETFs are in the air. They are in the DNA, to use an expression I don't much care for. They are the hot marketing idea."

Allocating aggressively among specialized asset classes or narrow sectors of the market in an attempt to boost returns is one way financial planners can justify charging their annual fees, typically 1 percent of assets or more. The advantage of this strategy is that using low-cost ETFs allows the total expense ratio—the adviser's 1 percent fee plus the ETF's minuscule fee—to be comparable to those of actively managed mutual funds. But one wonders if investors would even need such advice if they just listened to Bogle and kept it simple, owning just a balanced fund or a total stock market and total bond market fund. "The problem an adviser has is that it is very difficult to just say, 'Buy Vanguard Wellington Fund or buy a target-date fund, and I'll give you a call in 10 years and we'll see how we're doing,'" Bogle observes. "Buy and hold means, you don't revisit [the portfolio] all the time. So what are you paying the adviser for? Well, I say you are paying the adviser to keep you from doing something [foolish] because we get so wrapped up in behavioral issues."

It is obvious that some people will always need financial advice. But how many people would have been just fine if they had bought one of Vanguard's low-cost balanced index funds or the Wellington Fund 15 years ago and held on instead of hiring an adviser? These two funds have beaten the vast majority of their peers over the long term and are well diversified in both stocks and bonds. The advice adds an extra layer of fees that in some ways defeats the purpose of indexing—in fact, it adds a croupier intermediary to the mix. And many advisers are apparently trading a lot as well. Although turnover in Vanguard's ETFs is not nearly as high as it is in other shops' funds, it hovers around 200 to 300 percent, Bogle says, which is still pretty high and will no doubt lead to lower long-term returns.

Vanguard's decision to satisfy the adviser market, perhaps at the expense of individual investors, is a different and maybe less distasteful sort of conflict of interest from charging high management fees directly to all fund shareholders in that advisers are shareholders too. Still, fulfilling advisers' needs to drum up more business by offering them increasingly complicated specialized tools to play with doesn't seem to be in the spirit in which Vanguard was originally founded. Even though advisers who use ETFs or index funds don't charge loads or up-front commissions for their services, their fees still result in 1 percent less of assets in shareholders' pockets every year. The fact that individual investors can more effectively "do it themselves" at Vanguard without resorting to advisers or ETFs is almost certain.

Despite McNabb's claims to the contrary, there is also ample evidence that Vanguard does in fact want to do business with speculators. In May 2009, the company bid to acquire the ETF business of Barclays Global Investors, the largest ETF manager, whose financially troubled parent, Barclays Bank, sought to raise capital by divesting itself of this division. At the time, Barclays managed some 180 iShares ETFs, many of which were invested in highly speculative, narrow slices of the market and suffered from the extraordinary turnover of assets that Bogle is so critical of. Some of the extremely volatile sectors that Barclays ETFs indexed, to name just a few, included Asian real estate stocks, home builder stocks, oil equipment companies, silver bullion, and Brazilian stocks. Moreover, iShares generally had much higher expenses than Vanguard's ETFs and were run for a profit. How could such an acquisition possibly fit into the at-cost shareholder-oriented ethos of Vanguard?

Although he is quick to acknowledge that he has no real say in Vanguard's decision making anymore, so it's easier for him to be critical,

Bogle for his part did not approve of the deal: "I really worried about it as a business proposition. How can you have a low-cost line of ETFs and a high-cost line of ETFs? I don't know the answer to that. I don't think it's possible to raise the prices on the Vanguard ETFs, and, if we lower the prices on the Barclays ETFs, then the profits we bought vanish. So I was worried that it wasn't a sound business proposition, and I communicated those positions to management without particular comment."

At the time Vanguard had $51 billion in ETF assets and Barclays had $261 billion, so a deal would have instantly catapulted Vanguard into the front row of the ETF game. Perhaps McNabb, who had been in the CEO's post only since August 2008, thought that given how distressed the market was in general and Barclays Bank was in particular, it was a good time to buy a tremendous business on the cheap. And so again we have that dichotomy that what makes perfect sense from a business perspective for a fund management company does not always make sense for its fund shareholders.

Certainly, when I spoke to McNabb, he had weighed the pluses and minuses of the acquisition offer, which was rumored to be $5 billion, very carefully, but the fact that he even considered the deal is disturbing. "There's a lot of speculation about what we were up to," McNabb says. "Did we take a hard look at [Barclays]? Absolutely. At the end of the day, BlackRock bought all of BGI. We looked specifically at iShares. I'm a big believer in organic growth. I am a really big believer that market share is earned, not bought. And so there's a tremendous bias built into my thinking and our collective thinking around those principles. When you see something like the kind of consternation the world was going through and you see that the possible opportunities of acquiring iShares or any other entity would be a net positive benefit to our shareholders, you at least have to look at it and think about it. If at the end of the day you cannot make the case that it's going to benefit your existing clientele, then it's not something you should be doing."

Ultimately, New York–based mutual fund behemoth BlackRock acquired all of Barclays Global Investors, including its large institutional account business, in December 2009 for $15.2 billion in cash and stock, thus becoming the world's largest money manager, with $3.2 trillion. Vanguard shareholders probably should have heaved a sigh of relief. Not only would the speculative culture of Barclays have been a poor fit with Vanguard's, but because Vanguard is owned by fund shareholders, there was an extremely important question as to how the company would have paid for its offer.

Either Vanguard would have had to assume some form of debt that existing Vanguard fund shareholders would have had to pay, or, as Bogle speculates, in return for a cash outlay, Vanguard fund shareholders would have received some form of equity in the acquired company. "There is certainly no such thing as a free lunch," Bogle says. "But I'm not sure—and I'm a step removed from Vanguard—I'm not sure we would have had to take on debt. We could have carried the $5 billion or whatever we would have paid for that part of Barclays . . . on the books as an investment. And then every fund would own a tiny piece of Barclays."

Regardless of how the deal was financed, as Bogle observed, it would have created two kinds of Vanguard shareholders, one in the Vanguard Funds run at cost, who would pay for the acquisition, and the other in Barclays ETFs, who would be charged higher fees so that they could pay Vanguard's shareholders back. Meanwhile, what Vanguard shareholders would have been paying for was a fund shop that would have catered largely to speculators who trade even iShares' most broadly diversified ETFs fast enough to make traditional investors' heads spin. Despite their second-class status, Barclays' shareholders most likely wouldn't have noticed any change or would have benefited from lower costs over the long term.

But what would have been in it for Vanguard's existing shareholders except a potential liability that would need to be repaid? "Let's call it a marketing expense, an expense that is required to bring in additional assets, like an advertising expense," Bogle says. If the fees collected from Barclays' acquired ETF business covered the costs of acquisition and there was enough left over to return a "profit" to Vanguard's shareholders, then fees for Vanguard Fund shareholders overall would decline, and the "marketing expense" of the acquisition would be justified. And yet Bogle feels that the drawbacks would have exceeded the benefits, reaffirming his basic market-share-must-be-earned-not-bought philosophy. "I thought, we're going to be [$261] billion larger overnight if we do Barclays; but if we don't do Barclays, we are going to be [$261] billion larger five years from now, so what's the hurry and why would you pay for the advantage?"

The idea that increasing economies of scale would reduce costs is a valid one, but one that provides diminishing returns for shareholders as assets grow. In other words, the economies gained by $1 billion in new money for a fund shop with only $500 million in total assets are far greater than those gained from $1 billion of new money for a shop with $1.3 trillion. Many mutual fund costs are largely fixed, so as assets grow, those fixed costs are spread over a larger asset base, and expense ratios fall if fund management is willing to pass on those economies of scale to shareholders. Vanguard, to its credit, completely passes on those savings. But once you've reached Vanguard's immense size, the addition of new assets adds incrementally less and less percentage-wise to expense ratio savings, especially when the average Vanguard expense ratio is already a low 0.20 percent. And of course, in the Barclays case, any savings would have occurred only after the cost of acquisition was covered.

Bogle recognizes the difficulty in driving expense ratios much lower once you're a behemoth like Vanguard and questions whether the additional assets that ETFs will bring in are worth the potential harm done to the investors. "What limits are there to innovations?" he asks. "Let's assume the innovation of the ETF becomes profitable over time—it may be profitable today for all I know—but is that an adequate justification for something that upon first impression may not be helping the shareholders? It may be helping them to speculate rather than invest. That's a decision I leave to the management. I lean towards the facts." The key fact being, in Bogle's analysis, that ETF shareholders tend to underperform mutual fund ones over time.

Toward the end of 2009, an all-out war erupted in the ETF industry between Vanguard, Charles Schwab, Fidelity, and BlackRock. The opening salvo was fired by Charles Schwab in November, when it launched four ETFs that Schwab customers could trade commission-free, and then another four in December. To up the ante even more, some of the

Schwab ETFs had the lowest expense ratios in the industry, undercutting even Vanguard's. Of particular note was the Schwab U.S. Broad Market ETF, which, with a 0.08 percent expense ratio, was cheaper than the Vanguard Total Stock Market ETF's 0.09 percent. In addition, Vanguard's brokerage at this point charged most of its ETF investors $12 a trade, putting it at a distinct disadvantage to Schwab.

Fidelity and BlackRock stepped into the ring next in February 2010, inking a deal in which Fidelity agreed to sell 25 of BlackRock's most popular iShares ETFs commission-free in return for a revenue-sharing agreement with BlackRock. For the long-term buy-and-hold investor, such deals are actually detrimental because the costs of offering commission-free trades are borne by all ETF shareholders via higher total expense ratios to recompense Fidelity for the lost commissions that it would have earned otherwise. And since buy-and-hold investors don't do a lot of trading, they don't really see much of the benefits of free trades, while speculators get a windfall. In effect, one class of ETF shareholder—the rapidly trading speculator—is being subsidized by another—the buy-and-hold investor. To make matters worse, the deal created an unfair two-tier brokerage caste system in which shareholders trading iShares outside of Fidelity, be they speculators or long-term investors, had to cover the costs of free trading for Fidelity's brokerage customers. Of course, the enticement to speculate because the trades are "free" is perhaps most detrimental of all for long-term investors from a psychological standpoint, as it can easily lead to performance chasing and buying and selling "hot" ETFs at the worst possible time.

Given all of the above concerns, it was a bit of a shock to see Vanguard issue a press release on May 4, 2010, announcing that it was eliminating transaction fees on all 46 of its ETFs for Vanguard's brokerage clients. As a consequence, clients are now able to place 25 trades per year for each ETF without paying any fees. Although the 25-free-trades-per-ETF limit will act as a deterrent to the most aggressive day traders, if such a setup isn't an invitation to speculate, I don't know what is. And yet Bill McNabb was quick to dismiss such an idea, stating in the initial release, "To be clear, our commission-free offer is not intended to encourage the active trading of ETFs, which we believe is counterproductive and rarely successful. Rather, it enables investors to construct a balanced, long-term portfolio of low-cost Vanguard ETFs and add to the portfolio regularly."[7]

Although having commission-free ETF trades may be beneficial to long-term investors who seek to dollar-cost average by purchasing small numbers of shares at regular intervals over time, such free trades were already offered to Vanguard's mutual fund investors. In addition, the mutual funds have express safeguards in place to prevent excessive speculation, often including redemption fees on short-term trades and trading restrictions. The April 2010 prospectus for the Vanguard Total Stock Market Index mutual fund, for instance, highlights how different the company's attitude is toward speculators in its mutual funds from those in its ETFs: "Each Vanguard fund (other than money market funds and short-term bond funds) limits an investor's purchases or exchanges into a fund account for 60 calendar days after the investor has redeemed or exchanged out of that fund account. ETF Shares are not subject to the frequent-trading limits."

So was the decision to offer free ETF trades really in the best interest of Vanguard's long-term shareholders, or was it merely a ploy to defend and hopefully increase Vanguard's index fund market share from encroaching competition? Consider, for instance, that, just as in the case of the Fidelity/BlackRock deal, someone must pay for all those free trades, and that those buy-and-hold Vanguard shareholders who trade the least are effectively subsidizing those who trade the most. "The promotion of ETFs is a big marketing game, and I guess that if you want to be in the market, you have to compete, and if the competition is eliminating commissions, you have to eliminate commissions, too," Bogle says. "Would that be what Bogle would do? I'm not in a position to do it one way or another. Anything that has to do with a marketing base I'm always skeptical about, number one. Number two, there is no such thing as a free lunch. So this will make the ETF unit at Vanguard less profitable or more unprofitable. And that comes, therefore, at the expense of the remaining Vanguard shareholders who own these various enterprises we are in. Is that good or bad? You would have to ask someone other than me. That's the mathematics. It's not that something is all of a sudden free. Cost exists, revenues disappear, and there's not a bottomless pit here."

McNabb, for his part, defends the decision as merely leveling the playing field between Vanguard's mutual fund and ETF shareholders: "The idea is we don't want transaction fees that might make sense from a purely rational standpoint to get in the way of people making good decisions in the long run. We saw that happening. We saw people picking one vehicle over another simply because of an $8 [transaction] fee even though if you amortize the fee over 10 years, it was a rounding error. And frankly, the revenue you gave up wasn't that great. It makes the selection easier one way or another for the investor. We don't care essentially if someone buys an ETF or if someone buys a traditional open-end fund."

As for one type of Vanguard investor subsidizing the activity of another, McNabb acknowledges that this has occurred to some degree at the fund shop from the beginning and thinks of it as a largely unavoidable cost of doing business and an acceptable one as long as it doesn't get out of hand. "In every individual case, your fund pricing in general is a little bit of a communist approach," he says. "Everybody is paying the same fee, even though, if you call [Vanguard] twice, and I only call once, you are a more expensive client to deal with. Yet we're still charging you the same amount. If someone was trading hundreds of times [for free], though, and somebody else was trading once, the point would be fair. But we aren't seeing that at all. If we did, we would ask the person to go somewhere else. We are pretty clear about that."

Ultimately, I think that the commissionless trades will probably not hurt Vanguard's long-term mutual fund shareholders, as Vanguard should easily gain enough assets in its ETF business to cover the costs of such trading. The real damage will be to the ETF speculators themselves, who will now be enticed even more to trade when they shouldn't, and to clients of advisers who use these ETFs. Those are the people who in the long term will almost assuredly underperform buy-and-hold investors in the aggregate.

As for Vanguard's need to grow its market share regardless of whether long-term shareholders benefit or not, there may be two possible less-than-savory motives for this. One is that Vanguard's Partnership Plan bonus system is still tied to the net cost savings for shareholders, which increases along with assets so long as the fees that Vanguard charges are less than those of the competition. Since, to Vanguard's credit, its fees are always lower than the competition's, there is a perverse incentive to grow market share for Vanguard's lowest-cost products by any means necessary, even if that means indulging speculative investors' worst desires. So long as assets grow and investors are still saving money on the expense ratio side, Vanguard's executive bonus pool will expand too.

The other reason for Vanguard's pursuit of the ETFs business is a far more subtle psychological one involving the ethos of both of Bogle's successors. The fact is that no executive wants to be known as simply maintaining market share in his or her industry, to be, in effect, just the "caretaker" of John Bogle's legacy. The desire for growth is in every executive's blood as much as looking at the bottom line is part of every young MBA's executive training. But because Vanguard is such an unusual, mutually owned company, its goals aren't the normal ones, and a growth-at-all-costs philosophy simply isn't in the best interest of its shareholders. Brennan and McNabb surely have imbibed Bogle's market-share-must-be-earned-not-bought philosophy, but the desire to constantly expand and launch new products must be hard to resist for any ambitious CEO who wants to make a name for himself, even one schooled at Bogle the ascetic's knee.

But how much expansion is too much? For instance, what possibly could be the reason other than market share for Vanguard's June 24, 2010, announcement that it was launching a slew of 19 new ETFs, most of which would track the Standard & Poor's and Russell indexes, even though its existing ETFs already own largely the same baskets of small- and large-cap U.S. stocks. The move seemed like an exercise in redundancy merely to attract new shareholders wedded to more popular benchmarks, even if those benchmarks were no better and some might say inferior to the benchmarks that Vanguard's existing ETFs already track.

At the time when Vanguard launched its first ETFs back in 2001, it was having a legal spat with Standard & Poor's over the licensing fees for its ETFs. So Vanguard developed its own benchmarks with index designer MSCI's help, and after back-testing the results, Vanguard CIO Gus Sauter concluded that the new benchmarks were actually superior to the much stodgier S&P and Russell ones. But the popularity of S&P and Russell with institutional investors has led Vanguard to launch these new me-too products to compete with the likes of iShares and State Street. "We recognize that institutional investors and financial advisors may have a preference for certain benchmarks, and our goal is to offer them best-in-class funds and ETFs based on a choice of leading index providers, including FTSE, MSCI, Russell, and S&P," McNabb stated in a press release.[8] But such a decision prioritizes popularity and marketability over long-term performance for shareholders if Vanguard's own research on its custom benchmarks is correct. What's more, the new ETFs create an additional financial burden for Vanguard shareholders of covering the initial launch costs and licensing fees for essentially redundant products.

McNabb recognizes the redundancy issue but thinks that the launch was necessary to satisfy the wishes of Vanguard's institutional clients: "In a perfect world you would say [the new ETFs] aren't needed, but we don't live in a perfect world. What we have observed is there are a large number of users of index funds, in particular ETFs but funds too, who have very deep allegiance to a particular brand of benchmark. Interestingly, when we cocreated with MSCI their benchmarks, they were actually superior. The S&P and Russell have moved to correct that. So there's very little difference in terms of index construction. But many systems are built around—you know everything gets compared to Russell, everything gets compared to Dow Jones—and what we were hearing from lots of different clients is that 'we love your stuff, but we would love it even more if we didn't have to buy someone else's Russell product or S&P product because we know you guys could do it better and at a lower cost.' So that's really what drove that." In the meantime, though, any of Vanguard's existing shareholders who recognize that the new ETFs are redundant and have no desire to own them are footing the bill for the product launch.

And yet it's hard not to recognize that from a business perspective—as opposed to a shareholder one—all of Vanguard's recent decisions regarding ETFs make perfect sense. In fact, if anything, one wonders about the business sense of Vanguard's competitors. Why would anyone willingly engage in a price war with an industry leader that is run at cost? Surely, executives at Schwab and BlackRock must have known ahead of time that the Wal-Mart of the fund industry would be able to undercut them on price. In fact, just to throw an additional grenade into the mix, Vanguard's new S&P 500 ETF will have the lowest expense ratio in the industry at 0.06 percent. Internally, at Vanguard some executives seem to feel regret only for the fact that the company didn't enter the ETF fray sooner and allowed Barclays and State Street a head start. As one remarked: "Look, there is no question that ETFs have been a huge development in the industry, and we almost missed it. So, we all collectively said 'no, that's not a better mousetrap,' and to some extent we had to change our mind. We were proved wrong by market sentiments."

Vanguard's efforts have already been working, as its market share of the ETF space during the first seven months of 2010 increased by two percentage points to 13.8 percent, while BlackRock's share fell by 0.5 percentage point to 47.4 percent and State Street's 1.1 points to 23.2 percent.[9] Moreover, one month after the company announced that ETF trades would be commission-free, new brokerage account growth was up by 90 percent.[10] Whether such successful business strategies will translate into successful investment strategies for Vanguard shareholders remains to be seen.

CHAPTER 16

The Spirit of Mutuality

Perhaps Bogle's most important contribution to the mutual fund zeitgeist is not his well-known belief in low costs—or, more formally, his "cost matters hypothesis"—but his lesser-known, more subtle argument for mutualization and the fiduciary ethos it inspires. A key concept Bogle promulgated and championed is the idea that "strategy follows structure"—that Vanguard's mutualization led to its behaving as a true fiduciary for its shareholders and seeking to manage funds at the lowest possible costs.

Bogle's basic premise for mutualization alludes to a biblical precept in Matthew 6:24 that "no man can serve two masters"—that is, that funds that have both a management company with its own set of external shareholders and a separate but not equal set of fund shareholders will inherently have conflicts of interests. Because there are two sets of shareholders and two sets of directors, one of which is actively engaged in the management of the fund company while the other is passively handpicked by the management company, management will inevitably seek to maximize profits for itself and its shareholders at the expense of fund shareholders by charging as much in fees as the market will bear. Or, as the adage says much more poetically: "No man can serve two masters: for either he will hate the one, and love the other; or else he will hold to the one, and despise the other. Ye cannot serve God and mammon." As usual with St. Jack, you can replace the word "God" with "fund shareholders" and "mammon" with "fund management."

To avoid this inherent conflict of interest, Vanguard's mutualized structure has just one set of shareholders and one board of directors. And in some respects the importance of this structure supersedes, or rather precedes, the company's drive to cut costs. In fact, Bogle says that the salutary effects of having a mutualized structure are so great that it literally led him to create the first index fund. In a lecture he gave at his beloved Blair Academy in 2002, there is a section titled "Strategy Follows Structure" in which he describes this effect:

> Yes, we had the insight to recognize the opportunities associated with implementing a low-cost, index-oriented, structured-portfolio strategy. But, given the elementary mathematics of the market, that insight is so startlingly obvious that it *must* have been shared by many other firms in our industry. All of our rivals had the same *opportunity* but, just like the prime suspect in a murder mystery, we alone had the *motive*. Because of our very *structure*, the finger of guilt, as it were, pointed directly at Vanguard. We *sought* low costs; our rivals, because they earn their profits from the amount of fees they receive, aren't exactly eager for fee reductions.
>
> Our structure, then, played not only a vital, but essential, role in shaping our strategy. It established us as industry leaders, not only in index funds and bond funds, but in the then-burgeoning money market fund arena, where the link between lower cost and higher yield is virtually dollar for dollar. *Strategy follows structure.*[1]

Bogle, being a true missionary at heart, crusades for the industry to see the light and shift to Vanguard's mutualized structure, the irony being that such a shift would of course threaten Vanguard's business leadership in the industry by providing real competition. Not that the super-ethical Bogle really cares. Nor is he deterred by the fact that this transformation would be difficult to well-nigh impossible for smaller and newer players to do successfully because they wouldn't have the scale to compete against the industry leader. He has long hoped that some of the industry's big boys would suddenly decide to give up their immensely lucrative businesses in favor of Vanguard's austerity model.

What Bogle thought would be the impetus for such a shift was a serious bear market in which some of the major industry players would be so weakened that they would have to consider more radical alternatives to their current incestuous governance structure. When the dot-com bubble finally burst and the market timing scandals were exposed, he saw an opportunity to make his dream a reality. His target: Putnam Investments. In a November 2003 speech before the New York Society of Securities Analysts, Bogle cited market conditions similar to those that induced Vanguard's board to pass his proposal for mutualization, and he euphemistically referred to a number of fund families burned in the market-timing scandal by their cities or states of origin. So Janus Funds was "Denver," and Strong Funds was "Wisconsin." It was evident when he talked about another scandal-tainted firm known as "Boston," which was a "wholly owned subsidiary of a giant global insurance broker," that he was really referring to Putnam, as, at the time, the firm was a division of insurer Marsh & McLennan and under investigation by the Massachusetts U.S. Attorney's office. "Boston," he believed, was the best candidate for mutualization as "a firm whose recent circumstances reflect such remarkable parallels with those of the pre-Vanguard Vanguard funds."[2]

After detailing how poorly Putnam's funds had performed for shareholders while collecting immense fees for management, Bogle summed up his air-tight case for mutualization:

> If this combination of staggeringly high costs, aggressive marketing of speculative funds, large losses inflicted on fund owners, poor relative performance, immense compensation paid to executives, staggering profits channeled to Boston's absentee owners, scandalous behavior, and the opportunity for huge savings doesn't place "mutualization" at the top

of the agenda for the next meeting of Boston's fund board, it's hard to imagine what would. And, if Boston adopts that mutual fund governance model, I'm sure others will follow. "Come on in, peers, the water's fine![3]

But Bogle didn't just pound his bully pulpit and demand that industry sinners mend their evil ways this time. He actually approached the fund board of directors at Putnam with the mutualization idea and tried to convince them to do it. "I talked to the chairman of the board, who unfortunately used to work at Marsh & McLennan," Bogle recalls with some bitterness. "He used to work at Marsh & McLennan, and he's the chairman of the Putnam independent directors. And they brag and preen. One of the directors I happened to know resigned when they wouldn't do it. I talked to another director down here, and he said, 'I understand what you are saying, but it is Marsh & McLennan's property, and we have no right to take it away from them.'"

The fact that a fund director would assume that the funds are the management company's "property" instead of the fund shareholders' is telling of how bad conflicts of interest can be at most fund companies. Ultimately, instead of mutualization, Putnam was sold to Power Financial Corp., a Canadian financial conglomerate, for $3.9 billion in 2007. Meanwhile, former Putnam Management Company CEO Lawrence Lasser, whom authorities claimed knew about late trading and market timing at Putnam as early as 2000, received a $78 million termination settlement package, a clean employment record, and a promise by Putnam to pay all of his future legal bills after being forced to resign from the company in 2003.[4] That was, of course, in addition to the $163 million he made in total compensation from 1998 to 2002, while the alleged illicit activity was occurring. The end result infuriated Bogle. "Larry Lasser probably made 250 million bucks in salary. For what? For ruining the funds? For violating his fiduciary duty? For knowing that the funds' portfolio managers were trading against the funds and not informing the directors and more?" Ultimately, Lasser received, in Bogle's words, only "a crappy little flippin' fine" of $75,000 from the SEC in 2007 for allegedly allowing pay-to-play arrangements with brokers to entice them to sell Putnam funds.

Bogle believes that such egregious behavior in the fund industry is a more recent phenomenon and that in the decades immediately following the Investment Company Act of 1940, fund companies were true to their fiduciary principles. In one of his best speeches, "The Alpha and Omega," he described how the first open-end mutual fund, Massachusetts Investors Trust (MIT), was operated as a "truly mutual mutual fund, one organized, operated and managed, not by a separate management company with its own commercial interests, but by its own trustees; compensated not on the basis of the trust's principal, but, under traditional fiduciary standards, its income."[5] A few other funds in the industry's "golden age," such as State Street Investment Corporation and Incorporated Investors, also modeled themselves on the ancient idea of the loyal trustee, being more interested in portfolio selection and investment advice than in distribution and marketing. Such funds were "internally managed," meaning that their portfolio managers were employees of the funds themselves, as opposed to an external management company, so their interests were fully aligned with those of shareholders.

But something happened in 1958 to derail that positive trajectory. A court ruled that it was okay for fund companies to sell their management contracts to outside investors. Bogle describes this decision as a momentous though often overlooked event in the history of the industry in a speech titled "A New Order of Things—Bringing Mutuality to the 'Mutual' Fund": "The date was April 7, 1958, when the United States Court of Appeals for the Ninth Circuit ruled that the 1956 sale of shares in Insurance Securities Incorporated (ISI), at a price equal to nearly 15 times its book value, did not constitute 'gross misconduct' or 'gross abuse of trust' under Section 36 of the 1940 Act. The SEC had gone to court to oppose the sale, on the grounds that the excess price represented a payment for succession to the adviser's fiduciary office."[6]

Selling the management contract allowed fund companies to have external shareholders, the "two masters" that prevent the ethical execution of fiduciary duty. It also allowed management companies to go public and ultimately led to them being acquired by giant financial conglomerates. Although the spirit of the 1940 Act was opposed to such "trafficking" in management contracts—as the contract really belonged to the fund and fund shareholders, not to the management company—it never explicitly forbade such sales.

Bogle would describe the court's 1958 decision as one of the germs that helped spread the nation's pathological mutation from being an ownership society in which managers behave as true fiduciaries to an agency one in which managers are primarily out for themselves:

> Within a decade, many of the major firms in the fund industry joined the public ownership bandwagon, including Vance Sanders (now Eaton Vance), Dreyfus, Franklin, Putnam, and even Wellington (the firm I had joined in 1951, right out of college). Over the next decade, T. Rowe Price, and Keystone (now Evergreen) also went public. In the era that followed, financial conglomerates acquired industry giants such as Massachusetts Financial Services (adviser to the fund complex of which M.I.T. had become a part), Putnam, State Street, American Century, Oppenheimer, Alliance, AIM, Delaware, and many others. The trickle became a river, and then an ocean.[7]

Public ownership immediately created pressures from the management company's shareholders to produce profits at the expense of fund shareholders. This was especially so at financial conglomerates, where the fund management business was just one division among many at a larger bank, insurer, or brokerage firm seeking to meet its earnings estimates every quarter. With two sets of shareholders, the question became, to which group did management company employees have a fiduciary duty, especially when the interests of the two weren't aligned? Both groups sought high fund returns. But when it came down to fees, the two groups were diametrically opposed: the more fees collected, the higher the profits for management company shareholders; the less fees collected, the higher fund shareholders' returns were.

Of course, Vanguard's mutualized structure largely avoids such conflicts of interest by having only one set of shareholders of the funds who collectively own the funds and The Vanguard Group management company, much like a mutual insurer is owned by its policyholders. As a result, there is no drive to siphon off profits for outside management company shareholders via higher fees. With just one master set of shareholders whose interests come first, Vanguard is in most respects the ideal fiduciary, thanks to its structure.

Bogle would demonstrate the detrimental effects of public ownership and, in particular, conglomerate ownership of management companies in a study he conducted of fund complex returns, the results of which he discussed in his 2008 speech at George Washington University Law School. The study measured the percentage of funds at the 50 largest fund complexes with the highest and lowest Morningstar ratings. Morningstar's ratings of one to five stars are completely quantitative in nature, based on long-term risk-adjusted returns. Bogle subtracted the percentage of bottom-ranked one- or two-star funds from the percentage of top-ranked four- or five-star funds to come up with a single positive or negative number, the higher the better. Vanguard, of course, was the leader with a score of +54 percent, but the remaining results, as he described them, drove home his point about public ownership of management companies:

> Joining Vanguard among the top three are DFA and TIAA-CREF, both at +50. (More than coincidentally, all three firms are focused largely on index-like strategies.) At number four is T. Rowe Price (+44), followed by Janus (+38) and American Funds (+26). Honestly, I think most objective observers would agree that over the past decade, at least five of these six firms have been conspicuous in delivering superior risk-adjusted returns, a judgment that confirms the methodology. Again more than coincidently, this six-firm list is dominated by four management companies that are not publicly owned—Vanguard, DFA, TIAA-CREF, and American—and none are controlled by conglomerates.
>
> On the other hand, each of the bottom six firms are units of giant brokerage firms or financial conglomerates. Their ratings range from −40 for Goldman Sachs to an astonishing −58 for Putnam, with only 4 percent of its funds in the top category and 62 percent rank in the bottom category. Strik-

ingly, every one of the 17 lowest-ranking firms on the 50-firm list is conglomerate-held, while only one of the firms among the top 10 can be similarly characterized.[8]

Because of the conflicts of interest inherent in the two-master structure, Bogle has long lobbied for Congress to create a federal fiduciary standard that would force management companies to put fund shareholders first. Such a standard would codify into law the spirit in which the Investment Company Act was written. Although it would encourage mutualization as a more efficient structure, the standard would not enforce it, as Bogle recognizes that, for smaller funds that haven't reached the scale yet to be self-sufficient, such a transformation could be difficult.

Rather, the standard, in Bogle's words, would be a series of principles that would require money managers: "(1) to act solely in the interests of their shareholders and beneficiaries; (2) to observe due diligence and professional standards in their investment practices; (3) to honor their responsibilities as owners by active participation in corporate governance; and (4) to eliminate conflicts of interests in their activities."[9] If codified, such a standard would be likely to force the divestiture of fund management companies from financial conglomerates, as the conflicts of interest would be exposed as being too great if a strict fiduciary principle were applied. It would also enforce true participation in corporate governance by fund managers instead of the usual rubber stamp. A strict interpretation of eliminating conflicts of interest could even force funds' boards of directors to apply a "reasonableness standard" to fund expenses, wherein they would be required to compare them not just to other overpriced funds in the industry but to the fees the management company charges other clients, such as pension funds, which tend to be much lower.

Clearly, Vanguard's mutualized structure prevents many of the abuses that exist in almost every other large mutual fund complex. But the structure may also have led to certain unintended and perhaps undesirable consequences and may actually possess conflicts of its own that are unique in the industry. First and foremost, it is always important to remember that there is still a legal veil separating Vanguard's individual fund shareholders and The Vanguard Group management company. Collectively, the funds own The Vanguard Group; the shareholders do not, from a legal standpoint. But since the shareholders own the funds, they are the de facto owners of The Vanguard Group.

And yet because of the legal separation, there may be certain instances where conflicts of interest arise between Vanguard Group employees and Vanguard fund shareholders. Of major concern, as previously mentioned, is Vanguard's Partnership Plan bonus system, which rewards employees primarily for the amount of cost savings they generate for fund shareholders. Bogle often boasts of the "profits" returned to shareholders at Vanguard in the form of cost savings because of its mutual structure, but he doesn't often mention in the same breath that a small portion of those profits are siphoned off to pay executive bonuses, thus irrevocably linking the two together.

While cost savings are generally a good thing, there may be a saturation point at which the detriments to performance that come from scale in actively managed funds outweigh the benefits of lower expense ratios. But because Vanguard's bonuses are based more on cost savings than on outperformance, there is an incentive to let the funds become bloated in order to drive down expense ratios and reap as much bonus money tied to cost savings as possible. There is also an incentive to launch as many new products as possible to gather more assets and reap more cost savings, regardless of whether those products are beneficial to shareholders or not. So despite Bogle's and Vanguard's claims to the contrary, there is still a "dual orientation" in the company's objectives, although it is clearly not nearly as harmful to shareholders as are the conflicts of interest at externally managed funds.

When asked, Bogle does acknowledge this dual dimension to the profit sharing plan, stating that when he was CEO, three-quarters of the bonus was based on profits through cost savings, and only one-quarter was based on a fund's outperformance of its peer group. This means that the incentive to let funds get too big was three times as great as the reward for perhaps closing a well-performing actively managed fund so it could remain nimble and continue to outperform. Yet Bogle also notes that by 1992, bonuses for Vanguard crew members were limited in size to a percentage of their income because they were getting out of hand. "[The bonus plan] has a certain incentive to grow assets because if you multiply that 1 percent [in annual cost savings] that I gave you times a trillion dollars, you are going to get a much smaller number than if you multiply that 1 percent by 2 trillion," he says. "Enough people have reached, or had reached, the stop-out phase [in the bonus plan], so I don't think the rewards created by the plan were substantial."

While Bogle is no longer intimately connected with the design of the bonus plan since he ceased being Vanguard's chairman in 1999, according to editor Dan Wiener of the *Independent Adviser for Vanguard Investors* newsletter, the plan still offers a perverse incentive for Vanguard's senior management to gather as much in the way of assets as possible:

> **Over the 26 years since Vanguard founder Jack Bogle put the Partnership Plan together, the dividend has compounded at a 14.5 percent rate, which is a heck of a lot better than the 10.4 percent annualized gain for 500 Index. Although most Vanguard employees, or "crew members," are capped out in terms of the size of their annual bonus (30 percent of base compensation for older employees and reportedly just 10 percent for newer employees, hardly a bonanza given the parsimonious pay Vanguard is famous for), top executives still earn the bulk of their compensation from the Plan's dividends.[10]**

Vanguard CEO Bill McNabb says that adequate safeguards are in place to prevent asset bloat in that the outside subadvisers to Vanguard's actively managed funds receive performance-based management fees. If they feel that bloat might detrimentally affect their returns, they will ask that the fund be closed. "That structure really encourages the managers to raise their hands and say, 'No more,'" he says. "When you look at the swings in what [the performance-based fee] can do to your compensation, it's pretty effective overall on the quality side. If a manager feels like he or she is getting too much money, they are going to raise their hand, and the board is going to act accordingly. I think our track record is pretty good on that score. We have closed a large number of funds to new shareholders." But such subadviser incentives do not affect Vanguard executives' drive for scale, and it is relatively easy for them to tack on an additional subadviser to a fund if another one doesn't want to receive any additional assets. Nor do they prevent the temptation for Vanguard executives to launch products that are completely unnecessary so that they can gather more assets.

If strategy follows structure, how does a drive for scale and low costs being built into the architecture of a management company's bonus system affect the strategies of its funds? Bogle himself has described the deleterious effects of asset size on fund performance in *Common Sense on Mutual Funds*. For one, as assets grow, managers have greater difficulty buying and selling illiquid stocks because their trades in low-volume equities have increasing "market impact" costs on every purchase and sale. So it's hard to buy a microcap stock with a tiny float or low volume if you have billions to invest.

To absorb the additional assets and avoid market impact costs when funds grow unwieldy, managers must buy stocks with larger market caps, buy more stocks, or trade less frequently. To varying degrees, Vanguard has employed all three of these strategies to address the size issues of its actively managed funds, with varying degrees of success. Arguably its best actively managed funds—Windsor(s) I and II, Primecap, Wellington, and Dividend Growth—tend to specialize in large-cap stocks and practice low-turnover buy-and-hold strategies to minimize transaction costs.

Of course, Bogle and many other investment gurus have argued that active managers are better off practicing long-term buy-and-hold strategies anyway. But in Vanguard's case, the fact of the matter is that it really can't practice a high-turnover aggressive investment style with much success and achieve the kind of scale that Vanguard usually wants. In fact, the few Vanguard stock funds that have had high turnover ratios generally have been failures. Three with some of the highest ratios, Vanguard U.S. Growth (101 percent), Vanguard Growth Equity (98 percent), and Vanguard Mid Cap Growth (125 percent), have been category laggards for the last decade, Growth Equity and U.S. Growth in particular being among the worst performers in their fund categories despite rock-bottom expenses.

Interestingly, one exception at the company has been the recent success of Vanguard Capital Value Fund, and yet this is one of the only Vanguard funds that closed to new investors at a very manageable size of $742 million in October 2009. At the time, it had a startling turnover ratio of 300 percent, the highest of any Vanguard equity fund. When it closed, Bill McNabb said that it was experiencing a "cooling-off period" because too much hot money was flowing into the volatile fund, as it was having a banner year. The fund subsequently reopened in late 2010 and may become bloated soon like other Vanguard funds. Also of interest, in December 2009 Vanguard added another comanager to the fund named David Palmer who has a different, more conservative buy-and-hold investment style than the aggressive manager Peter Higgins, who attracted all the hot money. No doubt the fund will now be considerably tamer and less concentrated than it was when Higgins ran it by himself.

One can see the trade-off between asset bloat and low expenses most easily in two of Vanguard's most famous actively managed funds—Vanguard Primecap and Vanguard Capital Opportunity. Both funds are subadvised by the growth-oriented firm Primecap Management and have done extraordinarily well for many years. In their case, the fact that the fund managers invest somewhat aggressively still allows for Vanguard's scalable model because, though they buy tech and health-care stocks like most growth managers, they trade very infrequently, having minuscule turnover ratios (typically in the 10 percent to 15 percent range). This means that they hold each of their stock positions for several years. They also tend to purchase growth stocks that are temporarily beaten down, so that they are buying when other managers are selling, making it easier for them to trade. (Most growth managers do the opposite, practicing momentum strategies, which require them to buy popular stocks hitting all-time new highs, so they usually need to get in and out of positions quickly, and, as a consequence, their strategies are not scalable.) So even though Vanguard Primecap has a whopping $26.9 billion in assets and Capital Opportunity had $7.9 billion, the funds largely haven't lost their luster.

Be that as it may, it is crucial to note that, despite the fact that Vanguard closed the two funds to new investors arguably much too late in 2004, subadviser Primecap Management still wanted to gather more assets. So the same year Primecap opened three of its own branded funds outside of Vanguard. The results so far have been a testament to the fact that asset size matters a great deal to performance, especially when smaller companies are beating larger ones, as they have been doing in recent years. As of April 2010, the Primecap Odyssey Aggressive Growth Fund had just $640 million in assets. It has a very similar aggressive strategy of buying and holding rapidly growing companies as Vanguard Capital Opportunity, yet its expense ratio of 0.79 percent is significantly higher than Capital Opportunity's 0.50 percent. Despite this fact, over the past five years ending July 31, 2010, Odyssey Aggressive Growth has delivered a 31.3 percent cumulative total return compared to Capital Opportunity's 16.6 percent—almost double the performance, despite higher fees.

There are two likely reasons for the disparities in performance. The more obvious one is that Odyssey Aggressive Growth has a median market cap of just $2.2 billion because more than half its portfolio is in small- and micro-cap stocks, and these stocks have outperformed in recent years. Meanwhile, Capital Opportunity's median market cap is $13.4 billion, and only 8 percent of its portfolio is in small- and micro-cap stocks. In fact, Capital Opportunity has experienced what fund nerds derisively call "style drift" over the years because its bloated size prevents it from buying stock in smaller companies.

When Vanguard first hired Primecap to run Capital Opportunity in 1998, it was a tiny fund with less than $100 million in assets. Its February 1999 prospectus objective described the fund as investing "primarily in U.S. stocks, with an emphasis on small- and mid-capitalization companies that have rapid earnings growth prospects." Moreover, in the Primecap team's first annual report in October 1998, it mentioned that management had increased the fund's weighting from less than 25 percent to more than 50 percent in small caps with market caps less than $1.2 billion because it believed that smaller companies "currently offer the greatest value in the marketplace." And even as late as 2002, when the fund was about half its current size, it had a median market cap of just $4.8 billion.

Clearly, given how the newer and smaller Primecap Odyssey Aggressive Growth Fund is positioned, the team is still finding significant opportunities in small companies. And yet Vanguard Capital Opportunity simply cannot invest in these companies in any meaningful way. In fact, Vanguard has since changed the fund's prospectus so that it no longer mentions a small- and mid-cap emphasis. As of 2010, the prospectus reads: "The Fund invests mainly in U.S. stocks, with an emphasis on companies that are considered to have prospects for rapid earnings growth. The Fund does not focus on companies of any particular size."

The evidence of the strategy follows structure phenomenon—of Vanguard, because of its desire for scale and low costs, tending to do better with large-cap, low-turnover styles—is further corroborated by Vanguard Primecap, which, although it too has drifted over the years from more of an all-cap style to one that is almost exclusively large-cap now, clearly excels in this area. Consider that Vanguard Primecap, over the past five years, has beaten the higher-cost Primecap Odyssey Stock, which has a similar large-cap orientation. It gained 15.5 percent through July 2010 compared to Odyssey Stock's 12.8 percent. Surely, one day, when large caps are in favor again, the lower-cost Vanguard funds will beat all the higher-cost Primecap ones, but this in many respects is beside the point. The point is that the Primecap branded funds, because of their smaller asset bases, can buy any size company effectively, while Vanguard's Primecap funds can't.

But style drift is only one of the disadvantages of Vanguard's drive for scale. A much harder to quantify problem is market impact costs. For managers who trade frequently, the impact of their purchases and sales on stocks of smaller companies with limited volume can be dramatic. A 2010 asset capacity study conducted by growth fund manager Turner Investment Partners concluded that high-turnover managers with $1 billion in assets can lose as much as 10 percentage points a year in potential return when investing in small, illiquid stocks purely from market impact costs.[11]

Bogle has written about market impact costs in *Common Sense on Mutual Funds* in relation to a study published by his son John Bogle, Jr., who today runs a tiny Newton, Massachusetts–based money management firm called Bogle Investment Management and a mutual fund called the Bogle Small Cap Growth Fund: "After examining more than 20,000 trades, [John Bogle, Jr.] reports these costs: trades in value stocks, 0.6 percent of the dollar amount of the trade; trades in small-cap growth stocks, 1.8 percent; trades in which shares represent one-eighth of daily volume, 0.5 percent; shares representing two days' volume, 2.3 percent. He concludes that the hidden drag of transaction costs rises as the size of purchases and sales become a larger fraction of market volume—an effect that, he states, 'exists for every style, for every size and for every manager.'"[12] Bogle, Jr., has been known to close his mutual fund to new investors at the virtually unheard of level of $100 million to keep market impact costs to a minimum.

It is evident that value stocks are easier to trade than growth stocks because value managers, by default, buy what everyone else is selling, so willing sellers provide them with plenty of liquidity—an indication that Vanguard, with its immense scale, should probably do better with value managers than with growth ones. (The exception proving the rule is Vanguard's Primecap funds, for the aforementioned reasons.) Adding small caps and an aggressive trading style to a growth-oriented fund virtually ensures that the only way to execute such a strategy successfully as an active manager is to do precisely what John Bogle, Jr., has done and close a fund at a minuscule size. In fact, when I asked Bogle if Vanguard could execute a strategy similar to his son's at Bogle Small Cap Growth, he said, "It would be ridiculous."

It is also worth considering the effect of Vanguard's mutualized structure on fund all-in costs. Surely, Vanguard's expense ratios are the lowest in the industry percentage-wise, with an average of just 0.20 percent, but are the fees it collects the lowest in dollar terms? Given the company's immense size, the answer must be no. Bogle himself often recommends that investors not simply look at the percentage expense ratio for funds such as Fidelity Magellan because, despite its seemingly reasonable 0.74 percent ratio, it collects many millions in fees thanks to its $22 billion in assets. The same kind of dollar analysis, of course, can be applied to Vanguard. Consider, for instance, the Vanguard Explorer Fund, which invests in small-cap growth stocks. According to the fund's April 2010 semiannual report, it had $9.7 billion in assets and a low

0.54 percent expense ratio for individual investors and an even lower 0.34 percent ratio for high-net-worth investors in its Admiral share class. But, because the fund is so large, those percentages translate into $19.8 million in net expenses for the six months ending April 30, 2010.

Now compare that $19.8 million to the $4.3 million collected by the Champlain Small Company Fund in the six months ending January 31, 2010. The Champlain fund had only $626 million in assets as of its January 31, 2010, annual report, so that fee translates to a much higher 1.30 percent annual expense ratio. But one important distinction is that Champlain is closed to new investors. Even though the fund actually trades less than Vanguard Explorer, having a moderate 48 percent turnover ratio compared to Explorer's 95 percent, the managers at Champlain thought it was important to shut their doors so they could still invest in small caps nimbly and efficiently. And although the advantages of such a strategy cannot be proven with a mathematical certainty, like Vanguard's low expenses, in this fund's case, its 36.9 percent cumulative total return since its December 2004 inception through July 31, 2010, beat Explorer's 11.3 percent return by a wide margin.

This is not to say that a small asset size always trumps low expense ratios, but a more sophisticated analysis of Vanguard's actively managed funds would weigh the advantages of their low expense ratios against the drawbacks of their immense size—comparing, say, the dollars saved via low expense ratios versus the dollars lost because of higher market impact costs. As far as I know, such an analysis doesn't exist yet. But surely being small and nimble isn't everything. Despite John Bogle, Jr.'s tiny sub-$100 million asset base in the Bogle Small Cap Growth Fund, his fund lagged Vanguard Explorer in the last five years, as the downturn whipsawed his small- and micro-cap holdings, although over the longer term he has outperformed. Meanwhile, his semiannual expenses in dollar terms were a minuscule $576,233 as of the fund's February 28, 2010, report. That looks downright cheap next to Explorer's $19.8 million.

Unfortunately, Explorer, like Primecap, has experienced style drift, with its median market cap more than doubling from $860 million in 2002 to $2.0 billion in 2010 as assets also almost doubled during that time. So it is effectively shut out of investing in many of the micro-cap stocks John Bogle, Jr., prefers, or at least in any meaningful way. Although it has a good long-term record, in recent years it has begun to lag, and if assets continue to grow, I would expect that it will continue to struggle.

Bogle, for his part, thinks that having multiple subadvisers handling Vanguard's actively managed funds helps mitigate the problems of asset bloat. Explorer, for instance, currently has six different subadvisers running different slices of its portfolio, including Vanguard's own quantitative equity group. Surely, smaller subadvisers placing trades separately might lessen some of the market impact costs that only one management team handling a bloated fund normally pays. But so many diverging managers lead to a portfolio so diffuse that it resembles other bloated funds that have to invest in additional stocks to absorb all the new money they're receiving. In July 2010, Explorer had 841 stocks in its portfolio. That's only 181 fewer stocks than the Vanguard Small Cap Growth Index Fund, which has outperformed Explorer by a wide margin over the last 10 years and has a much lower 0.28 percent expense ratio. In fact, Explorer is so overly diversified that it could be called a closet index fund, as its correlation with the Russell 2000 Growth Index is 99 percent. So in many respects, having all the subadvisers defeats the purpose of active management. By way of contrast, Champlain Small Company Fund holds only 98 stocks.

Bogle believes in multimanaged funds since managers often fall in and out of favor during different time periods, so employing multiple advisers smooths out a fund's returns. "One year one of them is best, and the other year someone else is best, and they move up and down in the pecking order," he says. Because in aggregate they will not depart much from the average money manager's gross returns, he says that Vanguard will ultimately win after deducting expenses because of its superefficient operations and its subadviser fees that are negotiated at arm's length down to the bare minimum. And Vanguard tends to favor low-turnover managers, which gives it an extra edge on transaction costs. "Put all that together, and a Vanguard fund that performs as average will win by about 1½ percent a year or by 20 percent over a decade," he says. "So we win by 20 percent over a decade by being average."

But those sound like the words of a man who doesn't really believe in active management to begin with. The point of indexing is to be average and win on costs. The point of active management is to be extraordinary and win despite costs. Why would anyone pay more than an index fund for just average returns that will be less than the index's after expenses? I would argue that Vanguard's best actively managed funds continue to be those run by a solitary manager like Primecap or Wellington, which have the double advantage of being extraordinary and having low costs. And it seems that tacking on a new subadviser may be more a consequence of the shop's desire for scale than for superior returns.

Ultimately, the multimanager approach may also have to do with another "problem"—if one can call it that—which is unique to Vanguard. If strategy follows structure, what does Vanguard's low-cost structure mean to the recruitment of top active managers? Consider that all of Vanguard's outside managers have other lines of business that may often be of a higher margin than running Vanguard's low-cost funds, and you may begin to ask why such managers choose to run money for Vanguard at all. How does it look for a high-profile firm to be subadvising a Vanguard fund with, say, a 0.30 percent expense ratio and be simultaneously running a retail mutual fund in exactly the same style for 1.50 percent? Would there not be a risk of cannibalizing the assets of one's higher-margin products as investors flee to Vanguard's lower-cost ones?

It is always important to remember that although Vanguard is ostensibly run at cost as an ersatz "nonprofit," its subadvisers want to make as much profit as possible. So why would they sign up for the Vanguard experiment? "The economics of a mutual fund company, or a mutual fund on a standalone basis, are very simple to understand," says Arthur Zeikel, former chairman of Merrill Lynch Asset Management and a close personal friend of Bogle. "At some point the incremental profit margin becomes close to 100 percent. So it doesn't matter what the fee is. The net income is going to go up because it's a fixed-cost business." This is true only so long as the adviser doesn't cannibalize other higher-margin lines of its business in the process. And there are a few ways to avoid this problem. One is not to offer retail funds, and often Vanguard hires managers who run only institutional money, so there is no conflict with its retail products; this was the case, for instance, until recently with Primecap. But another way—a way that greatly expands the pool of available active managers for Vanguard—is to subadvise a multimanager fund. Since other managers are influencing the portfolio, the multimanager fund is unlikely to cannibalize the business of a branded fund run by a single external subadviser.

Given all the above quirks of or drawbacks to Vanguard's mutualized structure, what can we say are its unique advantages for actively managed funds? Obviously, the at-cost structure is tailor-made for indexing, and it seems that any firm that challenges Vanguard on this front is sure to be soundly defeated. But perhaps the greatest advantage a low-cost structure has for active managers is its inherent edge in risk management. Generally speaking, the less volatile the asset class or market sector, the more of an edge Vanguard funds will have over their peers. This can be predicted with an almost mathematical certainty because less volatile asset classes by their very nature have less variability in returns, meaning that most funds invested in that asset class will perform very similarly before deducting expenses. Hence, Vanguard, as the low-cost provider, wins after deducting expenses. But it also wins generally by taking on less credit and quality risk in its portfolio. This can be seen most easily in, say, a corporate bond fund. To produce the same yield after expenses as Vanguard's, other bond funds must take on more credit and duration risk to counteract the drag of their higher fees.

The flip side to this equation is that Vanguard is more vulnerable to defeat in the most volatile asset classes and sectors of the market—in, say, small caps, emerging markets, or individual sector funds. The equation is fairly straightforward here, too: the more variable the returns of an asset class, the less of an impact expenses will have on returns relative to the volatility of the asset class's price moves. If, say, in the micro-cap sector, some stocks are up 1,000 percent while others are down 90 percent, the fact that a money manager invests in one group or the other will be far more significant than whether his fees are 0.30 percent or 1.50 percent. In this regard, active management will have a greater effect on performance, but whether that effect will be positive or negative is often very hard to tell. So the advantage is still Vanguard's, but those active managers who do choose wisely will probably beat Vanguard by a mile.

Similarly, the more flexible an active manager's investment strategy is, the more likely it is to be able to beat a similar flexible fund run by Vanguard because again there is much more variability in possible returns in a portfolio that can invest in stocks, bonds, or cash than in a portfolio that can buy only short-term investment-grade bonds. Indeed, probably the biggest mistake most money managers ever made was to play the style box game against Vanguard, as it narrows the range of results. The old-school go-anywhere managers like Peter Lynch had a big advantage over today's narrowly defined money managers who can buy only large-cap growth stocks or long-term municipal bonds.

These structural advantages to and vulnerabilities of Vanguard as the industry's Wal-Mart have serious implications for the fund industry in general. If volatile asset classes are the one area of the fund market where a high-fee competitor can gain an edge over Vanguard and thus attract assets, then there will be a tendency for money managers to launch increasingly risky funds in order to compete. Consider, for instance, the fact that the global bond market is actually bigger in terms of total capitalization, at about $80 trillion, than the global stock market, which has about $50 trillion. One would think, given the available liquidity, that there would be at least as many bond funds as stock funds. So why is it that, according to Morningstar, there are only 1,518 bond funds compared to 6,268 stock funds? The answer seems obvious. Bonds tend to be less volatile, and so it is hard for most money managers to launch successful high-margin/high-fee products to invest in that asset class when a low-cost Vanguard fund will beat them every time. This industry penchant for the riskiest sectors is, of course, extremely harmful to fund investors, who get lured into increasingly volatile trendy products.

Despite Vanguard's inherent advantages, it is worth asking how much of its drive for scale and efficiency is due to its mutualized structure and how much is a result of its unique culture. In other words, are low management fees always a corollary of mutualization? "There is no such thing as a perfect structure," Bogle readily acknowledges. Or, as he often quips, to ensure that a company is run efficiently with shareholders, best interests at heart, it must have ethical principals as well as ethical principles. In fact, assuming that cost savings are guaranteed with mutualization is equivalent to believing that a government or nonprofit agency that provides a service at cost will always be able to run its operations more cheaply and efficiently than private enterprise will. Though such is often the case, it isn't always so, given the nature of bureaucracy and corruption. But eliminating the outside investor's parasitic desire for profit margins and conflicts of interests is surely an inherent advantage to the mutual structure.

CHAPTER 17

The Heart of the Matter

It seems as though everyone but Bogle is constantly worrying about his health. "He's had a lot of close calls," says his daughter Barbara. "When I was in college and when I was young and working and newly married—this was before caller ID, before cell phones, before all those things—if the phone would ring late at night or early in the morning, my heart would skip a beat cause I would think, there's my mom telling me that that's it. Because it was—he was so precarious for such a long time."

Though Bogle never seemed to break a sweat about his condition in front of his colleagues or family, clearly he may have been more frightened beneath the surface than he let on. At the time that Dr. Lown started to treat him in the 1960s, Lown had never seen a case of Bogle's rare genetic disorder before. His arrhythmogenic right ventricular dysplasia (ARVD), which caused his heart to suddenly accelerate to as fast as 180 beats per minute, wasn't even an officially recognized diagnosis yet. "When I examined him for the first time, I could tell he had a lot more dread than he was conveying to me," Lown recalls. "Clearly, other doctors had told him that he might not live past 40."

And yet after Lown devised a successful treatment plan for him, Bogle insisted on still playing squash, "I was vehemently opposed," Lown says. "While he listened to everything I said, he said, 'No way, I have to play. How do I manage it?' The only way was to bring a defibrillator to the squash court. He came back next time to see me, so pleased you can't imagine: 'I'm consistently winning. My opponents are so demoralized and fearful they'll have to resuscitate me, I beat them every time.'"

Perhaps Bogle shouldn't have been so cavalier about his condition. ARVD is one of the leading causes of sudden cardiac death among young athletes. Although it was undiagnosed at the time, subsequent research would reveal it to be a rare genetic, progressive heart condition in which the muscle of the heart's right ventricle is replaced by fat and fibrosis, causing rapid abnormal heart rhythms. The condition is thought to affect one in 5,000 people.[1] "With the displacement of the heart muscle by fatty and fibrous tissue, the ventricle becomes very thin and balloons and doesn't pump effectively," Lown explains. "That affects how the heart beats."

When Bogle was admitted to Hahnemann Hospital in October 1995 for a heart transplant, he was in such a deteriorated state that he could no longer travel to see Dr. Lown because he needed treatment locally almost every week. "At that point, his ARVD had progressed from a heart rhythm abnormality to actual failure of the heart muscle," says Dr. Susan Brozena, who was head of Hahnemann's heart transplant unit at the time. Bogle had already been to another specialist at Boston's Mass General, Dr. Roman DeSanctis, in 1992, who'd told him he must get on the transplant list right away. By 1994, DeSanctis had some worse news, Bogle recalls: "He said, 'Your heart is enormous . . . and in fact your right side of your heart has stopped working. You are operating on half of your heart, and if the left side stops, by the way, you're dead.'"

And yet as Bogle waited at Hahnemann for a transplant, he maintained an almost Zen-like sense of equanimity in the face of his potential demise. "I never thought I wouldn't survive," he remarks. "And I never thought I would survive. That was the whole point. I didn't think every day, will I or won't I? I had better things to think about." Mostly what seemed to keep him going was his faith—in God, in Vanguard, and most important perhaps, in the importance of his own labor. The fact that he kept working on Vanguard's annual reports, that he "pressed on regardless," kept his mind off the unpleasant realities of his physiological breakdown.

"I enjoyed writing the annual reports," Bogle says. "And you've got to do something every day when you are in a hospital situation. I find it very difficult to read a novel, as there's just too many damn distractions around. But when you're writing or doing something you are deeply involved in, or talking on the phone, it's much easier to get away from introspection. I'm a big believer in introspection, but not when you are waiting for a heart. You take each day as it comes. And you know you get into the hospital routine. It's not bad at all. There was no pain connected with it. I had to be lying down most of the time, because the heart not pumping well would mean I would get a lot of swelling if I was up and around. The body starts to break down because of the pumping failure. It was an interesting experience."

An "interesting experience" is just one of a number of euphemisms Bogle uses for nearly dying several times. Another euphemism for a heart attack, according to his son John, Jr., is "an unpleasantness." John, Jr., remembers also feeling the same dread that his sister did about phone calls in the middle of the night during Bogle's pre-transplant days in case there was another unpleasantness. But the transplant itself was no picnic either, contrary to what his father says. "Both periods were terrifying," John, Jr., remarks. "More terrifying was the heart transplant. It's such a monumental event with such risk that you know you are taking. You are voluntarily opting to do this clearly with the right objectives, but knowing you might not come out of there. I think at the time he did it, the risks were certainly smaller than they were ten years prior. But we all knew that it was a very risky procedure."

And yet there is a salve in rituals and routines that sometimes allows people to hold themselves together even when conditions seem unbearable, especially for a man as enamored of work as Bogle. He maintained a businesslike schedule for his days in the hospital, which helped keep his mind off the fact that death doesn't adhere to one. "It was such a long, long time he was in the hospital—four or five months," recalls his daughter Barbara. "I guess one thing I'll step back and say we are a very tradition-bound family, so when he was in the hospital, every Tuesday I would go in and have lunch with him, and we all had a particular schedule. He lived by the routine. That sort of made the time pass so much easier. But I think we just had such confidence in, you know, his prospects. It couldn't be any worse than it was before."

Bogle usually started working on his annual reports about 10:30 a.m., after the doctors had completed their rounds. He would continue until about 5:30 p.m., when his wife would arrive and stay with him until 7:30 p.m. When Eve left, he'd get back to work until 10 p.m. Then he'd read the *New York Times* till 10:45 p.m., take a sleeping pill, recite the 23rd psalm and the Lord's Prayer, and then do the *Times's* crossword puzzle until he drifted off to sleep.[2]

Bogle also had other heart patients to keep him company at Hahnemann Hospital. "We had our own heart failure unit," recalls Dr. Susan Brozena, Bogle's cardiologist. "It was self-contained, eight or nine beds in there, and 90 percent of the patients were waiting for transplants. They were all in the same boat as he was. They were all on these drips. We couldn't send them home, so it was like a little family up there. We had a little lounge and kitchen, and they basically lived there. Our visiting hours were not restrictive because it was a self-contained unit, and we wanted the families in. His family was there very frequently. He did have business associates come in too. He had his computer set up, his phone. He had his own office in there. It was amazing."

The transplant surgery itself takes three to four hours and is, as Dr. Brozena describes it, a ballet of organization. "First [the hospital] gets a call that there is a donor for a patient," she says. "The donor organ is matched with the blood type, body size, and status of the patient. What I mean by status is that if someone is stable at home and waiting for a transplant, they are considered status 2. If someone is in the hospital waiting, they would be a status 1. There are different categories of 1 depending on how sick people are. Once you are on [the list] long enough, when a donor comes in that matches a certain body size, that would be distributed to the person at the top of the list. One team goes to the donor hospital and retrieves the organs—organs because there is usually more than one retrieved from a donor—and the other team brings the patient to the operating room and they start to get him ready. But they don't start the operation until the donor harvest team calls and says, 'OK, it's a good heart.' You don't want to start an operation if there is something wrong with the donor. So then [the donor team] will call back and say they are on their way. But [the surgical team] won't open the patient until they know the heart is on site."

Once the new heart arrives, the surgical team must extract the old one. For at least an hour while they undergo cardiopulmonary bypass, patients have no heart in their body, instead being connected to a heart-lung machine that consists of a pump and an oxygenator that removes oxygen-deprived blood from the body and replaces it with oxygen-rich blood through a series of hoses. "Surgery is usually successful," Brozena says. "The problem with surgeries would be if someone had a previous heart surgery. Then just like when any incision heals, it heals with scar tissue. So it could take longer to dissect out the heart, and that causes more bleeding. That makes it more difficult. But [Bogle] didn't have open-heart surgery. He had had other procedures, but not that. The second issue would be bleeding, and he did not have problems with bleeding. The third issue would be if the patient had any other medical problems, like if their kidneys started to fail."

Once the surgery is complete, a patient has an 85 percent chance of survival for at least one year. "There is a 10-year survival rate overall of about 50 to 60 percent of patients," Brozena says. Since Bogle's surgery was conducted in 1996, he's "out pretty far," Brozena says, although she has transplant patients who have had their new hearts for more than 20 years. In Bogle's case, the fact that he had a genetic disorder rather than, say, arteriosclerosis brought on by obesity may have served him well. "He was blessed that he had no other medical problems other than his heart, so all of his other organ function was fine," Brozena recalls. "Theoretically he should have done well, and he did."

After the wait for a heart and the surgery are over, the final hurdles for transplant recipients are the body's potential rejection of the new heart or a general infection—a potential side effect of the immune suppression drugs patients are required to take so that the body doesn't reject the heart. The fact that these two potential reactions are interdependent creates a tightrope that transplant recipients and their doctors must walk in which a balance between defending against either eventuality must be established. "He did have a couple of infection episodes, pneumonia or respiratory infection, early on, but he did not have any early rejections at all," says Brozena.

Ironically, in older patients, the potential for rejection is less because the immune system is weaker. Infection, however, poses a greater threat. "Some people wake up after the transplant and feel immediately wonderful," Bogle says. "I did not. I probably had one of the poorer if not the poorest postoperative periods of any of my [transplant] classmates, but probably a better outcome. A lot of them retired. Several of them naturally died. Once you get past the first year, it's pretty good. I don't know what to say about it other than it's one more bump along the road of life, and you either cave in to it or you overcome it."

There was definitely some initial unpleasantness after the surgery, but Bogle took it in stride, stoically adhering to his faith in a higher power. "As I said many times, it was 'thy will be done, not my will be done,'" he recalls. "So my early weeks after the heart transplant were absolutely miserable. I could see my family, but they were only allowed to be in the room for an hour, and I could see them watching the clock, hoping it would run quickly so they could get the hell out. It was a real mess. But after a couple of weeks, I started to do very well. I ended up coming back to work at Vanguard sometime around April 1, 1996, and spoke in the analysts national meeting in Atlanta on May 8, 1996."

Bogle's speech before the Association for Investment Management and Research in Atlanta was called, "Six Things to Remember about Indexing, and One to Forget." In front of a hostile crowd of portfolio managers and analysts, he detailed the advantages of indexing over active management. It was as though—if you'll forgive the pun—his life had barely skipped a beat. To top it off, it was his birthday, and his son John, Jr., was on the AIMR panel at the conference. Could anything signify his complete revitalization better than this? As a present, John, Jr., gave him a squash racket. "My wife thought that was horrible, but I did get back to playing squash for quite a few years," Bogle says. "So [the transplant is] of course frightening in the abstract, but we human beings just keep pressing on, and there's no point in getting preoccupied. As I said to people at the time, you know, if I thought jumping up and down on the kitchen table screaming about the unfairness of life would help, I surely would have jumped up and down on the kitchen table and screamed about the unfairness of life. It occurred to me that it might make things worse rather than better."

In fact, all Bogle seems to feel is gratitude for being able to survive so long. In particular, he was thankful for all the effort Dr. Lown had put into keeping him alive for 20 years prior to even the existence of a diagnosis for ARVD. At a 2008 tribute to Dr. Lown upon the publication of Lown's book *Prescription for Survival*, Bogle had the following to say: "So here I am tonight, to report to you that the package of love, healing, care, intensity, focus, empathy, and professional skill provided by Dr. Lown was without parallel in my long struggle with cardiomyopathy, and enabled me to press on with my life." Having completed his speech, Bogle then uncharacteristically broke out into song, replacing the words to the Beatles' "Hey Jude" with his own rendition of "Ber-nard," making the world "better, better, better."[3] Recalls Dr. Lown: "He'd arranged a flautist or clarinet to play with him. The whole audience was stunned. This old gent with a croaking voice brought down the house. It was an event they would always remember." The week prior to the event, Bogle had actually been in the hospital and was still truly under the weather, but he made an effort to travel to Boston just to speak and sing the praises of the wondrous Dr. Lown.

Bogle also wanted to thank the family of the heart's donor. Although donors' names are generally anonymous, Bogle found out when he met the recipient of his donor's liver, whose wife happened to make the connection from a newspaper article she'd read about Bogle's transplant being on the same day as her husband's. They knew more about the donor than Bogle did. "He was a young man who was 26 and died in a motorcycle accident," Bogle says of the donor. "I wrote the family and never heard back. Maybe there wasn't any family, maybe they don't speak English, maybe the letter was a little high toned. Maybe they couldn't get over the shock of losing their child. Maybe anything. I never heard back for any more detail. And I just signed it anonymously because one doesn't know what they are getting into. But it's all done through the heart transplant association. So your anonymity is protected unless you want to sign the letter. They do the delivery."

While Bogle has been blessed with mostly good health since the transplant, he has had some serious complications in recent years. In 2008 he had a problem with the dosage of one of his anti-rejection drugs being too low, and his body started to reject the heart. "It took a while to get him out of that," Dr. Brozena says. "He had to be hospitalized for different therapies. Fortunately, it worked. I think he's a little more tired now since then. So it has slowed him down a little bit." But the problem with increasing the dosage of anti-rejection drugs is that the patient's immune system is weakened. "The immune system is always going to fight your [new] heart, because it never sees it as part of you but as foreign tissue," Brozena says. "So we had to increase his immunosuppression, and whenever you do that, you put people at a higher risk for infection. It's a double-edged sword."

In 2009, Bogle came down with a terrible infection that nearly killed him. "I got a disease called Listeria," he recalls. "It's a blood disease. The fatality rate is 50 percent if you are on anti-rejection drugs, which make you subject to all kinds of difficulties because your body does not have the power to get rid of the disease. And so I was in a coma for a few days. They were not sure if I would live or not. And it took me quite a while, maybe three or four weeks, to get over that. And they took very good care of me. I was at Penn Hospital, and then I came to the Hospital of the University of Pennsylvania. And I came out, and I wasn't getting any better. After a week at home, I was getting quite bad, felt miserable, felt like I was getting worse every day. So I went back to Bryn Mawr Hospital, and then I had a big organ shutdown. I had to have some surgery. I had to have dialysis. I was in the intensive care unit. I got out after about a month of that and about a week later got a blood clot and had to go back to the hospital. So it was a long while. But what are you supposed to do? You get into the hospital routine. You try to be good to the nurses. That's a pretty good rule to follow. You don't want the nurses mad at you. You try to be cooperative and pleasant enough, but it's hard when you cannot sleep at night, but you eventually get through it. My wife and family were just wonderful. They were there sleeping in the hospital room just in case. So after that [experience], I said it doesn't seem a good idea to bitch about some little thing like that when you are still alive and had these wonderful years of life."

A "little thing" like Listeria might go well with an "unpleasantness" for a heart attack in Bogle's vocabulary of euphemisms. But it is precisely such equanimity tinged with humility and self-denial in the face of seemingly dire circumstances that has allowed Bogle to triumph in so many areas of his long and productive life. "Doctors take a lot of credit, but ultimately it is the patient that lives or dies," observes Dr. Lown. "In this case, the miracle resides in John Bogle. His indomitable personality helped him survive all the hospital stays."

CHAPTER 18

The Future of Indexing

In the wake of two brutal bear markets, the efficient market hypothesis (EMH) came under attack. Since Bogle's beloved index fund is the purest expression of the market, it too came under scrutiny. It was a sign of the index fund's newfound preeminence that critics, instead of calling for its elimination, as they had in the past, actually sought to build a better mousetrap. From these complaints a number of newfangled indexes and products that track them emerged. And the future is sure to bring many more to market.

Although active managers had long groused about the hypothesis's deficiencies, academia remained solidly in the EMH camp. So it was a bit of a surprise when Robert Arnott fired one of the first post-dot-com-era salvos in the March/April 2005 edition of the esteemed *Financial Analysts Journal* by declaring that his newly designed "fundamental indexes" were superior to traditional market-cap-weighted ones. Arnott, a confirmed quant/academic and at the time the *Journal*'s editor, was not the typical active manager with gripes about settling for mediocrity.

His attack went straight to the heart of the efficient market hypothesis. He believed that the way the market valued stocks in popular indexes such as the S&P 500 and the Wilshire 5000 by their market capitalization led to distortions in which the most popular stocks were weighted the most heavily, regardless of the underlying fundamentals of the businesses those stocks represented. The argument had a particular resonance in the aftermath of the dot-com bubble, in which companies such as Cisco achieved larger weightings in the S&P 500 and Wilshire indexes than Exxon and GE, even though Cisco produced less earnings and cash flow than those old-economy companies. Arnott proposed weighting companies by their actual fundamentals— book value, sales, dividends, cash flow—rather than market cap. Such weightings, he believed, would more closely approximate the "true" intrinsic value of companies as measured by the present value of their future cash flows.

For Arnott, the fact that markets are inefficient is the primary reason he believes that his indexes will outperform traditional ones. He described what he thinks his fundamental strategy's advantages are in an interview and e-mail exchange with me: "If the market were efficient, the fundamental index methodology wouldn't produce superior long-term returns. Nor would [the fundamental index] have any reason for long-term underperformance. As a broadly diversified portfolio, it would be expected to essentially match the market over time. In a less than efficient market, we know that some stocks (and occasionally many) will be priced above or below their true fair value. Those that are priced above true value will have higher capitalization and higher valuation multiples than they should. And they'll eventually underperform. This leads to four patterns:

- "Some of the largest-cap companies deserve their large cap. But some are there because they're overpriced. There should be a slight preponderance of overvalued companies at the top of the market cap list; these will underperform, creating a 'size effect.'
- "Some of the highest multiple growth companies deserve their high multiples. But some are there because they're overpriced. There should be a slight preponderance of overvalued companies at the

top of the valuation multiple list; these will underperform, creating a 'value effect.'

- "As the market seeks to identify and correct its pricing errors, we should see long-horizon mean reversion. We do.

- "Market-cap weighting will have more invested in these companies than a hypothetical 'fair value weighted' portfolio, so the cap-weighted portfolio will have a return drag relative to this 'fair value weighted' portfolio."

Although it is not a total market index, Arnott compared the S&P 500—for which there was more historical data—to a large-cap index he designed that was weighted on stock fundamentals in his original 2005 study. He looked at a long 43-year historical record from 1962 through 2004 and found that the fundamental index outperformed the S&P 500 by 1.97 percentage points a year, and with slightly less volatility or beta. Nor could this record simply be attributed to the "small-cap" effect, in which smaller companies outperform larger ones, as the fundamental index, although having lower weightings in the largest, most popular companies than the S&P 500, still managed to beat an equal-weighted version index of the S&P 500—which invests more heavily in smaller companies—by an even wider margin of 3.09 percentage points. It wasn't long before Arnott's financial research and money management firm Research Affiliates had licensed the new indexes to ETF vendors such as PowerShares and fund company Pimco.

Bogle, of course, was almost immediately skeptical of the newfangled competition to his beloved S&P 500 and Wilshire 5000 indexes. In a 2006 op-ed he penned with fellow index advocate Burton Malkiel for the *Wall Street Journal*, he argued that fundamental indexing was really more of a fad than a "paradigm shift" for index investors. He also reiterated that the reason a total stock market index fund outperformed was not because of the efficient market hypothesis but because of his own cost matters hypothesis:

First let us put to rest the canard that the remarkable success of traditional market-weighted indexing rests on the notion that markets must be efficient. Even if our stock markets

were inefficient, capitalization-weighted indexing would still be—must be—an optimal investment strategy. All the stocks in the market must be held by someone. Thus, investors as a whole must earn the market return when that return is measured by a capitalization-weighted total stock market index. We cannot live in Garrison Keillor's Lake Wobegon, where all the children are above average. For every investor who outperforms the market, there must be another investor who underperforms. Beating the market, in principle, must be a zero-sum game.[1]

If the reason a total stock market index fund outperformed was lower costs and not efficiency, then there was no guarantee that a higher-cost fundamental index fund would necessarily beat it just because the market is inefficient. Bogle pointed out that not only did the new fundamental index fund products have higher expense ratios than conventional market-cap-weighted ones, but they would also in all likelihood have higher turnover ratios, leading to greater transaction and market impact costs than a total market-cap index fund, which basically buys and holds most stocks forever. Ultimately, what fundamental indexing represented, in Bogle's view, was really a style tilt in favor of value investing because the weightings of stocks that were overvalued relative to their underlying fundamentals would be reduced whenever the fundamental index rebalanced, while the weightings of undervalued stocks would be increased. Enacting such a tilt would lead to bouts of underperformance when the style is out of favor and to increased transaction costs brought on by the rebalancing.

But by acknowledging that the market may in fact be inefficient, Bogle opened a Pandora's box for traditional index funds. Because the question then becomes, how inefficient is it? If the market is inefficient enough that a fundamental index fund can exploit those inefficiencies to the point where it covers the additional costs of higher expense ratios and transaction fees, then the newfangled index funds might just be worthwhile. If one considers that the new Vanguard S&P 500 ETF has a 0.06 percent expense ratio, while PowerShares FTSE RAFI US 1000 Portfolio ETF, which tracks Arnott's large-cap index, has a 0.39 percent one, then it would be likely that the PowerShares ETF would beat Vanguard only so long as the historical 1.97 percentage point edge Arnott demonstrated the fundamental index had over the S&P 500 persisted.

Admittedly, Arnott's study results were back-tested and not adjusted for transaction costs. But Arnott designed the indexes to employ a low-turnover approach in which the portfolio would rebalance once a year. "Our fundamental index has a 10 percent to 15 percent turnover ratio, while cap-weighted indexes [such as the S&P 500] have 5 percent to 10 percent," Arnott says. "So we have a 5 percentage point higher turnover than the cap-weighted index." He also thinks that because the index tends to buy unpopular stocks while selling popular ones during the annual rebalancing, there is ample liquidity for such a strategy and that market impact costs would be minimal.

As for Bogle's cost matters hypothesis, Arnott agrees that it is mathematically irrefutable. He just thinks that the arbitrage achieved from mispriced securities being revalued correctly in an inefficient market will be greater than the cost savings—or expense arbitrage—generated by conventional index funds. "It is a truism—active management is a loser's game after deducting higher fees and expenses, despite the existence of overpriced and underpriced stocks," Arnott says. "The market can't beat itself no matter how bad the mispricings are! Someone has to lose, and someone has to win. This assertion, this worldview, is a far more useful theory to guide investment decisions than the efficient markets hypothesis. It sheds light on just how difficult the quest for alpha really is. . . . But are there some consistent losers in this zero sum game—the 401(k) investor who chases performance, the mutual fund manager who invests in comfortable growth stocks, the story stock believers, or the retail investor who buys a good company rather than a good stock? If we can exploit these 'fish' in a systematic, low-cost manner, we can achieve excess returns, even within the 'cost matters' world."

The question as to whether the so-called value premium can persist is the crucial one for determining whether fundamental indexes will continue to outperform in the future. When a bubble period in which there are great distortions in valuation ends, fundamental indexation will probably perform the best, as the gap between, say, overpriced biotech stocks and underpriced industrial ones will be the widest, yet shrinking so that undervalued stocks in the market will either rise as overpriced ones decline or fall less, thus closing the valuation gap. By contrast, when the broad market is close to fair valuation as measured by the fundamental index, the stock weightings in both the fundamental and conventional indexes will be very similar, and so fundamental index products, which have higher expenses, will probably lag conventional ones. In addition, as the stock market enters a bubble period and certain stocks become increasingly overpriced while others lag, fundamental indexes will also underperform as the gap between overpriced and underpriced securities widens.

While I agree with Bogle that the likelihood of continued outperformance by fundamental indexes is not nearly as certain as that of conventional ones, I do think that he contradicts himself philosophically on the subject. I say this because Bogle is, like many old-timers on Wall Street, a "fundamentalist" at heart who believes that stocks have an intrinsic fair value that is measured by the present value of their future cash flows. This philosophy, best expressed by the father of value investing, Ben Graham, abhors speculation of any sort in which stocks make gains not on their underlying earnings and dividends but on price movements alone. And Bogle is true to that philosophy, having devoted many speeches and whole chapters of his books to bemoaning the increasing speculation in the stock market.

In *The Battle for the Soul of Capitalism,* for instance, he asks in the wake of the dot-com crash why investment America went wrong. His answer: "Because it focused on the momentary precision of stock prices rather than the eternal importance of intrinsic corporate value, however difficult to measure. Because it ignored the critical importance of future cash flow, however difficult to predict with accuracy. Because it forgot that long-run stock values are created by the enduring economics of investment return rather than the transitory emotions of speculative return."[2]

But to renounce speculative returns in favor of the "eternal importance of intrinsic value" is to renounce much of the gains that occurred in the stock market and by proxy in Vanguard's own market-tracking index funds during the height of the Internet bubble. Bogle himself has well documented how much of the market's returns that occurred during the bubble came not from true earnings and dividend growth, but from speculative price increases. Those speculative gains on tech stocks with little or no or even fraudulent earnings in effect made the stock market dishonest and incredibly inefficient from a fundamentalist, Ben Graham viewpoint. And such outsized gains would not have been made by the fundamental index, as it would have given almost zero weight to stocks with no earnings such as Pets.com and much less weight to overhyped stocks such as Cisco as opposed to Exxon, which had more cash flow— or a greater intrinsic value.

So although the fundamental index isn't assured of victory over the market-cap-weighted one, it is the more honest benchmark from the perspective of a man who ostensibly doesn't approve of speculation. In other words, if we forget momentarily about the fact that fundamental index fund products have higher expense ratios and think of Arnott's creation purely as a benchmark, it better represents the spirit of the ownership society that Bogle envisions, in which stocks are valued based on the intrinsic worth of their underlying businesses. By contrast, with market-cap-weighted indexes such as the S&P 500, the possibility that stocks are valued merely based on speculation is always present and in fact probable. So if the S&P 500 or Wilshire 5000 wins in the long term against Arnott's fundamental index, it will be because the "eternal verity" of intrinsic value that Bogle subscribes to failed. Such a victory is quite possible, given that stocks are rarely priced at what Ben Graham would define as their fair value, but it would be a Pyrrhic victory because the traditional index's "edge" will prove to be purely a speculative one.

The only way the fundamental index would be a less accurate measure of the present value of future cash flows than a traditional index is if stock prices were a better predictor of future cash flows than actual historical cash flows, which is what the fundamental index measures. This again raises the question of whether the so-called collective wisdom of the stock market renders it perfectly efficient at allocating capital or not. Does the stock market simply "know" which companies have the best prospects and, rather than overvalue them, price them higher because it accurately predicts that those companies' future cash flows will be much better than those of other, lower-priced securities? Bogle points out that the historical cash flow of General Motors was hardly predictive of its future prior to its going bankrupt. And yet investors who lost their shirts on tech stocks with zero future earnings growth and nosebleed valuations in the 2000–2002 bear market probably don't think much of the market's predictions either.

If the dot-com crash was a stake in the heart of the efficient market hypothesis, the 2008 credit crisis was probably the final nail in its coffin. Critics asked how the market could be "right" in its assessment of business fundamentals and produce returns that move along the normal distribution pattern of a bell curve when the S&P 500 fell 57 percent from its October 9, 2007, peak of 1,565 to its low of 676 on March 9, 2009. Such extreme short-term results weren't supposed to happen in an efficient market, critics such as Nassim Taleb argued, claiming instead that the distribution of returns had what is known as "fat tails" in which extreme events were more likely than a classic bell curve would predict.

Critics didn't just expose EMH as wrong but said that it actually caused the financial crisis. Financial columnist Roger Lowenstein's attitude toward the crisis and EMH's relationship to it was typical of the time. In a review of a book about EMH, *The Myth of the Rational Market*, Lowenstein said that the upside of the 2008 crash was that it could "drive a stake through the heart of the academic nostrum known as the efficient-market hypothesis." He went on to say: "How did this faith in the supremacy of market group-think do us harm? For one, as the dot-com and other manias demonstrated, the crowd occasionally gets it wrong. The mistaken faith in markets turned regulators into fawning groupies. Notably, former Fed chairman Alan Greenspan doubted that he or anyone else could detect—or regulate—a bubble in advance."[3] Another article published in *The Times* of London near the bottom of the downturn in January of 2009 described the attitude of economists and world leaders toward EMH at the World Economic Forum in Davos, Switzerland, as downright hostile: "Asked which policy assumption had most contributed to the global financial crisis, the most popular answer by far was the belief that markets are self-correcting."[4]

The defenders of EMH responded to the attacks by saying that they never claimed that the "market got it right" or moved along a normal distribution pattern, only that it contained the current best estimates of what the right price was. Furthermore, they argued that if there was an identifiable way of proving that the market's estimation of equity valuation was wrong, why didn't more money managers exploit it and beat the market?

Typical of the hypothesis's defenders is Larry Swedroe. Director of research at Buckingham Asset Management and author of eight books on investing, Swedroe is an avowed Boglehead and major advocate of indexing and EMH. A mention of the accusations leveled at EMH enrages him. "The efficient market hypothesis never said anywhere that the market price is the right price!" he exclaims. "People misquote that all the time. All it says is that the market price is the best estimate of the right price. We don't know what the right price is until after the fact. Therefore, the best efforts to outperform are highly likely to prove counterproductive. Unless you can show me persistence of outperformance more than randomly expected, then you have all the evidence you need to believe that markets are highly efficient and efforts to try to outperform are likely to prove counterproductive. There are literally no studies that show [consistent outperformance by active managers]."

Swedroe's response echoes that of Harry Markowitz, one of EMH's founding fathers. Markowitz claimed in a 2010 Q&A with *Morningstar Advisor* that he never said that stock prices move in a normal distribution pattern on a bell curve, but rather that investors behave like utilitarians who strive to maximize their expected returns despite uncertain outcomes, and therefore the market prices contain the best estimates of rational investors: "I never assumed probability distributions were normal. I never justified mean variance analysis in terms of probability distributions being normal. My basic assumption is that you act under uncertainty to maximize expected utility."[5]

Despite these counterstatements, there are numerous quotes in Justin Fox's *The Myth of the Rational Market* (New York: HarperCollins Publishers, 2009) revealing that some members of the academic coterie behind EMH believed that the market did in fact get pricing right and moved along a normal distribution pattern. Certainly the way the financial services industry responded to the hypothesis was to make that assumption, and academics, who unfortunately often had financial ties to the industry, didn't seem too eager to disabuse the industry of this illusion. (As a business journalist with 15 years' experience, I can't tell you the number of presentations I've sat through by financial hucksters in which an efficient frontier was displayed as though it were the Ark of the Covenant.) Indeed, I am often surprised that no regulator or ethics committee has investigated the rather glaring conflicts of interest that arise from finance and economics professors turning their academic research into immensely profitable products sold on Wall Street. Would such academics willingly admit that their beloved hypothesis was flawed while products based on it were making them millions of dollars a year?

But even if a more accurate gloss on EMH is that the market contains the "best estimate" of stocks' fair values given all the publicly available information, I would still maintain that this is a grossly inaccurate assertion. I would argue that indexing works as well as it does not because some money managers can't find consistently exploitable inefficiencies in the market, but because most money managers have no real desire to find those inefficiencies. In other words, I don't believe for a minute that the money management industry, which now owns about 70 percent of the stock market's total capitalization, is even remotely interested in applying its best estimates for fair value when it invests in stocks. Rather, its primary goal is to gather as much assets as possible, and, if achieving that goal requires money managers to buy stocks they believe are grossly overvalued, they will happily do so to collect more fees, keep their jobs, and earn their bonuses.

In other words, indexing wins most of the time not because of market efficiency or even just simply low costs—although they certainly play a part—but because of the structural flaws and systemic conflicts of interest that Bogle has long identified as being endemic to the fund industry. It's important to remember that the vast majority of mutual fund management companies are compensated based on a percentage of assets, not on how much their funds outperform the market. Is it any wonder, then, that their primary goal is to gather assets? For example, suppose you're managing a tech fund with $500 million in assets at the March 2000 stock market peak. Now, suppose that in the back of your mind, you know that the dot-com stocks you own are totally overvalued, but your fund was up 100 percent last year and some institutional clients want to give you another $500 million to invest, thereby doubling your annual management fees collected from, say, $7.5 million to $15 million, even if the market is flat and your stocks go nowhere for the next year. Do you turn away that hot money because you think dot-coms are overvalued? Do you take it and hold it in cash and wait till tech stock prices come down, but risk the possibility that your overhyped stocks may continue to rally and that your clients will be dissatisfied and withdraw their money? The temptation to take the money and keep buying the same stocks despite your best estimates that they are grossly overvalued will be too strong for most money managers to resist.

There is ample evidence that the two-masters fund structure and the agency society that Bogle described prevents many money managers who would otherwise be able to beat the market from doing so. The most obvious proof of this phenomenon is in management fees themselves. Because management companies are more interested in pleasing their company shareholders than their fund shareholders, they will charge the highest fees they can possibly get away with. Would more managers be able to beat the market if expense ratios at actively managed funds were closer to those of index funds? Obviously, they would, as study after study has revealed that low-cost funds tend to beat high-cost ones. The hurdle rate for an active manager trying to beat the market with an expense ratio of 0.40 percent is much lower than one with the typical 1.5 percent.

But high expenses are only the most recognizable symptom of a much larger systemic problem. Consider, for instance, that most fund managers are employees of large fund companies or publicly traded financial conglomerates, and you will realize that the biggest risk such managers face isn't the stock market collapsing, but career risk. They don't want to lose their jobs. This, in effect, discourages managers from investing differently from the herd of other managers. The consequences, for instance, of being out of the market in 1999, even though tech stocks were reaching unheard of valuations, was lagging your peers and your benchmark by a wide margin, as the S&P 500 was up by 21 percent and the Nasdaq Composite was up by 86 percent. As a result, the pressure to invest just like everyone else was extreme, even though everything managers had learned about financial analysis should have told them that stocks were expensive. Only a few had the strength to resist that herd mentality, and most were punished for it. In fact, during the bubble, a number of very high-profile money managers either were fired or quit their jobs under duress because they refused to buy stocks that they felt were wildly overpriced, among them Fidelity's Jeff Vinik and George Vanderheiden, Oakmark's Robert Sanborn, Tiger Management's Julian Robertson, and Merrill Lynch's Chuck Clough. In retrospect, these men seem like heroes.

Such open dissent was very rare during the euphoria of the dot-com bubble. From 1998 through 2001, investment strategist Jeremy Grantham of GMO would take a poll of money managers at every conference he attended, asking them if the p/e ratio of the S&P 500 was too high. In 1999, all but 7 of 1,700 polled said it was, yet very few of them were avoiding large U.S. stocks. "The best way as a money manager to reduce your career and business risk is to make sure you're doing whatever else everyone else is doing, which by the way is the official definition of prudent," Grantham quips. "You follow Keynes's [maxim], 'Never be wrong on your own.' How can you guarantee that will not happen? You look around to what other people are saying and doing, and you, loosely speaking, fit into the pack. Now if you are wrong, that is not a significant reason to get fired." Grantham says that almost every manager he surveyed knew that the bubble was sure to burst, but almost no one did anything for fear of lagging their peers.

The sad fact is that managers can't beat the market unless they invest differently from the herd because the herd collectively is the market. Ultimately, managers who follow their peers' lead become closet indexers and thus can't overcome the index after deducting their exorbitant management fees. They lose their individuality and become like the average manager, and by doing so avoid getting fired when collectively they lag by a little bit. So, the idea that such sheep are putting forth their best estimates on stock prices when they invest is, in a word, ludicrous.

And yet even those managers who want to break away from the pack often don't have a choice. In fact, their decision not to employ their best estimates when buying stocks may involve no ulterior nefarious motive, conflict of interest, or even herdlike behavior on their parts. It may be that they're just doing their jobs. Since the fund industry started to slice and dice the style box, the manager with "large-cap growth" in his fund's name may really have no other choice but to follow his fund's mandate and buy large-cap growth stocks, even if he personally thinks that large-cap growth stocks are a stupid investment. The problems with such mandated investing are especially apparent with index fund managers. Even if the manager of an S&P 500 index fund thinks that U.S. stocks in general are overvalued, she still has to buy every stock in the index when shareholders add cash to the fund, or she will be forced to lag her benchmark. And it's important to note that many fund shareholders have applied automatic investing strategies in their 401ks that add to their position in the funds with every paycheck. If such mindless automated and prospectus-mandated investing is occurring in the stock market, how on earth can stock prices be said to contain the best estimates of rational investors for their intrinsic value?

Admittedly, the pressure to follow the herd doesn't come just from fund management but from fund shareholders as well, who also move in herds, chasing hot funds on the way up in a bubble and stampeding on the way out during a decline. Because of the open-end structure of most mutual funds, managing cash flow is a persistent problem. Investors throwing tons of money at hot funds force their managers to buy more of their favorite stocks that may quickly become overpriced or purchase additional stocks that aren't their best ideas. As more stocks are added to the portfolio, it begins to increasingly resemble its benchmark, and the fund becomes a closet index fund. By contrast, managers who don't follow the herd by being fully invested in stocks on the way up start to lag and suffer redemptions from irrationally exuberant shareholders and can lose their jobs (or their business if they own the management company). During a panic, the reverse becomes a problem. As shareholders dump the fund, managers are forced to sell stocks that are becoming more attractively valued in the decline, even if they'd much rather be buying them. So even if the manager has the best of intentions and does think differently from his peers, he has no choice but to follow the herd.

In Grantham's view, this herdlike behavior is the primary reason securities markets are incredibly inefficient and present opportunities for the true contrarian investor. "You wouldn't have bubbles unless you had a career risk for institutions and the madness of crowds for individuals—the pain of watching your neighbor get rich," he says. "It means you have massive momentum, massive chasing of asset classes, and almost no willingness to rotate into the less risky cheaper asset classes. There will always be that advantage, I think, for those institutions with long investment time horizons—particularly foundations and endowments—that can just extract this extra rent from the market [by investing in the cheaper, less risky asset classes] at the expense of the rest of the market, which feels compelled to keep dancing until the music stops."

In order to understand why most money managers fail to beat the market consistently, I think it's important to understand why one person, against all the apparent odds, has succeeded. No one fills that bill better than Warren Buffett. Although he is a brilliant investor with tremendous skill at stock picking, I would argue that it is the unique structure of Berkshire Hathaway that also gives him a significant edge over the average mutual fund manager.

Even before he took over Berkshire Hathaway, though, Buffett ran an investment partnership from 1956 through 1969 that was structured in a fashion far superior to today's average mutual fund. For one thing, his fees weren't based on a percentage of assets under management. Instead, he received no compensation unless his partners earned a return of 6 percent a year. Of any gains earned above that 6 percent minimum, he kept 25 percent. Thus he was incentivized on his performance, not by gathering assets.

In addition, the Buffett partnership allowed new investments or withdrawals only once a year, in December, so he never had to deal with hot money moving into and out of the fund, forcing him to buy or sell at inopportune times. Finally, he had almost all of his liquid net worth invested in the fund, thus aligning his interests with those of his shareholders. Most of today's mutual fund managers invest very little in their funds—another sign that they don't think much of what the funds own. Buffett's partnership beat the market every year until he liquidated it in 1969 because he felt there were limited investment opportunities. Given that he needed to earn at least 6 percent to get paid, he was strongly motivated to liquidate despite an incredible 13-year run if he felt opportunities were limited. Such would never be the case with today's asset-hungry mutual funds.

Berkshire was an improvement even on the partnership's superior structure. An operating textile company at the time, Berkshire provided Buffett with a steady stream of cash flow to acquire other businesses outright—newspapers, insurance companies, a bank—and make investments in the stock market. The insurance acquisitions in particular enabled Buffett to take a pool of long-dated assets—Geico's "float"—and invest that cash in stocks without worrying about hot money or shareholder redemptions. So, he could buy when everyone was selling and sell when everyone was buying without any pressure on him at all. Berkshire was also internally managed by him much like Vanguard and had no external management company to placate with fees to be extracted parasitically from shareholders. Regardless of what investors thought of Berkshire's stock, Buffett could do as he pleased with the cash flow from the underlying businesses. That flexibility proved incredibly advantageous during the 1970s, when stocks were beaten down to bargain basement prices. Asked how he felt at the time about the opportunities, he responded, "Like an oversexed guy in a whorehouse."[6] Mutual fund managers with massive redemptions weren't nearly so jubilant.

In addition, as an employee of Berkshire's shareholders as opposed to an external management company, Buffett received a modest salary compared to other top money managers, currently $100,000, not a fixed percentage of assets. Instead of extracting his pound of flesh in the form of fees, he invests in Berkshire's stock alongside his shareholders to profit from its growth. Having donated substantial amounts of shares to charity, Buffett still owned some $46 billion worth in Berkshire shares in 2010. Clearly, with such an alignment with shareholders' interests, he cares more about Berkshire's performance than about his own compensation from the company. He faces zero career risk but substantial fiduciary risk as a true steward of shareholders' capital. Finally, Buffett employs a concentrated go-anywhere style that allows him to not get locked into a square in the style box or even locked into stocks. His goal plain and simple is to produce profits for shareholders while minimizing the potential for permanent impairment of their capital. He will never intentionally become a closet indexer.

And yet even the great Buffett faced significant challenges as Berkshire grew so big that it became unwieldy. In a famous letter he wrote to financial historian Peter Bernstein in 1998, Buffett declared that "about 75 percent of the difference in our performance between now and in the distant past is accounted for by size. We have always known that huge increases in managed funds would dramatically diminish our universe of investment choices. . . . For the entire 1950s, my personal returns using equities with a market cap of less than $10 million were better than 60 percent annually. At our present size, I dream at night about 300 basis points [or 3 percentage points better than the market]."[7]

Bogle would cite Buffett's letter in his *Common Sense on Mutual Funds* as evidence of how difficult it was for even the best money managers to beat the market, since their success generally leads to a flood of assets. They are eventually faced with an even greater problem investing the new money than Buffett was because, in their case, the hot money tends to come all at once. In fact, because of the difficulty of successfully achieving excess returns in an open-end mutual fund format, Buffett himself even recommends that most investors are better off using index funds—a remarkable statement, given that he is indisputably the greatest money manager of all time.

Given the current corrupt system of mutual fund governance, widespread conflicts of interest, and the flawed structure of open-end funds, I would definitely agree that the index fund is the best choice for most investors. But I would add that it might be possible for an enlightened money manager to create a mutual fund with a structure similar to that of the young Berkshire Hathaway that would have a decent chance of beating the market. Indeed, some of the old internally managed closed-end funds such as General American Investors and Central Securities have a similar enough structure to Berkshire that they have managed to triumph over the market.

While it is important to note that Bogle's maxim on the zero-sum game of money managers investing in the entire stock market will hold no matter what, there is no justifiable reason from a fiduciary standpoint why active managers should have as terrible a record versus the market over the long term as they currently have. In one analysis Bogle conducted of the returns for 384 equity funds compared to the total stock market index from 1982 through 2009, he found that only 12 funds, or about 3 percent, beat the market by a significant margin.[8] That is an unacceptable and, I believe, wholly unnecessary level of failure.

If the total stock market index is unbeatable by the average stock fund manager, the same can be said for the total bond market index after deducting fund expenses. Lower fees, as always, are the index fund's key advantage, and yet here again we encounter similar problems with the way the benchmark is constructed to those Arnott identified when developing his fundamental stock index. The entire bond market is also market-cap-weighted, but with bonds, tracking the benchmark precisely with an index fund makes even less sense than it does with stocks. Equity at least is considered to be on the asset side of a company's balance sheet, but bonds are debt on the liability side. So why would an investor want to overweight the companies or bond issuers with the greatest amount of debt on their balance sheets? From a fundamental standpoint, investing the most in companies with the greatest market value of outstanding debt instead of the healthiest companies with the least amount of debt is a recipe for disaster, but that is how most bond indexes are constructed, including the total bond market ones.

From a historical perspective, though, Vanguard's Total Bond Market Index Fund held up very well during the 2008 credit crisis because it was heavily weighted in Treasury bonds and government agency debt, and there was a "flight to quality" that year in which the entire world sought the safe haven of Treasuries and the U.S. dollar during the meltdown. Since the U.S. government is currently the largest issuer of debt in the country, Treasuries had a 43 percent weighting in the index as of July 31, 2010. But excessive leverage on the government's balance sheet may one day ruin its credit quality and its standing as the safe haven for the world's assets.

Measuring the impact of government debt and the economic wherewithal of countries to pay it back can be challenging, though. Because governments don't have valuation metrics the way corporations do,

Arnott had to look at different stats when constructing a global bond index based on fundamentals instead of market capitalization: population, land mass (as a proxy for natural resources), gross domestic product (GDP), and energy consumption (as a proxy for economic advancement). To me, debt as a percentage of GDP seems the best measure of a country's overall credit quality. But be that as it may, Arnott's fundamentalist approach, which does not reward countries that borrow more than their peers, such as the United States and Japan, with a larger weighting in the index, outperformed market-cap-weighted government debt indexes by 0.9 percentage point a year from 1997 through 2009—a significant amount in the low-returning world of sovereign government debt.[9]

For corporate bonds, and, in particular, high-yield bonds, the advantages of a fundamental index approach are even greater. Arnott found that ranking companies based on more familiar corporate fundamentals—company assets, dividends, cash flow, and sales—would add a huge 2.6 percentage points a year to returns over market-cap-weighted indexes in the high-yield sector. And that makes complete sense because the last thing any investor would want to do would be to overweight the most overleveraged companies that are likely to default in the junk bond space. To Vanguard's credit, it doesn't index high-yield bonds, but employs a low-cost, actively managed style in this sector that tends to favor bonds with better credit qualities than the average junk fund. But other indexers, such as Barclays and State Street, do track market-cap-weighted high-yield benchmarks. They may be in for some competition. In 2010, rival PowerShares created an ETF to track Arnott's fundamental high-yield benchmark.

Vanguard's Total Bond Market Index Fund should also continue to do fine as long as the United States is perceived as the safe haven for the world's assets. But it might be time for the fund shop to consider a more global approach to bond indexing and to incorporate such fundamentals as GDP into its weightings of bonds, as opposed to market cap. Rivals such as Pimco have already developed such fundamental-based global indexes. If the United States ceases to be the dominant global economic superpower, Vanguard Total Bond Market Index may not hold up well in the next downturn. The bonds from a country with more GDP or less debt on its balance sheet might be the new safe haven.

There are other asset classes and sectors that every would-be indexer or fund company upstart has started tracking that Vanguard has thus far avoided. Certainly commodity futures have become one of the biggest index success stories from an industry perspective. Whether such products will be a success from a long-term investor's perspective remains to be seen. One of the biggest problems has been a condition called contango, in which the futures that indexers buy are always more expensive than the ones they're selling. Because of the short-term nature of futures contracts and the higher turnover of such products, front running is a major problem, especially for single-commodity funds in such sectors as natural gas and livestock. Many hedge funds and traders have earned handsome profits front running natural gas ETFs, which must buy the same futures contract every month at the same time.

Bogle, for his part, has no interest in commodities, as he sees investing in them as purely a speculative activity because commodities, unlike businesses, produce no cash flow. A barrel of oil produces no profits. It just sits there. So buyers of commodity futures are simply betting on a higher price for the commodity, not on an underlying business producing something and paying cash flow to them in the form of dividends or bond income. That is textbook speculation, in his view. Surely, a low-cost broadly diversified commodities futures index fund or ETF launched by Vanguard would attract great interest. Such broadly diversified indexes are harder to front-run, and there are already "financial engineers"—a term Bogle hates—working on solving some of the problems with contango.

Another area of intense interest in the industry is indexing hedge funds—a seemingly daunting task because hedge funds practice such specialized strategies and provide limited access to investors—but the financial engineers looking for their next score are, of course, up to it. Because nonqualified—that is, poor—investors can't buy hedge funds with million-dollar minimum investments, creating a low-cost retail index fund product presents some real challenges. Andrew Lo, a professor of finance at MIT, thinks he's found the solution by attempting to capture the beta—a measure of correlation—of hedge fund strategies via index futures. He is managing a new fund titled the Natixis ASG Global Alternatives Fund that implements his strategy, but it really is too soon to tell how effective the strategy will be. His fund has an exorbitant 1.61

percent expense ratio, but compared to hedge funds, which charge 2 percent of assets plus 20 percent of all profits, it seems almost reasonable.

Bogle, of course, is generally repulsed by almost everything about hedge funds—their outrageous fees, their excessive use of leverage, their speculative trading, and their false promises of outsized returns with little downside risk. And yet Vanguard CEO Bill McNabb has expressed interest in a workable hedge fund index. "We've had some experiments going on to see if we can replicate in an index fashion certain kinds of hedge fund returns and so forth," McNabb says. "I think the jury is still out. There's been a lot of academic research done on it, and we take the academic research and we apply it to see if it works, and if it does, we might do something, and if it doesn't, we won't." While certainly not a ringing endorsement, McNabb's statement reveals some of the interesting new directions Vanguard may take under his stewardship. Certainly, if it were possible to execute such an index effectively, Vanguard would do it much more cheaply than anyone else would.

Despite the plethora of index funds and ETFs, I think there is one investment solution that index investors still have a great need for that doesn't exist yet in a suitable form, and that is an effective asset allocation index. A landmark study by Gary Brinson in 1986 revealed that, if one ignores expenses (which of course in the real world one can't ignore), 93.6 percent of the variation in quarterly portfolio returns is due to the asset allocation of portfolios, not the individual security selection. And yet, because index funds are "unmanaged," they often seem like tools without a carpenter or an architect to put them to good use. Indeed, one of the greatest failings, I think, of the total stock market index—or, for that matter, any stock index—is that it doesn't answer the fundamental question of whether it's worth owning stocks at all. Bogle and Vanguard can tell investors that, after deducting expenses, the Vanguard Total Stock Market Index is better than the vast majority of equity funds, and it is. But they can't tell people in March of 2000 or October of 2007 that the stock market has peaked and is about to crash.

The efficient market hypothesis and its concomitant capital asset pricing model (or CAPM) were supposed to answer the "why-own-stocks" question via the notion of an equity risk premium—that investors are rewarded for the additional risks they take in stocks with greater returns than those on bonds. Therefore, those with long time horizons who can stand the greater volatility should always allocate more to stocks than to bonds, regardless of what the respective valuations of the different asset classes are at the time. Allocations under CAPM were determined based on past performance, past volatility, and past correlations—all of which are ultimately derived from the historical price movements of asset classes, not their current valuations or underlying business or economic fundamentals. And yet every mutual fund prospectus must carry the legal disclaimer: "Past performance is no guarantee of future results."

Of course, after the two brutal crashes, CAPM was also called into question, and I think justifiably so. It is my contention that CAPM and the efficient market hypothesis are really a political and religious ideology masquerading as a social science. Underlying them is a basic faith that in the long run, stocks always go up—that human beings are rational, efficient allocators of capital and that they will always be rewarded appropriately for the rational risks they take over the long term, just as in Christian theology God always rewards the faithful who follow His laws in the afterlife. When extrapolated to the larger society, as these theories were meant to be by their libertarian architects, they sought to validate via the scientific method a belief that capital markets get it right by themselves and that no government or social intervention of any sort is needed. The results of such extrapolation were disastrous, not only because individual investors are irrational and bad allocators of capital, but also because their corporate and financial agents have little interest or ability in rational allocation either.

In fact, CAPM's equity risk premium model has fared so poorly of late that over a 41-year period from 1968 through February of 2009, Arnott revealed in an article in the *Journal of Indexes*, stock investors earned no noticeable return premium over 20-year Treasury bonds at all, despite taking on considerable amounts of business risk and experiencing far more volatility in returns.[10] Nor is this to say bonds are better than stocks. After so many years of strong performance, bonds actually seem like a terrible investment in 2010, and yet just as with the stock bubble in 1999, investors are irrationally pouring tons of money into them. Rather, the question is whether there is a reasonable means for index investors to achieve an effective allocation of capital between stocks, bonds, cash, and perhaps alternative investments without getting caught up in bubbles.

While all the evidence indicates that short-term market timing doesn't work, there is something to be said for long-term strategic and tactical asset allocation moves that are based on the fundamental valuation principles that Ben Graham espoused. If such principles instead of EMH and CAPM had been applied in March 2000, there would have been no reason whatsoever to own overvalued large U.S. stocks at all when almost every other asset class and sector of the stock market— all bonds, small-cap stocks, REITs, foreign stocks, Treasury bills, and money markets—were so much cheaper on a fundamental basis unless stock index investors wanted to continue to participate in the speculative momentum that Bogle normally opposes. When the S&P 500 has a p/e ratio of 30, as it had at the March 2000 peak, the only real gains left to be had from it are speculative ones from the greater fool willing to throw more money at stocks, hoping that they will continue to surge. To put things in perspective, in March 2000, a risk-free one-year Treasury bill yielded almost 6 percent compared to the highly suspect 3.3 percent earnings yield on the S&P 500. That is 6 percent risk free versus 3.3 percent from companies that routinely like to goose their earnings with accounting tricks—the "rational" choice from a fundamental standpoint seems obvious in retrospect.

To Vanguard's credit, it does offer a number of asset allocation products, but most of them tend to have static allocations or age-dependent ones—its series of "target-date retirement" funds that are designed to have heavy weightings in stocks when investors are young and greater weightings in bonds when they're old. Such strategies leave relative fundamental valuation out of the picture. Underlying target-date funds are the same faulty assumptions of the capital asset pricing model—that, in the long term, stocks will always beat bonds because of the supposed equity risk premium. There is also the assumption that bonds are always safer than stocks, when they're not. A better analysis would seek to evaluate the present value of the future cash flows of each asset class and invest the most in those assets with the greatest expected cash flow yield and the least expected downside risk. In other words, look at the relative valuation of the different asset classes, the stability of their respective cash flows, their credit quality, and their duration risk. Then invest accordingly in the cheapest and safest assets. Insist upon a tangible cash flow yield premium on riskier assets, such as stocks, rather than simply assuming, based on past performance, that stocks will continue to deliver a premium in the future. This would prevent such allocation funds from automatically investing in stocks or bonds when there is a bubble in either asset class.

Of course, some might say that asset allocation decisions are what financial planners are for. But assuming that indexers should just simply hire a financial planner to do the allocating for them raises the question of what the purpose of low-cost indexing is in the first place. That's because hiring a financial planner adds another financial intermediary to the mix, another "croupier," in Bogle's words, who will reduce investors' returns typically by about 1 percentage point per year. So the question is whether it's possible to create an asset allocation fund that reaps all the potential gains that indexers normally enjoy without paying extra for financial advice. This seems to me to be the primary challenge for indexing going forward.

Vanguard has tried to address this problem somewhat in its Vanguard Asset Allocation Fund and Vanguard Managed Payout funds, but with little success. In Asset Allocation's case, the fund has the flexibility to invest in stocks, bonds, and cash in any amount, and it uses an indexed strategy to achieve exposure to its stocks and bonds. But the fund's prospectus objective is to deliver stock-like returns with less downside risk than the stock market, and it is generally benchmarked against the S&P 500 or an "asset allocation composite" of 65 percent stocks/35 percent bonds. Such an objective and benchmark give the fund a bias toward stocks and its managers an "equity-centric" mentality in which the goal is not to produce stable returns for shareholders but to beat the stock market. As a result, what the managers at the fund's subadvisor Mellon Capital consider their "neutral allocation" is a 65 percent weighting in stocks. Moreover, the fund can switch only between the S&P 500, long-term Treasury bonds, and cash. This limits the range of asset classes too much. Given the fund's stock bias, it was 100 percent allocated to stocks throughout most of 2008 and fell by 36.4 percent that year, just slightly less than the market itself.

Although the managed payout funds are relatively new and have the flexibility to invest in even more asset classes than the Vanguard Asset Allocation Fund, they too seem to be stock-centric, as they suffered sharp losses during the 2008 downturn and continue to hold hefty equity weightings even in the Vanguard Managed Payout Distribution Focus Fund, the most conservative of the three funds meant for retirees. The allocations in these funds are determined by an investment committee much like a pension plan or foundation, but the methodology employed remains largely a mystery, and so far an unsuccessful one. Would it not be better to create a straightforward rules-based asset allocation index that shifts between classes based on fundamental valuation, allocating more to the cheapest asset classes that offered the greatest yield? And would it not be better to end the equity bias once and for all and simply stress profits, or what the industry calls absolute returns, as the primary goal? Perhaps then when the next bear market comes, Vanguard will capture even more assets than it did during the last one.

CHAPTER 19

The Future of Vanguard

How could the future of the Vanguard Group as a business be anything but bright? The low-cost provider in a commoditized industry always wins, and contrary to what many of its exorbitantly paid executives may think, the mutual fund industry became commoditized with the popularization of the index fund. As long as Vanguard remains true to Bogle's founding principles, it should continue to be the Wal-Mart of the fund industry, undercutting all of its competitors on price. And unless one or more of those competitors wakes up and decides to convert from an external management structure to an internal mutualized one, they will always be one step behind the leader, always forced to rob Peter—fund shareholders—to pay Paul—the management company—with their higher fees inevitably causing them to lag. Ultimately, their two-master structure is a loser's strategy.

But because many millionaires have been made in the fund management biz, companies will not give up their gravy train so easily. So I wouldn't hold my breath for another mutualization. Over time, what will likely happen is a further bifurcation and consolidation of the industry in which only a few giant fish control most of the assets, while scores of tiny minnows manage higher-cost niche products. I would expect the mid-sized fund companies such as Janus Funds or Gabelli Funds to ultimately disappear, gobbled up most likely in an acquisition when index funds and ETFs consume their profit margins or assets rush out the door during the next downturn. Vanguard, in all likelihood, will be the biggest beneficiary of this asset rush.

With $1.4 trillion in assets and more than 12,000 employees, Vanguard can hardly be seen, if it ever could be, as the work of one man anymore. Still, a company's culture is often established from the top down, so it's important to understand a little about Bill McNabb to get a sense of where Vanguard is heading.

In many respects, McNabb seems like a more open, outgoing version of Jack Brennan. With a Wharton MBA and a love of team sports like rowing, soccer, and basketball, he seems unlikely to be someone who rocks the boat. Affable to a fault and media friendly, he is one of the few Vanguard executives to navigate the divide between Brennan and Bogle with relative ease. McNabb's relationship with Bogle is more grandfatherly and mutually respectful than Oedipal like Brennan's. "McNabb came down and had a personal visit with me on his first day in office," Bogle recalls. "He was very nice, very thoughtful. I try to comport myself to not give him any problems. If I have issues, one thing or another, and there are plenty of those things, I will talk to him about them. He's been very gracious." About the differences between Vanguard's three CEOs, Bogle says: "What I see, honestly, I am probably the consummate truster and Brennan is the consummate counter and Bill, I would have to say, is a reasonably decent combination of the two. By reasonably decent I don't mean anything that sounds negative, but halfway between us."

Although Jeremy Duffield, Vanguard's head of international planning and development, clearly could have been a contender for the CEO position himself, he thinks McNabb has the ideal balance of Bogle's and Brennan's best qualities. "I think of Vanguard as the house that Jack built," Duffield says. "So that Jack [Bogle] provided the vision and founded the company. And he provided the leadership and the principles and the values and got everyone behind him. But it was really Jack

Brennan—not just after he took over, but when he was understudying Jack Bogle—who built the team out and gave us all the processes and the modern thinking and the management capabilities to make it work. In that sense they were tremendously complementary. . . . [McNabb] has learned from both of them, which is fantastic—the idea that he's been around so long and he's worked with both and can see both sides. It's an opportunity to take the best of both and sort of blend it. What a great position and a great man to do it."

Unlike Bogle, who, despite his belief in shareholder democracy, likes to take charge of things, McNabb is definitely a delegator and team player, which in many respects is essential for effectively running an organization of such an immense size. It seems unlikely, though, that under his lead, Vanguard will do anything revolutionary to further upend the status quo in the fund industry. In all probability, it will remain conservative to a fault. If Bogle was like a bad-boy entrepreneur with a disruptive technology—the index fund—to shake the industry up, McNabb seems more like the genial CEO of a stodgy old-economy company with tremendous customer loyalty to products everybody knows and loves.

Whether or not the shareholders of Vanguard Funds will fare as well under McNabb as The Vanguard Group does as a business is another matter entirely. Their fate depends on the whims of securities markets because most of Vanguard's assets remain indexed to those securities markets. And it's evident that what's good for The Vanguard Group isn't always good for its fund shareholders. Consider the case of the commission-free ETFs. In the month of May 2010, when the free-trading program launched, trading activity in ETFs at Vanguard's brokerage division was up by 150 percent over the same month a year earlier.[1] All of that trading is great for Vanguard as a business, increasing the volume and popularity of its products. In fact, many financial advisers and institutional investors won't even touch an ETF unless it has a requisite level of daily volume indicating that it is liquid enough to trade. So the increased visibility of the products is vital to a business seeking to gather more assets. But Bogle might argue that a 150 percent increase in trading in one month is a sign that some dangerous speculation may be going on. That can be very unhealthy from an investor standpoint.

Going forward, the key question to ask when evaluating Vanguard and McNabb's management of it will be, is growth "the only evidence of life," as Bogle once claimed. Or can positive evolution also mean getting smaller, leaner, and smarter or even just thinking and behaving differently from the pack? At a certain point, the incremental expense ratio savings to be had from increasing assets become de minimis, and one must ask whether the sacrifices made to achieve that additional scale are necessary or even beneficial to Vanguard's existing shareholders. Is it worth, for instance, selling an inferior product like the Russell 2000 ETF when Vanguard already offers a superior small-cap one tracking an MSCI index that has outperformed the Russell by a significant margin? Sure, it will be popular with institutional investors who like to track familiar benchmarks, but at what cost to individual investors who don't know any better? And at what cost to Vanguard shareholders overall, who must subsidize the launch of the new ETF until it can achieve the scale necessary to pay for itself?

The two most questionable areas of Vanguard's expansion plans that will bear watching are its advertising budget and its new product offerings. One of its most high-profile ventures under McNabb has been an aggressive advertising campaign launched in March 2010 to promote "Vanguarding." According to a schmaltzy video with soaring inspirational music at the company's Web site, Vanguarding is "a behavior, a philosophy, a call to action." The ad, which can mainly be found online and in print, actually refers to Vanguard's at-cost structure. Vanguard's market share of the mutual fund industry in the United States is 13 percent, according to Bogle, so clearly there are some investors who haven't gotten the message yet, but since Vanguard is the largest mutual fund company, are such advertisements really necessary?

The fact that Vanguard hired a tony New York ad agency, Kirshenbaum Bond Senecal & Partners, and that the "Vanguarding" campaign was first tested with focus groups for its consumer appeal seems out of character for the ultra-efficient no-frills fund company. A *New*

York Times story about the campaign makes it sound as though it were scripted for central casting: "The genesis of the idea, according to Izzy DeBellis, executive creative director at Kirshenbaum Bond Senecal, was the phrase, 'Vanguard your money' which 'someone put up on the wall' during a brainstorming session. His reaction was, 'Oooh, I like that,' he said, because it took advantage of the fact 'that Vanguard has "guard" in it.' Further thought led to the concept of 'creating a platform by making Vanguard a verb,' Mr. DeBellis said, transforming it into 'a call to action, a philosophy.'"[2]

The images in the ad seem like kitschy allusions to middle-class comfort and security, with parents steering a toddler through the grass; a wholesome-looking African-American man being kissed on the cheek by his wife at his retirement party; a grandfather, father, and young son with wind-swept hair gazing blissfully at the sun setting over a craggy promontory, smiling and unafraid of the future. In true sanctimony, the ad even equates the highest religious value, "the Golden Rule," with Vanguarding. This is more Darrin Stephens than Don Draper. As one advertising blog put it, the soft-focus ad that strives for authenticity when the more authentic thing to do would be to not advertise at all actually "cheapens the Vanguard brand."[3] It also seems a little hypocritical to be using existing shareholders' capital to attract new shareholders via a marketing campaign that trumpets the firm's shareholder-first attitude. The only way such a campaign can be justified from a fiduciary standpoint is if it attracts enough assets to reduce the overall costs for existing shareholders.

Bogle, for his part, doesn't seem too fond of the campaign, not that he's ever been fond of any form of marketing. Aside from his obvious objection to the costs involved, he's even offended as a strict grammarian by the term Vanguarding. "I'm not so sure about turning nouns into verbs or adverbs," he remarks. "But I hope Merrill Lynch doesn't try it. Have you considered Merrill Lynching?"

Is this a case of market share being bought via slick ad-speak, not earned via low costs and outperformance? McNabb doesn't see it that way. He says the costs of running the ad are "a rounding error," adding, "I don't remember the exact number [Vanguard spent on advertising] 20 years ago, but we just looked at this recently, and what we are spending as a percentage of revenue or assets is dramatically lower. Absolute dollars it's more because we are a lot bigger." He also thinks that it is essential to explain to the investing public how Vanguard's mutual at-cost structure is different from all of its competitors, and that this ad could facilitate that.

Yet Bogle finds the calculating of marketing costs as a percentage of assets troubling because he believes that investors should be looking at the total dollars spent instead. "That campaign is said to cost $50 million as reported in the *New York Times*," he says. "Sources here tell me that it's more than that. People who run the campaign say generally our advertising costs had been running about $20 million a year [prior to the Vanguarding campaign]. . . . It comes back to the fact that we are spending many, many, many times what we were, although it is at least possible we are spending a smaller ratio. . . . But people should look at the dollars, not the ratios—fund management fees versus fund expense ratios, advertising expenditures versus ratio of advertising expenditures, total expense ratios compared to total expenses. All of that is important, yet we somehow deluded everybody into thinking the ratios are what count." Bogle observes that when Vanguard managed $300 billion, its funds had an average expense ratio of about 0.30 percent or total annual operating expenses of about $900 million. Today the expense ratio is lower at 0.20 percent, but Vanguard has $1.4 trillion, leading to total operating expenses of $2.8 billion. That doesn't seem like significant economies of scale, in his view.

In fairness to Vanguard, although the initial costs of the ad campaign have already been spent, McNabb says that if it isn't working—that is, bringing in enough new assets to reduce overall costs for existing fund shareholders—then he will simply cancel it. "One of the things we did when we launched this campaign is we created it in such a way that if we don't think it's resonating or doing the things we want it to do, we can turn it off quickly," he says. That makes perfect sense, but existing shareholders may wonder whether it was worth spending their money on such a venture, which really has nothing to do with them, since they already know how great Vanguard is, if it doesn't ultimately reduce their total costs but increases them instead.

Similarly, going forward, shareholders must ask whether Vanguard is living up to its fiduciary principles with each new product launch.

Vanguard now has 182 mutual funds and ETFs, according to Morningstar, and many more ETFs are on the way. How much is too much, especially when the firm's founder believes that a total stock market index fund is the optimal choice for equity investors? Do investors really need individual sector ETFs that are exposed to heightened levels of volatility and industry concentration risk? Do they need the newly launched Vanguard Explorer Value Fund, a multimanaged small-cap fund, when the firm already offers a perfectly good small-cap value index fund that will probably beat the new fund over time?

There have been a number of notable failures among the company's new product launches that appear in retrospect to be real head-scratchers. The company acquired Laudus Rosenberg U.S. Large/Mid Capitalization Long/Short Equity Fund and converted it into the Vanguard Market Neutral Fund in November 2007, dividing its assets between its original manager, Axa Rosenberg, and Vanguard's quantitative group. The fund keeps equal amounts long and short and attempts to have a zero beta, or a correlation that neutralizes the effect of the stock market. It instead depends on the effectiveness of the managers' stock picking skills to generate returns. From a cultural perspective, the concept of market neutrality at the fund industry's biggest index shop seemed a poor fit to begin with, especially because Bogle doesn't think that the vast majority of money managers can beat the market. So once the market's effects are neutralized, how much "alpha," or excess return, is left for shareholders? If the efficient market theorists can claim even a modicum of accuracy, wouldn't the return for a market-neutral fund after deducting costs be less than zero?

Bogle feels that the Market Neutral Fund was more about marketing and gathering assets from investors who have become increasingly interested in hedge funds than about actually offering a useful product. "The managed payout funds and the market neutral funds have just simply not done a good job," he says. "I don't know how to describe them. . . . I would say the test is—is this better than the index fund? Can it be better? The answer to that is, honestly, no. The index is the gold standard." Since Vanguard acquired the fund in 2007, it has produced negative returns in a volatile market where such strategies are supposed to protect investors' capital.

The three Vanguard Managed Payout funds also seem to have been launched to satisfy a marketing need and jump on the bandwagon of a hot new kind of fund. At the time when they were opened in May 2008, endowment funds like David Swensen's at Yale University were getting a lot of media play for producing spectacular returns by investing in all sorts of alternative asset classes, such as commodities, hedge funds, and private equity. As a consequence, the idea of creating a "Yale portfolio" was all the rage. The three Vanguard funds promised annual distributions to shareholders of 3 percent, 5 percent, or 7 percent over three-year periods, but because returns were so poor during the bear market, payouts had to be cut, and some portion of them were really a return of capital and not genuine returns. Much of what was inside the funds was a varying mixture of plain vanilla index funds and, surprise, Vanguard Market Neutral Fund—hardly a Yale endowment type of portfolio.

McNabb himself is hesitant about launching too many new products. But there are two key areas of interest to him—ETFs in general and non-U.S. investments. "ETFs we are going to continue to build out," he says. "It's a structure that works for certain kinds of investors and proves easier to administer for certain kinds of platforms, and it has taken the index story to a whole new constituency. . . . The second area that you should expect over time is probably a more robust set of non-U.S. more global investments for our U.S. investors. That's an area we could probably be richer in."

Although the timing couldn't be worse, if there is one mainstream investment product that Vanguard does seem to be lacking, it is some sort of international or global bond fund or ETF. The foreign bond market is bigger than the bond market in the United States, so it would make sense that the biggest index fund shop would offer an investment vehicle for gaining exposure to the foreign market. Many countries also have better economic and fiscal health than the United States, so investing in their bonds could provide necessary diversification if the United States slips back into a recession. Since competing management companies tend to overcharge for foreign funds and ETFs even more so than for domestic ones, Vanguard could provide some real value added for its shareholders and new investors by offering such funds with much lower costs. That said, bond yields were minuscule all over the world in

2010, and if inflation suddenly spikes and interest rates go up, the bond bubble will probably pop in the worst possible way, not just in the United States but everywhere.

Bogle, for his part, doesn't see the need for many more new fund products and even hates the word "product" to begin with because he thinks of the relationship between a fund management company and its investors as a fiduciary one built on trust, not a commercial one based on selling products. "I banned the use of the word 'product' here back in the early 90s or late 80s," he says. "After I left, that ban vanished. . . . I look at [a mutual fund] more as a trust service. It's a trust account [meant for the long-term investor]. Products, by contrast, often appear on the whim of the market. The most fundamental thing we do about marketing, which is the most abused term in business, is finding out what people want and giving it to them. That is the fundamental principle to marketing. If you are trying to give them something they don't want, change what you are giving them until it suits them. Of all the idiotic ways to invest money, that has got to be at the very top of the list."

Nor does Bogle think that Vanguard needs to launch any new "products" to continue to grow at a rapid pace. "We continue to maintain the highest growth rate in the mutual fund industry. About five years ago, we were $400 billion behind Fidelity, and now we are $400 billion ahead of Fidelity. That's an $800 billion swing! I don't see that we need more growth than that. I think we should be very chary about growth. Growth, as I've said in my speeches, should be organic and not forced. Grow because you are doing the right thing for your clients."

So if Vanguard already has all the funds and ETF products it needs, how can an ambitious new CEO of America's biggest mutual fund company make his mark? One real area of promise that even Bogle now agrees makes sense is overseas expansion. In the past, he was hesitant because of the costs involved with building a business from the ground up in a new country with a different competitive landscape and different securities laws, but now that Vanguard has the scale and resources he thinks are needed to accomplish such a task, he's all for it. "Anybody with half a brain—I pretend to have at least that much—knew we were moving into a global world," Bogle quips. "And one way or another we would have to compete internationally. It was a matter of timing more than anything else. I was ready to do it. Back when you were in the late 80s, to pick a date, we didn't really have the resources to do it." Still, Bogle let his right-hand man Jeremy Duffield return to his Australian homeland in 1996 to try to duplicate the Vanguard experiment in the land Down Under. By 2010 the Australia subsidiary managed $70 billion and was the country's fifth largest asset manager.

It's quite clear that overseas expansion is an essential part of Bill McNabb's business strategy. In addition to Australia, Vanguard now has offices in Belgium, France, Switzerland, the Netherlands, Korea, Singapore, Japan, and the United Kingdom. Yet he doesn't see Vanguard's foreign ventures just as growth opportunities. Like Bogle, he possesses a missionary zeal for low costs and indexing. So he doesn't call the transatlantic expansion a business strategy; he calls it a "non-U.S. aspiration" to differentiate Vanguard from other multinationals. "Many companies diversify overseas because they have to," he explains. "Coke and Pepsi are looking to grow, and they can't sell that many more cans of sodas to U.S. consumers, so they go to China. For us, the mutual fund business is a very fragmented one, and you could make a great argument that just stick to your knitting in the U.S. and you will have enough opportunities to continue to grow and prosper, and that would be a very fair argument. And that's probably why we were reluctant to expand overseas. But over the last few years, as I've wandered around either as a guest at Harvard Business School for one of their advanced management programs or traveling the globe, I cannot tell you how many different people from different countries have come to me and said, 'When is Vanguard going to come to my country, my region, or my area because we need what you guys stand for.'"

With only about 8 percent of its assets overseas, Vanguard definitely has room to grow in this area, so even from a "nonaspirational" purely business perspective, McNabb's plan provides a great way for him to really make his mark as a CEO. But the road will not be an easy one.

There are regulatory obstacles, additional costs, entrenched competition, and a simple lack of brand recognition in many foreign markets. And yet McNabb is hopeful: "Will we be able to go to the Chinese individual investor market in the short run? Probably not. But we are seeing a lot of interest from Asia, especially in Singapore and Hong Kong. And we are continuing to see interest from Europe, in the U.K. and the Netherlands in particular. And Australia has been pretty robust. It's probably 10 countries in all where we've had pretty good business."

Still, if McNabb wants to leave a great legacy behind, not only for The Vanguard Group as a businessman, but also for Vanguard fund shareholders as a true steward of their capital, there is one radical step he could take that might make him as famous and well-regarded even as Bogle. That would be to become a true shareholder activist. If the average mutual fund company votes 84 percent of the time in favor of management-sponsored proposals regarding executive compensation, imagine the impact Vanguard would have on the industry if it started routinely voting against compensation proposals and against directors who support excessive compensation schemes. As the largest mutual fund company, it would simply put its competitors to shame by doing so, and the pressure for them to follow suit would be immense. What's more, McNabb would be declared a hero, and investors would love Vanguard even more for behaving as a true fiduciary.

Bogle thinks that it's inevitable that Vanguard and other fund companies will become more active in the role they play during proxy voting. "Good corporate citizenship is going to be demanded, either by response to the call for a federal statute on fiduciary duty, which is a long way away at the moment, or the fact that investors are going to care how their money is managed," he says. "They are going to take it to people who vote actively on their behalf." As an indexer, which must buy and hold stocks forever, it would behoove Vanguard most of all to start really caring about corporate governance to improve its shareholders' long-term returns. Bogle hopes that one day the company will ally itself with other indexers and lead the charge for a more activist shareholder base: "Given the competitive nature of things, there will probably be some consortium of large index managers BlackRock/Barclays, State Street, and Vanguard being in the vanguard of that move."

Given Vanguard's immense size and the esteem with which investors hold it, there seems little reason for the company to remain passive regarding corporate governance. If there is a concern that the company could lose some institutional 401k or pension fund business from the executives it might vote against in a proxy, it's long past the time that such fears should be set aside for the benefit of fund shareholders. "Corporations have to show a little maturity here," Bogle observes. "What is a company's board of directors going to say when someone picks Vanguard to run their pension plan, tells them Vanguard is the best manager in the world but Vanguard votes against reelection of some director? Will the manager say we are going to fire [Vanguard]? You cannot do that, and it would be a grave error to do that explicitly. And if you do it passively, people won't know why you are doing it. Reason prevails somewhere along the way. So as we go down the road, I think people are going to have to get used to owners of stock behaving as owners of stock. And they are also going to have to get used to [the agents of] owners of stock acting in the interest of the people who they represent."

To further burnish its image, Vanguard could also increase the level of disclosure it has as a mutually owned fund company. If Vanguard willingly chose to disclose its top five executives' salaries and bonuses and exactly how much every senior executive, money manager, and director had invested in its funds without waiting for regulators to coerce the fund industry to do so, it would prove once and for all that it was really a mutually owned fund company in which there is no corporate veil separating management from its shareholders. It would put pressure on Vanguard's competitors to do the same. The increased transparency would be seen as a major competitive advantage—a selling point. The same could be said for changing the structure of Vanguard's board of directors so that it is 100 percent independent and spending the money to allow that board to have independent experts advise it. This too would further strengthen the image of Vanguard as shareholder-owned and shareholder-controlled as opposed to shareholder-owned but management-controlled.

All the above suggestions would enable the company to remain in the vanguard of the fund industry in terms of stewardship and fiduciary duty. While Bogle has advocated and fought for many of these changes in the industry at large, it's hard to say whether he would implement them himself if he were still in charge of Vanguard. As he often remarks, it's a lot easier for him to be critical now that he's not sitting in the executive suite of the world's largest mutual fund company. But if McNabb wants to ensure his legacy as a great man—as opposed to just a great businessman—such changes would be worth considering.

Bogle's legacy, of course, is as assured as Vanguard's. He will always be seen as a great man by those who knew and loved him. And the ranks of these are many, not only because of his inventiveness and his advocacy, but also for his genuine sense of humanity. During one of the last times I spoke with him, he reiterated that, when he was in charge, almost every Vanguard employee had hanging in his or her cubicle his quote, "For god's sake, let's always keep Vanguard a place where judgment has a fighting chance to triumph over process." Although, given the company's ungodly size, bureaucratic process must inevitably triumph, he couldn't be more sincere about his sentiments and his belief in individual recognition and achievement.

"He has always made a point to connect with anybody whose path he's crossed," notes his son John, Jr. "I remember it made a strong impression on me as a kid, that whenever I would go with him to his office during the week or on the weekend, and we would walk in to the building, a security guard would be there, and he would know that security guard by name. He knew if one of the guard's kids was sick, would ask about his child, or wife, and this was a part-time security guard at the lowest level of the organization who is not there much of the time, and my dad knows this guy well. He knows and cares about this guy. Until the company was thousands of people, I think he probably would have been able to have known just about everybody by name. He just instinctually wants to make connections with people, and I can see him being disappointed that he no longer would be able to do that when Vanguard reached a certain size."

No less a personage than Bill Clinton thinks that Bogle embodies what's best about the American spirit: an ethos of hard work, square dealing, and doing things for the greater good. In the foreword to the latest edition of Bogle's *Enough,* Clinton wrote: "John Bogle is a brilliant and good man, and every concerned citizen can learn and benefit from the important lessons he shares in *Enough.* It is a reminder that what Alexis de Tocqueville said about our nation so long ago remains true: America is great because America is good, and if she ever ceases to be good, she will no longer be great. *Enough* is about reclaiming both."[4]

Of course, it was Bogle who was eager to point out to me that Bill Clinton wrote that intro to his book and that he has more awards and honorary degrees than he can count. His ego does sometimes get in the way of his better parts. He's also fond of saying, "Who else but me speaks out?" and yet he's correct that no one else in the fund industry as far as I can tell does. But does that say more about the quality of Bogle's character or the lack thereof in the fund industry? That's a tougher question to answer.

Just to please him and name a few of the many accolades he's received—are you reading this, Jack?—here's a much abbreviated list of a few highlights: *Time* magazine named him one of the world's 100 most powerful and influential people. *Fortune* magazine called him one of the investment industry's four giants of the twentieth century. Princeton University gave him the Woodrow Wilson Award for distinguished achievement in the nation's service. He's been inducted into the Fixed Income Analysts Society Hall of Fame. (Perhaps if they ever do a display of hall of famers, they can include a prospectus and slide rule in Bogle's case.) He also has received honorary doctorate degrees from Princeton University, University of Delaware, University of Rochester, New School University, Susquehanna University, Eastern University, Widener University, Albright College, Pennsylvania State University, and Drexel University.

And yet if there is one great public legacy Bogle leaves behind to society, it may not be found in all the awards he's received or the books he's written or the speeches he's delivered or even in Vanguard itself. It is in the investors he's helped. During a dinner he hosted for Bogle at his condo in Miami, Boglehead cofounder Taylor Larimore, like

Jeremy Duffield, remarked that it was "the house that Jack built."[5] Only Larimore wasn't referring to Vanguard. Call it Bogle's other house. His better one. Between the two—Vanguard's and Larimore's—the agents running this behemoth of a financial institution must always remember that it is the little houses Jack built all across the nation that count, more so than the big. And just as long as they do, they will truly be preserving Jack Bogle's legacy for posterity.

ACKNOWLEDGMENTS

I would like to thank John Bogle first and foremost for graciously providing me with so much of his time. I truly believe he is in the vanguard of the entire fund industry and worthy of great praise and admiration. I also would like to thank John's assistants Kevin Laughlin, Emily Snyder, and Sara Hoffman, all of whom were indefatigable in helping me dig up stats and finding me contacts to call. Jack's brother William "Bud" Bogle was also a great help, as were his daughter Barbara Renninger and his son John Bogle, Jr., in explaining Jack's persona and history. Tucker Hewes of Hewes Communications was invaluable in helping me set up interviews with Jeremy Grantham and Rob Arnott, both of whom I am grateful to as well. Several Vanguard crew members both past and present were also generous with their time, among them Jeremy Duffield, Gus Sauter, Jim Riepe, Ralph Packard, Raymond Kaplinsky, Barbara Scudder, John Neff, and, perhaps most of all, current CEO Bill McNabb. Eliot Spitzer, it was great talking to you. Also thanks go to Lawrence Wilson, Burt Malkiel, Chandler Hardwick, Joe Torsella, Rick Stengel, Arthur Zeikel, Dan Wiener, Larry Swedroe, Taylor Larimore, and Gary Weinstein. My former *BusinessWeek* editor Jeff Laderman helped set this project up, and for this I am grateful. And I am also thankful for the insights of my current editors Gary Krebs and MaryTherese Church. Finally, I want to thank my family and my wife, Tanya, most of all, without whose love, support, and assistance this book would never have been written. And to my little dog Lucy—thank you for being by my side every single day. As the above list reveals, a book isn't the work of one man. It takes a village.

NOTES

Note: Materials not otherwise cited are personal communications.

PREFACE
1. John C. Bogle, *The Battle for the Soul of Capitalism* (New Haven, Conn.: Yale University Press, 2005), pp. 29–30.
2. John C. Bogle, "Uneasy Lies the Head That Wears the Crown," Speech at First FUSE Research Network Award for Lifetime Impact and Commitment to Investors, Boston, Mass., October 26, 2010.
3. John C. Bogle, *The Battle for the Soul of Capitalism*, p. 43.

CHAPTER 1
1. John C. Bogle, *Enough* (Hoboken, N.J.: John Wiley & Sons, 2009), p. 3.
2. Quoted in "A License to Bunk," *The Insurance Monitor*, vol. 65, May 1917, pp. 164–165.
3. "Says Insurance Co. Was Built on Wind," *New York Times*, December 4, 1907, http://query.nytimes.com/mem/archive-free/pdf?res=FA0D1E FD3C5A15738DDDAD0894DA415B878CF1D3.
4. "A License to Bunk," pp. 164–165.
5. Arthur Ignatius Judge, "A History of the Canning Industry," *The Canning Trade*, vol. 37, no. 21, 1914, p. 96.
6. John C. Bogle, "Leaving the Things That You Touch Better than You Found Them," speech before the Union League of Philadelphia, April 10, 2007.
7. "Remarks by John C. Bogle, '47," The Hollerith Lecture Series at Blair Academy, Blairstown, N.J., April 2, 2002.
8. "The Economic Role of the Investment Company," in *John Bogle, on Investing: The First 50 Years* (New York: McGraw-Hill, 2001), p. 355.
9. Ibid., p. 360.

CHAPTER **2**

1. "A Mutual Fund Pioneer Looks Ahead," *Invesment Dealers' Digest,* February 1960, unpaged.

CHAPTER **3**

1. Walter Morgan, interview, May 4, 1995.
2. Ibid.

CHAPTER **4**

1. Information obtained from records at Blair Academy.
2. Jack Bogle, interview, July 13, 1995.
3. Ibid.
4. Ibid.
5. Robert Doran, interview, June 26, 1995.
6. Jack Bogle, interview, May 8, 1995.
7. Ibid.
8. Ibid.

CHAPTER **5**

1. Jack Bogle, interview, August 15, 1995.
2. Barbara Hauptfuher, interview, August 3, 1995.
3. "Vanguard: A Fund Family for the 1990s," *Fortune,* December 31, 1991, pp. 80–88.
4. Memo written by Charles Root, August 20, 1970.

CHAPTER **6**

1. Jack Bogle, interview, May 8, 1995.
2. Ibid.
3. "Bogle's Do-It-Yourself Mutual Funds," *Sunday Bulletin Business,* February 9, 1975.
4. Karen West, interview, May 4, 1995.
5. Ian MacKinnon, interview, May 3, 1995.

CHAPTER **7**

1. Jack Bogle, interview, May 3, 1995.
2. Robert Doran, interview, November 20, 1995.
3. Ray Klapinsky, interview, May 4, 1995.

4. Jan Twardowski, interview, July 26, 1995.

5. Phil Fina, interview, May 15, 1995.

6. Jack Bogle, interview, August 17, 1995.

CHAPTER **8**

1. Jack VanDerhei, Sarah Holden, and Luis Alonso, "401(k) Plan Asset Allocation, Account Balances, and Loan Activity in 2008," *EBRI Issue Brief*, no. 335, October 2009, p. 16.

2. John P. Freeman and Stewart L. Brown, "Mutual Fund Advisory Fees: The Cost of Conflicts of Interest," *Journal of Corporation Law*, December 16, 2003, p. 633.

3. Lynn O'Shaughnessy, "Investing; A 401(k) Picks a Mutual Fund. Who Gets a Perk?" *New York Times*, February 15, 2004, http://www.nytimes .com/2004/02/15/business/investing-a-401-k-picks-a-mutual-fund-who -gets-a-perk.html?pagewanted=1.

4. "Equity Ownership in America 2005," a study by the Investment Company Institute and the Securities Industry Association, p. 1.

5. Lee Walczak, "The Mood Now," *BusinessWeek*, August 27, 2001, http:// www.businessweek.com/magazine/content/01_35/b3746601.htm.

6. Andy Serwer, "A Nation of Traders," *Fortune*, October 11, 1999, http:// money.cnn.com/magazines/fortune/fortune_archive/1999/10/11/267 017/index.htm.

7. Alexis M. Herman and Katharine G. Abraham, "Employment Cost Indexes, 1975–99," Bulletin 2532, U.S. Department of Labor, September 2000, p. 8.

8. John P. Freeman, "Statement of John P. Freeman, Professor of Law, University of South Carolina Law School, before the Senate Governmental Affairs Subcommittee on Financial Management, the Budget, and International Security," January 27, 2004, p. 6.

CHAPTER **9**

1. Ross Kerber, "Bogle Reversed on Pay Issue," *Boston Globe*, May 12, 2006, http://www.boston.com/business/articles/2006/05/12/bogle _reversed_on_pay_issue/.

2. Ibid.

3. Craig Stock, "'Yes, Virginia': The Compensation Question," Vanguard blog, April 27, 2010, http://www.vanguardblog.com/2010.04.27/yes -virginia-the-compensation-question.html.

4. Daniel Wiener, "Partnership Still Beats Indexing," *Independent Adviser for Vanguard Investors*, vol. 19, no. 7, July 2009, p. 16.
5. Ibid., p. 15.
6. Charity Navigator 2009 CEO Compensation Study, August 2009, www.charitynavigator.org, p. 1.

CHAPTER 10

1. Jennifer Boden and David Kovacs, "A Tale of Two Markets—and the Best Stocks in Them," *Taking Stock*, Turner Investment Partners, fourth quarter 2009, p. 1.
2. David M. Blitzer and Srikant Dash, "The Tale of an Index in Bull and Bear Markets: S&P 500 from 1997 to 2002," Standard & Poor's study, August 24, 2002, p. 3, http://www2.standardandpoors.com/spf/pdf/index/090502.pdf.
3. "Introduction to Secular Bear Markets," http://www.prudentbear.com/dmdocuments/secularbear.pdf.
4. Paul Krugman, "An Economic Legend," *New York Times*, June 11, 2004, http://www.nytimes.com/2004/06/11/opinion/11KRUG.html.
5. *2010 Investment Company Institute Fact Book*, 50th edition, p. 126.
6. Alvin Sargent, monologue from film *Other People's Money*, 1991, http://www.americanrhetoric.com/MovieSpeeches/moviespeechother peoplesmoneypeck.html.
7. As quoted in Maggie Mahar, *Bull! A History of the Boom and Bust, 1982–2004* (New York: HarperCollins, 2004), p. 95.
8. John C. Bogle, *The Battle for the Soul of Capitalism* (New Haven, Conn.: Yale University Press, 2005), p. 163.
9. Ibid., pp. 154–155.
10. *2010 Investment Company Institute Fact Book*, 50th edition, p. 143.
11. John C. Bogle. "Three Odysseys—The Long Adventurous Journeys of the Stock Market, the Mutual Fund Industry, and Vanguard," remarks before the Wisemen's Group, New York City, November 15, 2001.

CHAPTER 11

1. As described in Justin Fox, *The Myth of the Rational Market* (New York: HarperCollins, 2009), pp. 111–112.
2. Ibid., p. 130.
3. Ibid., p. 129.
4. Paul Volcker, "The Time We Have Is Growing Short," *New York Review of Books*, vol. 57, no. 11, June 24, 2010, p. 12.

5. Benjamin Graham and David L. Dodd, *Security Analysis*, 6th ed. (New York: McGraw-Hill, 2009), p. 70.
6. Lewis Braham, "Vanguard's Arachnophobia," Fund Watch column, SmartMoney.com, March 23, 2000.

CHAPTER **12**

1. Hal Lux, "Can Vanguard Stay the Course?" *Institutional Investor*, vol. 33, no. 8, August 1, 1999.
2. J. M. Lawrence, "Frank Brennan, 93; Banker Had an Honest, Caring Way," *Boston Globe*, April 8, 2010, http://www.boston.com/boston globe/obituaries/articles/2010/04/08/frank_brennan_93_banker_had _an_honest_caring_way/.
3. Amy Barrett, "Vanguard's New Boss: 'Being Famous Was Never on My Agenda,'" August 21, 1997, http://www.businessweek.com/1997/35/ b3542124.htm.
4. Hal Lux, "Can Vanguard Stay the Course?"
5. Peter Samson as quoted by Hal Lux in "Can Vanguard Stay the Course?"
6. Jerry Edgerton, "Vanguard's New Skipper Will Push High-Tech Service and Index Funds," *Money*, July 1, 1995, p. 53.
7. Paul Adams, "Mutual Fund Innovator Bangs Drum for Reform," *Baltimore Sun*, December 13, 2003, http://articles.baltimoresun. com/2003-12-13/news/0312130216_1_bogle-mutual-eliot-spitzer.
8. Sandra Ward, "Hardly Shy or Retiring," *Barron's*, August 16, 1999, p. F3.
9. Hal Lux, "Can Vanguard Stay the Course?"
10. Brenda Buttner, "Memo to Vanguard: You Need to Win Back My Confidence," TheStreet.com, August 19, 1999, http://thestreet.com/ funds/underthehood/774892.html.
11. Jerry Edgerton, "Vanguard's New Skipper Will Push High-Tech Service and Index Funds."
12. Hal Lux, "Jacks of One Trade," *Institutional Investor*, vol. 33, no. 8, August 1, 1999.
13. Joe Bousquin, "Vanguard's Bogle Miffed at Board's Stance," TheStreet .com, August 12, 1999, http://www.thestreet.com/story/773289/ vanguards-bogle-miffed-at-boards-stance.html.
14. Here is an interesting footnote to this story. One Vanguard board member told me that the board ultimately decided to cancel the pension because Vanguard generally voted against proposals for directors' pensions at corporations the funds were invested in. So for Vanguard directors to then have pensions seemed hypocritical.

15. Richard A. Oppel, Jr., "Vanguard Founder Declines an Offer to Stay as Director," *New York Times*, September 18, 1999, http://www.nytimes .com/1999/09/18/business/vanguard-founder-declines-an-offer-to-stay -as-director.html.

CHAPTER **13**

1. John C. Bogle, *Common Sense on Mutual Funds: Fully Updated 10th Anniversary Edition*, preface to the original edition (Hoboken, N.J.: John Wiley & Sons, 2010), p. xix.
2. Ibid., pp. 530–531.
3. John C. Bogle, "Losing Our Way: Where Are the Independent Directors?" in *John Bogle on Investing: The First 50 Years* (New York: McGraw-Hill, 2001), pp. 208–209.
4. John C. Bogle, "The Silence of the Funds: Mutual Fund Investment Policies and Corporate Governance," in *John Bogle on Investing: The First 50 Years*, p. 198.
5. As quoted in John C. Bogle, *The Battle for the Soul of Capitalism* (New Haven, Conn.: Yale University Press, 2005), p. 142.
6. Amey Stone, "Scandal Finds the Funds' Sly Secrets," *BusinessWeek*, September 4, 2003, http://www.businessweek.com/bwdaily/dnflash/ sep2003/nf2003094_8736_db058.htm.
7. John C. Bogle, "Statement of John C. Bogle to the United States Senate Governmental Affairs Subcommittee," November 3, 2003, http://www.vanguard.com/bogle_site/sp20031103.html.
8. Ibid.
9. Ibid.
10. J. Lawrence Wilson, letter to SEC chairman, January 7, 2004, found at http://www.sec.gov/rules/proposed/s72703/s7-27-03-71.pdf.
11. Vanguard directors, letter to SEC Secretary Jonathan Katz, March 10, 2004, posted at http://www.sec.gov/rules/proposed/s70304/ vanguarddirectors031004.htm.
12. John J. Brennan, letter to SEC Secretary Jonathan Katz, March 10, 2004, posted at http://www.sec.gov/rules/proposed/s70304/ vanguard031004.htm.
13. John C. Bogle, "Mutual Funds in the Coming Century . . . While We're at It, Let's Build a Better World," speech presented to the SEC, May 25, 2004, posted at http://www.sec.gov/rules/proposed/s70304/ s70304-175.pdf.

14. John C. Bogle, "Re: File Number S7-03-06 Executive Compensation and Related Party Disclosure," letter to SEC Secretary Nancy M. Morris, April 10, 2006.
15. John C. Bogle, "Re: File Number S7-12-04," letter to SEC Secretary Jonathan G. Katz, May 21, 2004.
16. Heidi Stam, "Re: Disclosure Regarding Portfolio Managers of Registered Management Investment Companies; File Number S7-12-04," letter to SEC Secretary Jonathan G. Katz, May 26, 2004.
17. John C. Bogle, *The Battle for the Soul of Capitalism*, p. 201.
18. Ibid, p. 169.
19. John C. Bogle, "Mutual Fund Secrecy," *New York Times*, December 14, 2002, http://www.nytimes.com/2002/12/14/opinion/mutual-fund-secrecy.html.
20. John J. Brennan and Edward C. Johnson, III, "No Disclosure: The Feeling Is Mutual," *Wall Street Journal*, January 14, 2003, p. A14.
21. Ibid.
22. John C. Bogle, *The Battle for the Soul of Capitalism*, p. 80.
23. AFSCME, "Compensation Complicity: Mutual Fund Proxy Voting and the Overpaid American CEO," The Corporate Library and Shareowners.org, p. 11, http://www.afscme.org/docs/AFSCME-2009-Report_Compensation-Complicity.pdf.
24. John C. Bogle, *Jones v. Harris* Amicus Brief, Summary of Argument, June 2009, p. 5.

CHAPTER **14**

1. Taylor Larimore and Mel Lindauer, "Meet the Bogleheads," in *The Bogleheads' Guide to Retirement Planning*, ed. Taylor Larimore, Mel Lindauer, Richard A. Ferri, and Laura F. Dogu (Hoboken, N.J.: John Wiley & Sons, 2009), p. 315.
2. Art Carey, "Market Moralist," *Philadelphia Inquirer*, October 19, 2008, p. A18.
3. John C. Bogle, *Enough* (Hoboken, N.J.: John Wiley & Sons, 2009), p. 139.
4. John Kenneth Galbraith, *A Short History of Financial Euphoria* (New York: Penguin Books, 1993), p. 20.
5. John C. Bogle, *The Battle for the Soul of Capitalism* (New Haven, Conn.: Yale University Press, 2005), p. 5.

6. Max Weber, *The Protestant Ethic and the Spirit of Capitalism*, 3rd ed. (Los Angeles: Roxbury Publishing Co., 2002), p. 17.
7. John C. Bogle, *Enough*, p. 224.
8. Art Carey, "Market Moralist," p. A19.
9. John C. Bogle, *Enough*, p. 126.
10. Ibid., p. 121.
11. Max Weber, *The Protestant Ethic and the Spirit of Capitalism*, p. 115.
12. Ibid., p. 119.

CHAPTER 15

1. John C. Bogle, "As the Index Fund Moves from Heresy to Dogma . . . What More Do We Need to Know?" The Gary M. Brinson Distinguished Lecture, Washington State University, April 13, 2004.
2. Michael Maiello, "Vanguard Steps Up to the Plate," *Forbes*, 2008 Fund Guide, January 28, 2008, http://www.forbes.com/forbes/2008/0128/084.html.
3. Matt Hougan, "Bogle: Investors Are Getting Killed in ETFs," *Index-Universe*, June 17, 2009, http://www.indexuniverse.com/sections/news/6012-bogle-investors-are-getting-killed-in-etfs.html.
4. Ibid.
5. John C. Bogle, *The Little Book of Common Sense Investing* (Hoboken, N.J.: John Wiley & Sons, 2007), p. 164.
6. Ibid., p. 170.
7. "Vanguard Offers Commission-Free Trades on Its Family of Low-Cost ETFs," Vanguard press release, May 4, 2010.
8. "Vanguard Plans Broad Expansion of Index Offerings," Vanguard press release, June 24, 2010.
9. "ETF Snapshot: July 2010," *State Street Global Advisor*, pp. 4–5.
10. Mark Jewell, "Vanguard's Free ETF Trades a Big Early Hit," Associated Press, June 23, 2010.

CHAPTER 16

1. John C. Bogle, "Entrepreneurship and Economic Progress," Hollerith lecture series at Blair Academy, Blairstown, N.J., April 2, 2002, http://www.vanguard.com/bogle_site/sp20020402.html.
2. John C. Bogle, "Corporate Governance and Mutual Fund Governance—Reflections at a Time of Crisis," Corporate Governance Conference, New York Society of Securities Analysts, New York, November 21, 2003.

3. Ibid.
4. Beth Healy, "Lasser Will Get $78M Payout," *Boston Globe*, June 11, 2004, http://www.boston.com/business/globe/articles/2004/06/11/lasser_will_get_78m_payout/.
5. John C. Bogle, "The Alpha and the Omega," an address to the Boston College Law School, January 21, 2004.
6. John C. Bogle, "A New Order of Things—Bringing Mutuality to the 'Mutual' Fund," 27th Annual Manuel F. Cohen Memorial Lecture at the George Washington University Law School, Washington, D.C., February 19, 2008.
7. Ibid.
8. Ibid
9. John C. Bogle, "Restoring Faith in Our Financial Markets," *Wall Street Journal*, January 18, 2010, http://online.wsj.com/article/SB100014240 52748703436504574640523013840290.html.
10. Daniel P. Wiener, "Partnership Still Better than Indexing," *Independent Adviser for Vanguard Investors,* vol. 20, no. 7, July 2010.
11. Turner Investment Partners, "Asset-Capacity Study for Turner's Stock Portfolios," first quarter 2010, http://turnerinvestmentpartners.com/index.cfm/fuseaction/commentary.detail/id/3036/csid/386/commentary_section/index.cfm/fuseaction/documents.detail/CID/3035.
12. John C. Bogle, *Common Sense on Mutual Funds: Fully Updated 10th Anniversary Edition* (Hoboken, N.J.: John Wiley & Sons, 2010), p. 363.

CHAPTER 17

1. The Johns Hopkins Right Ventricular Dysplasia Program, reference at http://www.arvd.com/q_a.html.
2. John C. Bogle, "Telltale Hearts," in *John Bogle on Investing: The First 50 Years* (New York: McGraw-Hill, 2001), p. 321.
3. John C. Bogle, "A Tribute to Bernard Lown, M.D.," Boston, September 13, 2008.

CHAPTER 18

1. John C. Bogle and Burton G. Malkiel, "Turn on a Paradigm?" *Wall Street Journal*, June 27, 2006, p. A14.
2. John C. Bogle, *The Battle for the Soul of Capitalism* (New Haven, Conn.: Yale University Press, 2005), p. 115.

3. Roger Lowenstein, "On Wall Street, the Price Isn't Right," *Washington Post*, June 7, 2009, http://www.washingtonpost.com/wp-dyn/content/article/2009/06/05/AR2009060502053.html.

4. David Wighton, "Efficient Market Hypothesis Is Dead—for Now," *The Times (London)*, January 29, 2009, http://business.timesonline.co.uk/tol/business/columnists/article5607960.ece.

5. Paul D. Kaplan, "What Does Harry Markowitz Think?" *Morningstar Advisor*, June/July 2010, p. 45.

6. As quoted by Roger Lowenstein in *Buffett: The Making of an American Capitalist* (New York: Main Street Books, 1996), p. 161.

7. Excerpted from Warren E. Buffett's letter to Peter L. Bernstein, *Economics and Portfolio Strategy*, June 1, 1998.

8. John C. Bogle, *Common Sense on Mutual Funds: Fully Updated 10th Anniversary Edition* (Hoboken, N.J.: John Wiley & Sons, 2010), p. 290.

9. Brett Arends, "How to Beat the Bond Market," *Wall Street Journal*, May 14, 2010, http://online.wsj.com/article/SB10001424052748703950804575242823816476484.html.

10. Robert Arnott, "Bonds: Why Bother?" *Journal of Indexes*, May/June 2009, p. 10.

CHAPTER 19

1. Mark Jewell, "Vanguard's Free ETF Trades a Big Early Hit," Associated Press, June 23, 2010.

2. Stuart Elliott, "The Verb Treatment for an Investment House," *New York Times*, March 15, 2010, p. B6.

3. "Vanguard Group Goes Mavericky with 'Vanguarding' Campaign," BrandCultureTalk, April 20, 2010, http://www.brandculture.com/blog/2010/04/vanguard-goes-mavericky-with-vanguarding.

4. William J. Clinton, foreword to *Enough* by John C. Bogle (Hoboken, N.J.: John Wiley & Sons, 2010) pp. vi–vii.

5. Taylor Larimore and Mel Lindauer, "Meet the Bogleheads," in *The Bogleheads' Guide to Retirement Planning*, ed. Taylor Larimore, Mel Lindauer, Richard A. Ferri, and Laura F. Dogu (Hoboken, N.J.: John Wiley & Sons, 2009), p. 322.

INDEX

Index

Index

Oakmark Funds, 179–181
Online trading, 77, 108, 149
Open-end fund, 16–17, 18
  (*See also individual fund companies*)
Operating expenses:
  asset size *vs.* expense ratio, 108, 217,
    230–238
  cost matters hypothesis, 124, 128, 221,
    253–254, 255
  Vanguard as low-cost leader, 63–64, 71–72,
    79, 81–82, 88, 113–114, 219, 240, 275
Ownership society, 157–162, 166, 172, 190–191,
  226

Paine, Stephen, 39
Palmer, David, 232
Partnership Plan, 88–96, 170–173, 216–217,
  229–230, 286
Passive school of investing, 123, 124
  (*See also* Index funds)
Pension fund management, 33–34, 42, 76–77
PowerShares, 254–255
Press relations, 96–99, 136–137, 147–148,
  162–163
Princeton University, 8–12, 16, 21, 200
Principal-agency relationship, 173–174, 178,
  190, 226, 261
Private company, Vanguard as, 59, 88–89, 90–91
The Protestant Ethic and the Spirit of Capitalism
  (Weber), 192
Protestant work ethic, Bogle as embodiment of,
  191–197, 202
Proxy vote disclosure, 173–179
Public ownership of fund management
  companies, 225–228, 226, 227–228
Putnam Investments, 223–224

Quakerism, 191–192
Qubes, 204

A Random Walk Down Wall Street (Malkiel),
  123
Real estate funds, 111
Regensteiner, Max, 70
Regulation, 69, 76, 167, 189, 190
  (*See also* Securities and Exchange
  Commission)
Renninger, Barbara Bogle (daughter), ix, 25,
  145, 243–244
Research Affiliates, 253
Revenue Act (1978), 76
Riepe, Jim, 87, 140–141, 194
Root, Charles, 47, 54
Rule 12b-1, SEC, 70–71

Sales loads, 63
Samuelson, Paul, 10, 120
Sauter, George "Gus," 121, 129–130, 204–205,
  219
Savings rates, decline in, 104, 107
Scandals, financial, 163–167, 187–190
Schroder Capital Management International, 68

Scudder, Barbara, 140, 146, 201
Sector funds, 111, 207–209
Securities and Exchange Commission (SEC), 51,
  55, 58, 66, 69, 168, 170, 177–178
Shareholder democracy, 157–162, 166, 172,
  190–191, 226
Shareholders (*see* Fund shareholders)
Sherrerd, Eve (Mrs. Jack Bogle) (wife), 25,
  195–196
Sherrerd, Jay (brother-in-law), 30
"Silence of the Funds" (Bogle), 163
Sinquefield, Rex, 131–132
Smith, Richard, 50, 54
Snyder, Emily, 154–155
S&P 500 Index, 102–103, 110, 120, 122, 130,
  253, 254–255, 258
Speculation:
  chasing market share and, 211
  debt's role in, 187–189
  dot-com bubble, 78, 107–109, 110, 164, 174,
    256–258, 261–262
  Great Crash of 1929, 4, 17–19, 24
  inevitability of, 190
  intrinsic *vs.* speculative value, 124, 125–128,
    256–258
  role in bull market (1982–2000), 102
  (*See also* Exchange traded funds)
Spiders, 204
Spitzer, Eliot, 164, 165
Stam, Heidi, 171–172
State Street Global Advisors, 132, 203, 218
Stengel, Rick, 200
Stevens, Jerald L., 141
Stewardship, 197–198, 200, 286
Stock, Craig, 94–95
Stock Market Crash of 1929, 4, 17–19, 24
Subadvisers, 237–239
Swedroe, Larry, 259

Taleb, Nassim, 258
Thesis, Bogle's college, 11–12, 21, 26
Thorndike, Doran, Paine & Lewis, Inc.
  (TDP&L), 33–35
  (*See also* Boston partners)
Thorndike, W. Nicholas, 34, 38, 42, 58, 65
Torsella, Joe, 199
Transaction fees for ETFs, Vanguard's
  elimination of, 213–216
Trustee relationship, fund management–client,
  97
Tsai, Gerald, 37
Twardowski, Jan, 67, 121, 122
12b-1 rule, SEC, 70–71
Two-masters fund structure:
  Bogle's mutualization and, 221–222
  fund managers' conflict in, 261–264
  management company *vs.* funds, 36, 44–45,
    46, 163, 224–231
  Vanguard's compensation disclosure issue
    and, 90–91

Value, intrinsic *vs.* speculative, 124, 125–127,
  256–258
Value premium, 255–256